D1063318

PENGUIN BOOKS

636

ALEXANDER POPE

BY

EDITH SITWELL

Owing to production difficulties it is impossible to maintain large stocks of our publications, and the titles available change so rapidly that the complete catalogue is of little value as a means of knowing what books are available. If you are not already on our mailing list and would like to know when new books or reprints are added, please send in your name and address on a postcard.

Suggestions for additions are welcomed.

ALEXANDER POPE

BY

EDITH SITWELL

PENGUIN BOOKS
HARMONDSWORTH · MIDDLESEX

FIRST PUBLISHED 1930
PUBLISHED IN PENGUIN BOOKS 1948

*Made and printed in Great Britain for Penguin Books Ltd,
by Balding and Mansell Limited London and Wisbech*

To

HELEN ROOTHAM
AND ALLANAH HARPER

with gratitude for their help in various matters connected with this book

AUTHOR'S NOTE

In writing this book the author has been specially indebted to the *Life and Works of Alexander Pope* with Introduction and Notes by J. W. Croker, the Rev. W. Elwin and W. J. Courthope (John Murray), to *The Life of Pope* by Robert Carruthers (G. Bell & Sons, Ltd), and to *Social Life in the Reign of Queen Anne* by Mr John Ashton (Chatto & Windus). She wishes to thank Messrs Chatto & Windus for their permission to quote from the last-named book in her chapter on 'Fashionable Life'.

CONTENTS

CHAPTER I

Introduction

If we consider the poetry written in this present age, and the standard of values given to us by those who would be our guides, we shall find that there is a general misapprehension of the aims and of the necessities of poetry; and this misapprehension has arisen in part from the fact that many respectable persons, but very few poets, are encouraged to write it. For this reason, among many others, the task I have given myself is a dangerous and formidable one; since whatever I say must of its very nature injure the personal susceptibilities, and make evident the lack of sensibility towards poetry, of some of our more eminent bores. Again, so many exhaustive, learned, and delightful studies have been made of the life of Alexander Pope, and there is so much diversity of opinion about the most ordinary facts of that life, that it is extremely difficult to disentangle the evidence. I do not hope to discover the truth about all his quarrels – more learned people than I have failed to do that – but I hope to exhibit him in his true light as a good and exceedingly lovable man.

Before we examine the life history of the small, unhappy, tortured creature, who is one of the greatest of our poets, and who is, in his two finest poems, perhaps the most flawless artist our race has produced, it will be better to examine the prevailing attitude towards his poetry, and indeed, towards poetry in general. The reputation of Pope is safe among the poets of this time; but it is a fact, also, that a large section of the public has not yet recovered from the cold, damp mossiness that has blighted the public taste for the last forty, fifty, or even sixty years; and to these people, Pope is not one of the greatest of our poets, one of the most lovable of men, but a man who was deformed in spirit as in body. How false this estimate has been, I shall hope to show. This general blighting and withering of the poetic taste is the result of the public mind having been overshadowed by such Aberdeen-granite tombs and monuments as Matthew Arnold – is the result, also, of the substitution of scholar for poet, of school inspector for artist.

The ground having been prepared for the pre-eminent bore, we were then obsessed by what, for want of a better name, I will call the Jaeger School of Poetry,* the school advocating health at all costs. Under these unhappy circumstances it cannot be expected that the purest of our artists, the man who, in his two greatest poems at least, would not be decoyed from his path by any will-o'-the-wisp of Science, interest in human nature, the wish to reform, or other poetry-wrecking influences, should be honoured or understood. At this time and in our age it has become the fashion for a poet not to be regarded as a poet unless he attempts to cure human ills, to comfort the dying world, unless he preaches sermons, or becomes a photographer, telling human nature to look pleasant; unless he produces panaceas for all ills, as the conjurer produces rabbits out of his hat, though the magic and the illusion surrounding the conjurer must be absent. In short, the poet must not be a poet, he must be some sort of moral quack doctor.

For the most part it is not poetry, but a moral message that is being given us, and a moral message in a blighted or in a shrivelled form. (Almost invariably the poem is deformed by this need for comfort, the shape is muffled in woollen shawls.) Indeed, at this time any person who for any reason whatever finds himself in an emotional state, regards himself, and is regarded by others, as a poet. It should not be imagined for a minute that any poet advocates lifeless poetry, or poetry that is written by people who take no interest in life. But it cannot be said too often or too clearly, that verse written by a person who is not a poet, no matter how worthy his motives may be, is not poetry. This truth, though it is one of the humblest of platitudes, unfortunately has not been understood or accepted by the mass of human beings. The poetry of today has been much debased by the Wordsworthian ideals of those versifiers who were fashionable from 1900 until about five years ago, and

* This is not meant in any sense of disrespect to Messrs Jaeger – but what is beautiful in wool is not always beautiful in verse!

who are, indeed, still read in certain quarters. To these men, rhetoric and formalism were abhorrent, partly no doubt, because to manage either quality in verse the writer must possess a technical capability. But in addition to this technical fault, we find in the verse of that time (as in much contemporary verse) the fault of an exaggerated praise of worthy home life, which alternated with swollen, inflated boomings and roarings about the Soul of Man. These reigned triumphant, together with healthy, manly, but rather raucous shouts for beer, and advertisements of certain rustic parts of England, delivered to the accompaniment of a general clumsy clodhopping with hobnailed boots. Yet in spite of this, the business man's careful logic was never absent, though it was combined, strangely enough, with the legendary innocence of the country clergyman. (This last trait is dedicated to the unfortunate Wordsworth.) Those stronger members of the populace who enjoy adventure, could be taken for short rides in Walt Whitman's powerful steam-roller. (He could be more than a steam-roller, I admit, but at his heaviest, crushed even the stoniest roads.)

Then sex was discovered; and it was at the same time that the Jaeger School of verse arose. Many things were discovered in quick succession. In fact the only thing that was not discovered was poetry. At the same moment a school of American-Greek posturants, resembling not so much marble statues as a white-tiled bathroom, exuded a thin stream of carefully-chosen, watery words. Added to this misfortune, we are now afflicted by the shrill moronic cacklings of the Sur-Realists – laying never so much as an addled egg – and the erotic confidences of rich young ladies, suffering less from an excess of soul than from an excess of distilled spirits. All, or most of these persons, have theories or battle-cries. These theories are all very well in their way, but they do not produce poetry, if we may hold that Shakespeare, Milton, Dryden, Pope, Keats, Coleridge and Shelley wrote poetry. How, under these circumstances, can the genius of Pope be appreciated at its proper worth–that genius which is the result of order and inspiration?

The state of poetry has become not better, but worse, since

the time when Byron wrote his defence of Pope in the preface to *Don Juan,* and complained that 'the Edinburgh Reviewers ... and Hunt and his School, and everybody else with their school, the dilettante lecturers at institutions, and elderly gentlemen who translate and imitate, and young ladies who listen and repeat, baronets who draw indifferent frontispieces for bad poets, and noblemen who let them dine with them in the country, the small body of the wits and the great body of the blues have latterly united in a depreciation of which their fathers would have been as much ashamed as their children will be.' In the same preface, Byron wrote: 'The great cause of the present deplorable state of English poetry is to be attributed to that absurd and systematic depreciation of Pope, in which, for the last few years, there has been a kind of epidemical occurrence.'

That statement, which was hardly true of the year 1822, since it was one of the great ages of poetry, is undoubtedly true today, when we are surrounded by formless licence and disorder, when inspiration is regarded with suspicion, and form is derided as old-fashioned, as if there could be fashion in poetry: such an idea degrades the art to the level of a dress-maker's shop.

It is a terribly informing task to read any anthology published during the last fifty years; to read, let us say, *The Oxford Book of English Verse.* How strange is the contrast between the beginning of such an anthology, with the great poems of the past, included, no doubt, because it is not possible for anyone, however insensitive to the structure and texture of poetry, to exclude them, and the poems which follow. The former are now generally accepted; they have passed into the consciousness of our race, though nobody, with the exception of those few people who care for poetry, would dream of thinking about them. Having read those poems, let us read some of the poems which were written shortly after the time of Swinburne, and which may have been admitted to the book in a spirit of fatigue or despair. What do we find? Matthew Arnold's chilblained, mittened musings, and T. E. Brown's appalling poem,

'A garden is a lovesome thing, God wot ...' (Yes, and God wot the fate that T. E. Brown would have met with, had Pope lived to see him. The poem leaves me with a feeling of having been hit over the ear, with no excuse and without provocation.) How then is it possible for a nation which has had its sensibilities blunted and coarsened by such gross stuff as the poem from which I have quoted, to realize the greatness, the fire, the supreme music and variation of the poems of Alexander Pope? The public, reading the homespun-dressed, pedestrian, worthy-citizen type of verse that is held up for their admiration in certain of the more imposing weekly papers, imagine that poetry, to be good, must be stupid and uninteresting. On the other hand, exhibitions of weak hysteria and hymn-singing are encouraged by certain of the daily papers, and that section of the public whose taste is formed by these papers, rushes to enjoy the spectacle of poets foaming at the mouth and writhing with 'passion', in much the same spirit as that in which a crowd gathers to watch the pleasing spectacle of an epileptic having a fit in the street. Under the circumstances, pure poetry must necessarily, it seems, be judged as heartless and soulless, no matter how much the poet's life and actions may prove the contrary.

Such a judgment as this, founded on false premises, on little logic, and no understanding, is meted out to Alexander Pope, of whom I may say, with the deepest humility, what Pope is reputed to have said of Dryden: 'Had I been born early enough, I should have known and loved him.' Never was a man worthier of love than this most misunderstood man, this great and – at his best – flawless poet.

The English people are incited to be kind and coarse in their view of this unhappy little creature of genius. In a preface to one of the most widely-read editions of Pope's works, I find this passage (the italics are my own): 'To realize the personal malice and the keen edge of the satire, we must again call up the London of 1720, and *the figure of this imp of a poet, grotesque and sinister, as he appears in Doctor Johnson's unsparing pen-portrait.* "The person of Pope is well known not to have been formed on the nicest model. He has, in his account of the Little Club, compared himself to a spider, and by another is described as protuberant behind and before ... His stature was so low that to bring him to a level with common tables, it was necessary to raise his seat. But his face was not displeasing, and his eyes were animated and vivid. We are told he was so weak as to be extremely sensitive of cold; so that he wore a kind of fur doublet, under a shirt of a very coarse warm linen with fine sleeves. When he rose, he was invested in a bodice made of stiff canvas, being scarce able to hold himself erect till it was laced, and he then put on a flannel waistcoat. One side was contracted. His legs were so slender that he enlarged their bulk with three pairs of stockings, which were drawn on and off by the maid; for he was not able to dress or undress himself, and neither went to bed nor rose without help ... His hair had fallen almost all away, and he used to dine sometimes with Lord Oxford privately, in a velvet cap. His dress of ceremony was black with a tye-wig, and a little sword." ' 'Unsparing!' Unsparing to whom or to what? To our feelings, if we have any heart or any humanity. For sympathy with Pope's character and for his sufferings shines through every page of Doctor Johnson's essay, though the poet's faults are not glossed over. I do not know how anyone could fail to be saddened by the tragedy of this man, whose body was too frail for the terrible burden of genius, and whose life was one long torture of pain and weakness and the humiliation caused by the knowledge of his deformity – a knowledge that had been forced upon him at a most impressionable age by the unspeakable Dennis. Pope had a heart like other men: he was young and romantic-minded, and from the moment of Dennis's attack upon him he saw himself doomed to live his life through without love. He had, perhaps, the most subtle and sensitive feeling for beauty of form possessed by any artist that our race has produced; yet he realized, how fully I dare not think, that his own outward form raised feelings of mocking amusement or coarse pity in the beholders. Indeed, his very weakness was a subject for ridicule.

I do not know why the unhappy Pope's under-lying beauty

of character and kindness have not been more commented upon, since his life's record is one of loyalty to his friends, unchanging love where that love was not betrayed, financial generosity, and, where that generosity was extended, the most extraordinary delicacy and kindness. Was this man filled with nothing but hatred and malice? His letters to his friends are among the most touching letters that any great man has written; his devotion to his parents and to his old nurse was beautiful and flawless; it lasted through their lives and after their deaths, unchanged and undimmed. Those whom he loved, he saw only with the eyes of love; he was angry once because Martha Blount, at the age of forty-eight, and with nothing left of her former beauty but her bright blue eyes, had not been invited to a ball; for in his sight, though in his alone, she was beautiful eternally, and age could cast no shadow on her. He reverenced great men throughout his life; he defended them with fire and vigour, and his friendship with Dean Swift was a monument of what friendship should be. The delicacy and patience shown in his dealings with the unhappy, ragged, and ungovernable Richard Savage, were beyond all praise; he persevered in trying to help this wretched creature after all others had given him up in despair. He has been acccused of thinking the miserable inhabitants of Grub Street beneath compassion. Never was there a baser libel on any great man: the instances of his kindnesses are not recorded as actions worthy of praise, but as the ordinary business affairs of every day. We are not allowed by his biographers to think of him as a good man. Matthew Arnold, on the other hand, overawes us with his goodness, yet I do not know that any special act of kindness is ascribed to him, save that of being remotely concerned (if an uncle can be held in any way responsible) in giving us Mrs Humphry Ward.

It is otherwise with Pope, and there is scarcely anything in his life that has not been made the subject of the most unreasoning calumny. His beautiful love for and friendship with Martha Blount has been deformed and reduced to the level of a common and sordid intrigue. How false that is, I shall hope to show. His warm-hearted longing that his friend Dean Swift should spend his declining years in Pope's house at Twickenham, sharing Pope's wealth with him, has been distorted by one biographer into an insincere and safe offer, made when Pope knew that such a project was impossible; his kindness and generosity have been slurred over, and hardly commented on. Only his small misshapen body, and the fits of fury to which the sufferings and illnesses of that body made him liable, have remained to us. I am moved almost to tears when I see Richardson's portrait of Pope in the National Gallery – the wide, visionary eyes, that have a look of almost childish anguish and loneliness, the wide and beautiful brow, the worn cheek-bones, and the sensitive pain-stricken mouth. I am moved beyond words when I read Doctor Johnson's description of his sufferings, and the passage which says: 'Pope was from his birth of a constitution sickly and delicate, but is said to have shown remarkable sweetness and gentleness of disposition. The weakness of his body continued through his life, but the mildness of his mind perhaps ended with his childhood. His voice, when he was young, was so pleasing that he was called in fondness, "the little nightingale".' It moves me also to think of that grotto at Twickenham, which housed such dreams of romance; of his dog, the Great Dane 'Bounce,' on whose grave he would have liked to inscribe the words, 'O rare Bounce', if it would not have seemed disrespectful to the memory of Ben Jonson. Why did the mildness of that mind end (if it did) with his childhood? Ask the vile and unspeakably disgraced Dennis, who lives, now, only in the poetry of the man to whose mind and heart he did so appalling and irrevocable an injury.

Why then is a man of such beauty of character distrusted? He was, it is true, formidable and terrible in anger; and many people have been so blinded with the malice they feel at seeing so frail a man, and so great an artist, able to defend himself against a thousand venomous little scribblers whose bodily powers were greater than his, that they are unable, or unwilling, to realize his tragedy, and the misery contained in such lines as these:

Late as it is, I put myself to school,
And feel some comfort, not to be a fool.
Weak though I am of limb, and short of sight,
Far from a lynx, and not a giant quite;
I'll do what Mead and Cheselden advise,
To keep these limbs, and to preserve these eyes.
Not to go back, is somewhat to advance,
And men must walk at least before they dance.

It is imagined, for some reason, that it is perfectly right and proper for persons of small wit, and a dreadful little slick talent, or indeed, for persons of no wit and not even that pimpish talent, to attack, and try to injure, any creature possessed of genius. It does not matter how low and foul the attack, it does not matter by what cunning, hatred, and malice it may be prompted, nor how under-brained and dirty the attacker may be. The quarry is possessed of genius, and is therefore meant to be hunted and half-killed. But let a man of genius reply, and the whole populace rises up to protect the original aggressor. The man of genius, it is understood, in protecting himself, and consequently his work, or in protecting his personal reputation, is a creature actuated by malice. He is cold-hearted, he is serpent-like. He should have allowed himself to be hunted into the grave, like Keats; starved into the grave, like Chatterton; driven out of England, like Shelley. And the malice is proved by the fact that, being a man of genius, he is naturally able to deliver harder blows when attacked, than the majority of his aggressors are able to administer to him.

In the time of Pope, the populace had not yet been deprived of the chivalrous and manly joys of bear-baiting, and had not, therefore, so much leisure in which to protect the little hounds who attacked their contemporary men of genius; but in these times, artist-baiting is one of the national sports, and although Pope lived so long ago that his genius might be remembered, and his return battle with his persecutors forgiven, he has not yet been excused for the fault of turning on them, and hurting them as they deserved to be hurt.

Why is he to remain thus unforgiven? The accusations that

are brought against him, are those of bad temper (when attacked, or when fearing attack), and of coarseness in an age when this fault was universal. So petty are the charges brought against him, that he is actually accused of not providing enough wine at his dinner-parties! What a charge to bring against a great man! He was savage, we are told. Yet, at a time when cruelty to animals, of the most unspeakably horrible kind, was exhibited daily, and was held to be no disgrace, this savage wrote an essay, reproaching such cruelty in the most moving terms. It needed no small amount of moral courage to do this. The fact is, that he is hated because he, being the great poet that he was, hated inferior poetry. He is disliked, too, because he wrote two admittedly unpleasant lines about a certain Sappho, and his enemy Lady Mary Montagu, that dreary rattle, conceived them to be inspired by her. We shall never learn all the truth about that quarrel. But we know, at least, that Pope denied that the couplet referred to her, and that he had written of her with great dignity, saying: 'My only fault towards her was leaving off her conversation when I found it dangerous'. She, on her side, is eternally disgraced by her own story: that Pope had made her a declaration, and that she had laughed at him. Nobody, it appears, has considered in its true light, the vulgar and murderous cruelty of such an act towards this little, deformed creature of genius, whose sensitiveness towards his deformity was so acute that even now, after these centuries, it is painful to contemplate. There are many instances of this suffering, exhibited under touching and human circumstances; witness the passage in a letter to the Misses Blount, in which he says: 'I have heard, indeed, of women that have had a kindness for men of my make'. Indeed, if that couplet was inspired by Lady Mary Montagu, I think she deserved it, coarse though it was.

We must remember when reading certain of the biographies and certain criticisms of Pope's life and of his work, that the authors were schoolmasters and scholars, not poets, and that no matter how great their learning and how deep-rooted their kindness, they could scarcely be expected to understand that to this man, who was one of the greatest poets England has produced, whose sense of texture in poetry was so excessively delicate that it has never been surpassed, and, I think, has scarcely been equalled, to this fine and sensitive artist, inferior poetry and clumsy texture in verse were an agony, and must have had almost the effect of a physical rupture.

Again, his bodily martyrdom (which inspired in Doctor Johnson one of the most moving passages in our literature) and the cruel and humiliating sneers to which that martyrdom exposed him, made him liable to bursts of fury which would have been held within bounds by a stronger frame. There is nothing cold about Pope's poetry; we are buried beneath a torrent of lava, but we are not walled up in ice. The effects of his rage, and this I cannot deny, were terrible towards his enemies, and even towards some quite harmless persons whom he believed to cherish designs against him. For the lamentable fact is that he loathed bad poetry – that the cause of poetry affected him as the sound of a bugle is supposed to affect a war horse. The bugle sounds, the war horse charges, and the village idiot is knocked down. The fact that he was almost a more perfect artist (by which I mean a man formed for nothing but his art, living by that art, spinning it out of himself as a spider spins a thread) than any other artist of our race, did not help to make so frail a body less subject to fits of irascibility.

In his lifetime, he could not be forgiven for his fame. Yet though it may seem an illogical trait in Pope's character when combined with this primary need for poetry – the very fact of his fame was an irritating factor. He longed to be regarded as a human being – to be loved as an ordinary man; and his deformity made this seem impossible to him. He was nailed to the outer walls of the city as Mr Pope the famous poet, Alexander Pope the crippled hunchback. His friendship conferred a favour, because he was famous; but the fame which fell to him, the deformity which he endured, made it seem impossible that he should suffer like other men, or feel pleasure like other men. Do we not find this need and this suffering over and over again, in his letters and in his poetry? It is seen, above all, in the poem which had been the cause of more hatred towards him than all his other poems – the 'Prologue to the Satires':

> There are who to my person pay their court:
> I cough like Horace, and, though lean, am short.
> Ammon's great son one shoulder had too high –
> Such Ovid's nose – and 'Sir, you have an eye'.
> Go on, obliging creatures, make me see
> All that disgraced my betters met in me.
> Say, for my comfort, languishing in bed,
> 'Just so immortal Maro held his head;'
> And, when I die, be sure and let me know
> Great Homer died three thousand years ago.
> Why did I write? What sin to me unknown
> Dipp'd me in ink? my parents', or my own?
> As yet a child, nor yet a fool to fame,
> I lisp'd in numbers, for the numbers came.
> I left no calling for this idle trade,
> No duty broke, no father disobeyed:
> The Muse but served to ease some friend, not wife,
> To help me through this long disease, my life;

and again:

> Oh let me live my own, and die so too!
> (To live and die is all I have to do:)
> Maintain a poet's dignity and ease,
> And see what friends, and read what books I please:
> Above a patron, though I condescend
> Sometimes to call a minister my friend.
> I was not born for courts or great affairs:
> I pay my debts, believe and say my prayers;
> Can sleep without a poem in my head,
> Nor know if Dennis be alive or dead.
> Why am I asked what next shall see the light?
> Heavens! was I born for nothing but to write?
> Has life no joys for me? or (to be grave)
> Have I no friend to serve, no soul to save?

It is evident from these lines, that Pope wished to be regarded as a straightforward and truthful man. He has been held to be something quite different. His principal fault was that he suffered from a constitutional inhibition against speaking the truth, save on those occasions when, if we except the æsthetic point of view, the truth would have been better left unspoken. But I have so often found both these faults in myself, that I do not dare to blame them; it is no doubt otherwise with some of his biographers, and they feel they have a right to do so. I do not deny that he was occasionally tortuous in his dealings, nor can it be denied that he was capable of suppressing or altering passages in his letters which might not exhibit him in the light in which he wished to appear. He did alter many of his letters before he allowed them to be printed. But although this behaviour may be called uncandid, yet the reasons for it – and even the excuse – are obvious. Pope knew only too well to what slanders a great man is exposed during his lifetime, from those who are envious of his fame. From what calumnies, then, might he not suffer after his death, when he could no longer defend himself against them. He had a passionate and genuine longing for friendship, and to be understood by his friends; he was in the habit of opening his heart to them in his letters. But those letters were meant for the eyes of none but his friends.

After the publication of his letters to Henry Cromwell – letters which were sold by Cromwell's impoverished mistress without the poet's knowledge, we find Pope writing thus to his friend Hugh Bethel: 'After publishing my boyish letters to Mr Cromwell, you will not wonder if I should foreswear writing a letter again while I live; since I do not correspond with a friend upon the terms of any other free subject of this kingdom. But to you I can never be silent, or reserved; and, I am sure, my opinion of your heart is such, that I could open mine to you.'

The truth is, that Pope had a longing to be regarded not only as a great poet, but as a great and good man, and really I do not know that it is a very unworthy wish. Sometimes the goodness and the benevolence wear a little thin, and natural irritability shows itself, as in the following amusing letter to Hugh

Bethel: 'I thank you for your repeated offer in relation to my sister. I furnished her with £150, and she has lost it, being cast in the law suit (or rather, I believe I have lost it) but I shall be able to make a shift till more of my rents come in. It is right, sometimes, to love our neighbours not only as well, but better than ourself, and to retrench from our extravagances to assist them in theirs, for it was mere folly of not making proper articles, that subjected her to this loss'. But though in this case, a certain patient irritation can be felt, the goodness undoubtedly was there, and so was the £150 – until it was lost.

It seems, therefore, as if Pope's character has been misunderstood because he was, primarily, a great artist, and lived first and foremost for his art. One of his biographers has said that no man ever lived more for fame than he. I can find no evidence of it, nor any evidence that he thought fame worth having. It seems that even his whole-hearted, fiery-souled devotion to poetry had to be subjected to the same calumny as the rest of that most unhappy life.

CHAPTER II

Pope's Birth and Early Childhood

ALEXANDER POPE was born in London, on the 22nd of May, 1688; and I must admit that there is a slight discrepancy between Pope's account of his ancestry and the actual facts. Like everything relating to his life, endless mystifications have been cast round this ancestry; the facts have been altered by various legends, some romantic, some not; and of these legends, some were circulated by his enemies, others were invented by himself, and were spread by his friends. For the small enchanter lived, and still lives, in an atmosphere of spells, enchantments, and fairy tales.

The actual facts seem to have been that Pope's grandfather was a country clergyman, who held the living of Thruxton, in Hampshire, and that the poet's father, who was born in 1645, was placed as a boy with a business firm in Lisbon, where he became converted to the Roman Catholic religion. We do not know what storms this conversion may have raised in the peaceful household at Thruxton. But perhaps the Reverend Mr Pope was as indulgent a father as, many years afterwards, his son proved to be. However this may be, the younger Mr Pope remained for some time in Lisbon, and then, returning to England, became a linen merchant in Broad Street, and married his first wife. This lady, who died in 1679, left one daughter, Magdalen, the sister referred to in the letter which I have quoted already as an example of Pope's intermingled kindness and irritability. Magdalen afterwards married a Mr Charles Rackett, of Staines in Middlesex, and became the mother of three sons; and Pope loved the whole family with great devotion, 'retrenching from his extravagances in order to assist them in theirs'. He showed every proof of love for them, helping the mother and her children during his lifetime, and making provision for them in his will, though his legacy to Martha Blount involved Mrs Rackett in another lawsuit.

After the death of Magdalen's mother, Mr Pope moved – some said to Lombard Street and others said to the Strand; and soon after his removal he married Edith Turner, the daughter of a small landowner who held property at Worsborough in Yorkshire. Of this marriage Alexander Pope was born. It was a marriage between two kindly, comfortable, and plain middle-class people of middle age; but their son, in the case of the story of his birth as in every other circumstance of his life, showed an invariably romantic imagination. This longing for romance haunted him throughout his life, and brought him to disaster again and again, as we can see from the history of 'the unhappy lady', and from his amused, half-fascinated, half-mocking flutterings round Lady Mary Wortley. This longing for romance, so cruelly thwarted by the shape and sufferings of his miserable body, caused him to endow his parents with a purely mythical noble birth.

His father, he declared, belonged to a family of which the Earl of Downe was the head. This, I am afraid, was completely untrue. His mother's family afforded him more food for romance, since of her three brothers, one was killed, another died in the service of King Charles the First, and the third was made a general officer in Spain; and from him Mrs Pope inherited the very small fortune that 'sequestrations and forfeitures had left in the family' (I quote from Doctor Johnson). Mrs Pope's sister, Christina, married the miniature painter, Samuel Cooper, who had painted Charles the Second, but whose best work was a portrait of Cromwell – a fine example of tact and adaptability. He was evidently a man of taste, and had been a friend of Butler, the author of *Hudibras*. Mrs Cooper acted as godmother to the poet, taught him his first lessons, and remembered him in her will with a legacy of a painted china dish, with a silver pot and a dish to set it in. To this she added the reversion of her books and pictures.

Pope, as Doctor Johnson has said, liked better to imagine fables about his father's ancestry, and to remember his uncle, who was a general officer in Spain, and those romantic dashing uncles who died for King Charles the First, than to remember his father's success in trade. But it is to his everlasting credit that, though he had undoubtedly romantic feelings about noble birth – was, in fact, more than a little snobbish – he was never ashamed, even at the height of his social success, of his honest, kindly, middle-class father, nor of his loving, sensible, rather ill-educated mother. He loved them and prized them tenderly all through their lives, and they loved him. They were his refuge against the cruelty of the world – and he had but few refuges. The household was a most happy and contented one. And it must be remembered that the snobbishness to which I have referred was, in part, a protection. It made the poet feel safer with himself. When insulted, in the horrible and pitiless manner to which he was accustomed, about his physical weakness, his tiny deformed body, he remembered his social success, and thought, perhaps, that his deformity was not so obvious as his enemies had suggested, or, at any rate, that it mattered less. Though he was tiny, tall people crowded round him. Though he was deformed, people with beautiful shapes surrounded him, were proud of knowing him – if he did not make love to them. And only too soon, he learned not to do that. The thought of his deformity was always with him after John Dennis's unspeakable attack upon him (Pope was twenty-three years old at that time). We find the poet writing to Judith Cooper, in 1722, saying that he will be glad to count her as a friend if she can overlook the fact of his ugly body; and there is a far more poignant passage in the letter to Teresa and Martha Blount which I have quoted already.

It is probable that Pope inherited at least some tendency to deformity from his father, who suffered from a slight curvature of the spine. It is quite undoubted that he inherited from his mother those terrible headaches that made his later life a martyrdom. But his half-sister, Mrs Rackett, told Spence that he was a pretty little boy, with the happy laughter, clear eyes and round rosy cheeks that healthy children have. He had, too, a gentle and affectionate disposition, and it was as a small child that the sweetness of his voice earned for him the loving name of 'the little nightingale'.

Poor little creature! While he was still in petticoats, he was attacked by 'a wild cow', who knocked him down, trampled on him, and wounded him in the throat with her horns. Mrs Rackett told Spence: 'The accident of the cow was when my brother was about three years old. He was then filling a little cart with stones. The cow struck him, carried off his hat and feather with her horns, and flung him down on the heap of stones he had been playing with'. Though this accident was thought to be of little consequence at the moment, it may have left some injury which was the cause of his ill-health in after life.

This was the only dark spot in that otherwise happy childhood, for he was much loved at home, and does not seem to have been tormented at school. And the fact that he was a Roman Catholic by creed saved him from the roughness and horrors of life at a public school.

The childhood of a poet is in nearly all cases a strange weaving together of the ecstasy that the poet knows and the helpless misery that is known by a child who is lost in the unfamiliar street of a slum. He is in a foreign place, and the faces around him are dark and strange. Even if they try to speak to him kindly, their language is one that is unknown to him. He must suffer within his heart the mad tempests of love for the beauty of the world of sight, sense, and sound, and the mad tempests of rage against the cruelty and blindness that is in the world. But he must suffer these dumbly, for among the tall strangers there is none to understand him, and among the small strangers there is nothing but noise and buffeting. The children are terrifying to him; their eyes are on a level with his own, but they are like the blind and beautiful eyes of statues – they see nothing. He loves them, and longs to be loved in return, but he knows that they, too, see him as a statue throwing some long strange shadow, or as a little foreigner dressed in mourning for someone they have never known, or playing an unknown game he has learned in far-off gardens. Yet in his home, this child was not a foreigner.

From the earliest age, Pope appears to have had the longing

for poetry which throughout his life was his ruling passion. He was a strange, learned little boy, and from the age of eight, when he was sent to a school in Hampshire, where he was under the care of a Romish priest called Taverner, he was in the habit of reading Ogilby's *Homer* and Sandys' *Ovid*. Pope's admiration for Ogilby was a childish one, and did not outlast his boyhood; but his youthful admiration for Sandys lasted throughout his life, and in his notes to the Iliad he has stated that English poetry owed much of its present beauty to Sandys' translations. As we know, Pope could not be sent to a public school; he was debarred from this, as well as from many other civil rights, by his religion. The fact that he could not be sent to a public school may have saved his life, delicate as he was. But who can tell how many of the faults in Pope's character, how many of the suspicions and fears which haunted him, may not have come from the fact that he was a member of this hated and persecuted sect – a sect that was distrusted politically as well as religiously. If we read any history of the time, we shall see that Roman Catholics might not pursue their religion openly; no pretext was too small as an excuse for persecuting them. It was held on every side that they were involved in Jacobite plots, and their neighbours feared them on this account. They were actually obliged to pay double taxes; and they could hold no Government position. What effect could these unseeing and brutal persecutions have upon one who was as little and as weak as Pope? Would they not have the effect of making him run underground for fear of being hurt? Add to this the anguish he felt as a very young man, on being forced to realize the fact that his deformity was the subject of mocking laughter, of cruel sneers, and of even coarser pity, and you have the whole reason for the faults which have been so unreasonably blamed in this otherwise benevolent and warm-hearted character.

On leaving the care of Mr Taverner, Pope was placed at a school at Twyford, near Winchester. From this school, I am shocked to say, he was removed, after a well-deserved whipping, because he had written a satire on his master. For even at this time the naughty little boy showed his propensities in more than one direction. We do not know much about his career at Twyford, but he seems not to have remained there for very long. Afterwards he joined a school at Hyde Park Corner, kept by a Roman Catholic of the name of Deane, an unhappy, raggle-taggle creature who spent a large part of his time in prison, or in the pillory, as a result of his religious convictions. He was evidently a most incompetent teacher, hopeless in this as in all the other aspects of his miserable life; but the Roman Catholic gentry thought it right to support their co-religionist by sending their sons to his school. But though the county families approved of him Doctor Johnson disapproved of him, and indeed administered to him one of his most awful reproofs: 'How Mr. Deane could spend, with a boy who had translated so much of Ovid, some months over a small part of Tully's *Offices*, it is now vain to enquire'. And he continues majestically: 'of a youth so successfully employed, and so conspicuously improved, a minute account must be naturally desired; but curiosity must be contented with confused, imperfect, and sometimes improbable intelligence. Pope, finding little advantage from external help, resolved thenceforward to direct himself, and at twelve formed a plan of study which he completed with little other incitement than the desire of excellence'. My opinion is that poor Mr Deane, whose nerve had already been broken in the pillory as a reward for his religious convictions, was terrified of so successfully employed a youth, and that he was not sorry to see him removed at the age of thirteen to Binfield, Mr Pope's house in the forest. However that may be, it is pleasant to think that in 1727, when Mr Deane was, as usual, in prison, his 'conspicuously improved' former pupil offered, with his usual delicacy and kindness, to make him a small allowance.

Meanwhile, during Pope's stay at the school at Hyde Park Corner he was able to visit the theatre, a form of entertainment which was more inspiring to artists than it is now. Under the influence of this inspiration he wrote, at the age of twelve, a play taken from Ogilby's Iliad, into which he turned some original verses of his own; and this was acted by the other little boys and by Mr Deane's gardener, who took the part of Ajax. What a delightful eighteenth-century version of the play-acting-scene in the *Midsummer Night's Dream* this must have been, with the little boys, their cheeks round and rosy as the gardener's apples, playing the part of long-dead heroes in that green garden. How great must have been Pope's excitement and anxiety and nervousness! how strange the world in which the gardener found himself – that green world where he could wander

> By the hero's armed shades,
> Glitt'ring thro' the gloomy glades,
> By the youths that died for love
> Wand'ring in the myrtle grove.

I wonder if, in after life (Pope's fame was established while he was very young) the echo of that fame reached the gardener, and he remembered being Ajax for one night; or if, to the end of his days, Pope was remembered dimly as an odd little boy who took the gardener away from his fruit trees, and planted him among heroes casting a more tremendous shade than these?

Pope was a strange little boy even at that time. There was no bee-winged glittering light of summer, buzzing drowsily in the garden, whose wings did not bring him the strange airs of poetry. And the snow, falling softly and suddenly as the first shadow of age upon some golden cheek, brought him its cold air of remote and unattainable beauty. He 'lisped in numbers'; nor could he remember the time when he did not write poetry. Doctor Johnson, with great beauty, applied to him the legend that was murmured about Pindar, saying that as he lay in the cradle, the bees swarmed about his mouth.

Even at this childish age, Pope had an enormous knowledge of, and insight into the nature of English poetry. He had a wide acquaintance, not only with those poets of the past and of his time who were known and widely read in that age, but also with those earlier poets whose readers were few and scattered. In later years, he intended writing a History of English Poetry; but unfortunately this project was abandoned. Waller and

Spenser were perhaps his favourite poets in this early spring, and to these, a little later, was added Dryden. In after life he stated repeatedly that everything he knew about versification he learned from Dryden, and that even at the age of twelve he could distinguish the difference between softness and sweetness in the texture of the several poets; for his feeling for this most important matter of texture was so phenomenally sensitive that had the verses been transformed into flowers, he could have told lily from rose, buttercup from cowslip, no matter how starless and moonless the night, merely by touching one petal. In these matters, he found Dryden to be softer, Waller sweeter; and that the same difference, the same subtle distinction, separated Ovid from Virgil. He believed the *Eclogues* of Virgil to be the *sweetest* poems in the world, and I wish that this could be remembered by those persons who, giving us thorny and stony wildernesses of verse, accuse Virgil of being their master.

Dryden, at this time, was still living, and could be seen; and to this child the dream of seeing Dryden was like the dream of seeing poetry in some bodily form. It meant all romance, all fable, all heroic glory, and Fame in the ilex-grove with her bright helmeted hair. It was while he was still at the school at Hyde Park Corner that Pope, in his passion for Dryden's poetry, induced some friends to take him to the coffee-house where Dryden was usually to be seen, that he might please himself with the sight of the old poet. 'I saw Dryden', he told Spence, 'when I was about twelve years of age. I remember his face well, for I looked upon him with veneration, and observed him very particularly.' He told Wycherley that though he had seen him but this once, he remembered that he was 'plump, of a fresh colour, with a down look, and not very conversable'. It may be remarked, at this time, that poets have rarely been great talkers, excepting when driven by excitement. It is sad to think that Dryden died when Pope was little more than twelve years old, and never knew the greatness of the poet whom he had inspired with such veneration – never knew the identity of the little boy who had once stared at him so earnestly

– if, indeed, Dryden noticed him at all. Many years after, there was to be a strange variation of this incident, when Pope was at the height of his fame, and an unknown and obscure boy gazed upon him as he had gazed upon Dryden. Northcote, in his *Life of Reynolds,* tells us that when he was a young boy Reynolds happened to attend a public auction, at which there was a great crowd. Presently he was surprised by a sudden murmur and humming sound, like that of bees approaching their hive. It was the excited murmuring of the crowd who, leaving the pictures and looking towards the door, left an avenue, through which a tiny deformed figure walked. It was Alexander Pope, who had thus unexpectedly made his appearance. 'Every hand', said Northcote, 'was thrust out to bid him welcome, and the future Sir Joshua Reynolds, then a youth, succeeded, by thrusting his hand under the arm of another person, to catch hold of that of the poet.'

Shortly after the incident in the coffee-house, which, with the performance of the play taken from the Iliad, must have been the two supreme moments of Pope's childhood, he was taken away from school, and went to live with his parents at Binfield, in Windsor Forest. And with this change, his life in the service of poetry began.

CHAPTER III

The Youth in The Forest

WHEN Alexander Pope was six years old, his father retired from business with a small fortune (Doctor Johnson said the fortune was of twenty thousand pounds; Martha Blount, Pope's lifelong friend, said it was ten thousand pounds). Leaving London, Mr Pope bought a small house and twenty acres of ground at Binfield, a happy, sleepy, country place, in the forest, in the neighbourhood of many of the Roman Catholic gentry. Pope has given us a picture of this little country house where he spent the happiest years of his life, those years of childhood and early youth in which he knew not that great men can be envied, or that fame brings its revenge of hatred.

> A little house with trees a-row
> And like its master very low.

Kind, simple Mr Pope and his wife were liked and welcomed by the neighbourhood, and soon became on friendly terms with the other families. Mr Pope devoted much of his time to gardening, and was particularly successful in growing artichokes, a formal and beautiful vegetable whose shape and dignity seems especially suitable to the age of Queen Anne. He was evidently a man of considerable personal quality, and original in his own way. Highly excited by his little son's poetical gifts, he was in the habit of helping this queer child, this little loving changeling, with his poems, correcting them, and sending them back with the message, 'this is a good rhyme', 'this is a bad rhyme', 'for thus', Mrs Pope told Spence, 'my husband called poems.'

Doctor Johnson tells us that, determined not to entrust his money to a Government which persecuted his religion, the old gentleman locked up his £20,000 in a chest, taking from it, bit by bit, such money as was necessary for the household expenses. He lived to be very old, and by the time he died, according to Johnson, there was not much money left. But Sir Leslie Stephen tells us, in contradiction of this story, that Mr

Pope was not quite so helpless about money matters, since he had investments in the French *rentes*, and had, as well, other sources of income. He had, for instance, a property at Windlesham in Surrey, and a yearly charge upon the manor of Ruston in Yorkshire.

Whatever the truth may be of Mr Pope's possession of money or lack of money, whatever the truth may be of much or little money left to his son, never was inheritance more wept over when it came; never was any father more tenderly loved by the humblest son than was this father by this great man.

Mrs Pope, that much-loved mother, to whom her son and his friends referred with tender disrespect as 'the old woman', must have been a simple, modest, kindly woman of great good sense. Not well-educated, she seems to have possessed the tact which comes from a simple soul and a warm heart, for her son's friends, judging by their letters, and even his enemy, Lady Mary Wortley Montagu, appear to have liked her, though Lady Mary was unable to resist making a comparison between Mrs Pope's good sense and her son's entire lack of it. It must have been difficult sometimes, in after life, for homely Mrs Pope to fit into the pattern with her son's friends with all their incredible differences of character, nature, and upbringing – to remain on smooth terms with people so different as Bolingbroke, the great, the terrifying Sarah Duchess of Marlborough, the fractious, vain, and acquisitive Sir Godfrey Kneller, and that rank, terrible, and pitiable man of genius, Dean Swift; but she managed it: and only on one occasion, as far as we know, did she confess herself beaten. That occasion was the time when Voltaire, visiting the house at Twickenham, shocked her so much with his conversation that she left the room. Mrs Pope's portrait shows a homely, shrewd, household face, the kind of aspect that makes us think of all kind homely things – of cold sheets and of home-made bread and butter, and sweet dews on a field of cowslips, and moonlight that is smooth and cold as amber. Her son loved her so much that he allowed her to copy his translation of the Iliad for him, though she spelt everything wrong, and the manuscript had invariably to be written out again, in secret.

But these were early days, and Mrs Pope was untroubled by either the Iliad or Sarah Duchess of Marlborough.

Here, as at every other time in his life, Alexander Pope was surrounded by poetry and the rumours of poetry and the far-off echoes of poetry. Never had trees sheltered a lovelier nightingale than the shades of this forest: for it was not many years since Milton had lived at Horton, where during five years of peacefulness and solitude, he had written 'Lycidas' and 'Comus'.

It is a strange fact that during most of Pope's childhood, Sir William Temple's estate of Moor Park, which lay only twenty miles from Binfield, sheltered that dark, solitary, and terrible madman of genius, Dean Swift, with whom Pope was to form in after life one of the most famous of all literary friendships. Yet they never met at this time. That terrible pedestrian who in his times of madness would 'eat [his meat] walking; for he continued his old habit, and was on his feet ten hours a day', never walked as far as Binfield.

As far as we know, Pope learnt his lessons alone while at Binfield, and at this time 'the successfully employed youth' was, according to himself occupied thus. He told Spence:

'The epic poem, which I began a little after I was twelve, was *Alcander, Prince of Rhodes*. There was an under-water scene in the first book; it was in the Archipelago. I wrote four books toward it of about a thousand verses each; and had the copy by me till I burnt it by the advice of the Bishop of Rochester, a little before he went abroad'. (I am afraid that the reference to Atterbury's advice was one of Pope's less successful flights of imagination. This is proved by one of the Bishop's letters to Pope, though it is equally certain that the poem was not admired in that quarter.) 'I endeavoured', said he (Mr Pope) smiling, 'in this poem to collect all the beauties of the great epic writers into one piece. There was Milton's style in one part, and Cowley's in another; here the style of Spenser imitated, and that of Statius; here Homer and Virgil, and there

Ovid and Claudian!' 'It was an imitative poem, then, as your other exercises were imitative of this or that story.' 'Just that!' (Mr Pope wrote verses imitative of sounds as early as in this epic poem.

> Shield, helms, and swords, all jangle as they hang,
> And sound formidinous with angry clang.)

'There were also some couplets in it which I have since inserted in some of my other poems without any alteration. As in the Essay on Criticism:

> Whose honours with increase of ages grow,
> As streams roll down enlarging as they flow.

'Another couplet in the Dunciad:

> As man's meanders to the vital spring
> Roll all their tides, then back their circles bring.

'In the scattered lessons I used to set myself about that time, I translated above a quarter of the Metamorphoses and that part of Statius which was afterwards printed with the corrections of Walsh.My next work after my epic was my "Pastorals".

'I translated Tully's piece De Senectute in this early period, and there is a copy of it in Lord Oxford's Library.

'My first taking to imitating was not out of vanity but humility. I saw how defective my own things were, and endeavoured to mend my manner by copying good strokes from others. My epic was about two years in hand, from thirteen to fifteen.'

* * *

Being of a nature both fiery and obstinate where poetry was concerned, the fifteen-year old poet, at about this time, determined to leave Binfield for a while, and make a stay in London for the purpose of learning the French and Italian languages, so that their poetry might become known to him. It is not surprising that his family held up their hands in horror at this suggestion; but in the end they gave way to him in this, as in everything else. Perhaps they felt that it was useless to reason with him where any question concerning poetry was involved, for they were accustomed to his obstinacy in this matter. Indeed, Edmund Smith, whose poetry is now almost, if not quite, forgotten, is himself remembered because, having seen Alexander Pope when the poet was aged about fourteen, he became of the opinion that the boy would 'either be a madman or a great poet'.

London does not appear to have helped Pope as far as the French and Italian languages were concerned; for Voltaire, after the notorious occasion when Mrs Pope was so shocked by his stories that she left the room, said that Pope knew nothing of French. He could, however, *read* it, even if he could not speak it fluently, and his ambition was limited to the reading of the language. London life, at that moment, did not attract him, and he remained there only for a few months, after which he returned to Binfield and to his own poetry. But alas, overwork and the successful employment which was so much approved by Doctor Johnson, had produced their effect, and Pope became ill with a nervous breakdown. This may have affected his health in after life, but at the time, though he undoubtedly suffered, he also enjoyed the suffering, to a certain degree. At least he enjoyed writing noble and pathetic letters to his few acquaintances, announcing his approaching dissolution. The family, in all probability, assisted at, and were worn out by, a hundred affecting death-bed scenes. The doctors could do nothing for the invalid, or indeed with him. They could discover no cause for the young poet's illness, for it seemed that he did not suffer from any of the fashionable maladies, which at that moment included such various ailments as (I quote from a contemporary list of deaths from all causes): Age, Ague and Fever, Appoplex and Suddenly, Bleach, Blasted, Scouring, Burns and Scalds, Calenture, Gangrene and Fistula, Wolf, Canker, Soremouth and Thrush, Colick and Wind, Dropsie and Tympany, Excessive Drinking, Falling Sickness, Flux and

Smallpox, Gart, Grief, Headache, Jaundice, Jaw-faln, Imposture, King's Evil, Lethargie, Leprosy, Livergrain, Spleen and Rickets, Lunatick, Megrim, Measles, Mother, Palsie, Plague, Plague in the Guts, Purples and Spotted Fever, Quinsie and Sore Throat, Scurvy, Spleen, Stitch, Stone and Strangury, Sciatica, Swine Pox and Tissick.

From none of these, unless it were from Headache and Lethargie, had the poet elected to suffer.

But happily among the recipients of the farewell letters was an exceedingly practical, sensible Catholic priest of the name of Thomas Southcote, and he, on receiving the letter, set off at once to enlist the help of Dr Radcliffe, a famous physician with a reputation for eccentricity. This good man had no hesitation in telling patients when they had nothing the matter with them. In fact the reputation for eccentricity, and the fact that he was not Court Physician, had been gained partly by his answer in reply to a message from Queen Anne, then Princess Anne, calling him to her bedside. At the moment the Doctor was sitting in his favourite tavern enjoying a bottle of Tokay, and he did not intend to be disturbed by any lady, no matter how important. He therefore sent back a message saying that her Royal Highness's illness was due to nothing but fancy, and that she was as well as anybody else. The Princess, not unnaturally, failed to appreciate the message, and flew into one of her rare rages, and he was dismissed from his post as Court Physician. When, however, Queen Anne was dying, he was summoned to the Palace again, and once more refused to attend her, saying that 'he had taken physic and could not come'. The public was much astonished at such behaviour.

On this occasion, he did not prescribe the worms boiled in milk, and taken lukewarm – that favourite medicine of the eighteenth century – a dose that was administered to those whose illness could not be diagnosed. Instead, he prescribed the simplest and healthiest of all cures – the poet was to work less, and he was to ride every day in the forest. The cure worked marvels, and it is pleasant to think that even twenty years afterwards Pope remembered Southcote's kindness, and on hearing of a vacant abbacy at Avignon, induced Sir Robert Walpole to obtain from Cardinal Fleury this appointment for the old priest.

It was shortly after this illness that Pope began those beautiful Pastorals which, throughout his life, he considered his best work from a technical point of view. And it is true that they are of an astonishing perfection, with their lovely and skilful use of liquids, and their complete absence of overweighting. The elder Mr Pope helped with advice, as was his habit from his son's earliest childhood, and it was the view of these Pastorals, as yet unpublished, that gained for Pope his first friend in the outer world.

Sir William Trumbull, this friend, was a retired statesman of about sixty years of age. Virtuous and kind, he was a man of great culture and learning, and had had as well a distinguished career. For he had been Ambassador at the Porte, and at Venice, and had occupied afterwards the position of Secretary of State to King William III. After his retirement he went to live at his country place, Easthampstead, and here he made the acquaintance of his new neighbour, Mr Pope, and became greatly attracted by the artichokes. Indeed, many presents of these ornamental and formal vegetables passed between the two old gentlemen, and Sir William was in the habit of complaining that he had not the magical touch with artichokes that Mr Pope possessed. That was how the friendship began. But it did not end there, for Sir William Trumbull was a man of great taste in poetry, and realized the genius of the sixteen-year-old poet before any of the outer world had done so, showing a fatherly anxiety and care for his future, watching over him and corresponding with him during his absence.

The sixty-year-old statesman and the sixteen-year-old poet rode together, day by day, in the forest, talking of the great poets of the previous age, and of those who had been dead for a thousand years. Pope taught Sir William to love Milton, that strange new-fangled poet; and in later days it was Sir William Trumbull who first suggested to Pope that he should translate the Iliad.

So time passed, slowly and imperceptibly.

Life in the forest and among the great gardens was so still, so clear, that it seemed, almost, as if everything were taking place under some limpid lake, in the afternoon of a dream. The days passed in solemn beauty, with the young poet and his ancient and experienced friend riding among the great shining leaves of summer, and beside the lake that was so still it appeared like Mr Pope's greenhouses, where, in the heat, the mirage flowers and blazing fruits spread themselves in silence.

But time was not spent in dreaming only, for life was there, waiting to be lived by the youth. There were many large houses shining like heaven among the dark huge trees of the forest, for besides Easthampstead, where Sir William Trumbull, that scholarly retired statesman lived, among his libraries and walled gardens, there were other great gardens where the laughter sounded like rain falling among the leaves, and where, seen through the trees, the white dresses seemed the last trail of snow, or of summer mist. Mapledurham stood in the dark forest, and Whiteknights, where, two years after this time, Pope was to meet Teresa and Martha Blount – Martha, who for the rest of that sad life was to him the dew of the evening, the garden in the forest, the summer days whose warmth seemed the infinite beauty and goodness of God.

CHAPTER IV

The First Battle

It must have been at about this time that Pope became acquainted with William Wycherley, who was then aged sixty-four, and who presented the appearance of an overblown and ancient nodding Roman ruin. Pope said that 'he had the nobleman look' – and certainly nothing in those sixty-four years of carelessness and change and rakishness had sobered him – neither his failure to make both ends meet, through the medium of his friendship with the Duchess of Cleveland (with whom he had scraped acquaintance when, attracted by his handsome appearance, she shouted 'rascal' at him from her chariot window), nor his marriage with the jealous Lady Drogheda, whom he had met in a bookseller's shop, and who would not allow him to continue at Court, nor his seven years' imprisonment in the Fleet, from which he was rescued by King James II, or partially rescued, for Wycherley feared to ask too much, and so mentioned only a part of his debt, and was pulled from the Fleet, eventually, by his grumbling and long-suffering father.

But all these events were forgotten, for he had lost his memory years ago, after an illness; indeed, for forty years before his death, he was without a memory, and relied for this, as for everything else, on chance.

Portraits of Wycherley show a coarse, 'fine' (in the stock sense), overblown face, with a trusting, rather bovine eye, a stupid, Jove-like, bull-strong brow (one expects to see curls like those on the brow of a bull, surrounding that forehead), and a rather pathetic air of careless boldness, the air of a superannuated Goliath who was soon to be stunned by a small and unsuspected David. He was still a wit and a beau, but was himself conscious of the hollowness of the fine-fronted Roman ruin. His memory had gone, and cold winds whistling through his empty head, brought tags of other people's poetry and wit and blew them round and round till he believed them to be his own;

for the poor old man was in the habit of reading himself to sleep, nodding over the works of Montaigne, La Rochefoucauld, Seneca, or Gracian. Always an optimist, his ruined memory helped him in this respect, and by the time the morning came, those nocturnal readings had become works of genius issuing from his own brain.

Wycherley was the first author of repute with whom Pope was acquainted; he had known Dryden; he had been, it was believed, irresistible as a young man; it was certain that he had been a courtier and had lived in the most fashionable world; and it is therefore not to be wondered at that the seventeen-year-old Alexander Pope was dazzled by the idea of him, ruined though he was – ran after him, wrote him letters, believed in him, until, alas, Wycherley, in a reckless fit, asked the youth to assist him in correcting his poems for a new edition. The reasons for this request were that, in his bovine and staring way, he had been much struck by his young friend's ability, and that he knew that his own volume of *Miscellanies* had been a failure. Now he was faced with preparing a revised edition of this for the press, and feeling that his impaired brain was at moments too apt to fly away, and at other moments too sleepy to allow of the unaided preparation of any edition whatsoever, he begged his young friend to look over that 'damned Miscellany of mine, to pick out, if possible, some that may be altered that they may appear in print'. The elder Mr Pope, that wise and shrewd man, saw the perils of the undertaking; but there was nothing to be done: the bugle had blown, and the war horse had charged. At first the charge seems to have offended nobody. 'You have', said Wycherley, 'pruned my faded laurels of some superfluous, sapless, and dead branches, to make the remainder live the longer; and thus, like your master Apollo, you are at once a poet and a physician.' Encouraged by this injudicious praise, Pope pruned the laurels still more drastically, though he still pretended to find the leaves green. He had merely contracted some of the poems, he said, 'as we do sunbeams, to improve their energy and force'; whilst with other verses, he pruned them away altogether, 'as we take branches from a tree to add to their fruit'. But the worst was still to come: for others, he said, he had 'entirely new expressed and turned more into poetry'.

Wycherley did not like this; yet he thanked his young friend, if rather sulkily: 'Let them undergo your purgatory'. And he added, with rather a warning, menacing note, that he hoped the young critic's 'great, vigorous and active mind would not be able to destroy his little, tender and crazy carcase'. However, Pope continued remorselessly with the pruning, and from this time the letters between the old dramatist and his young friend became more and more hollow in tone. Wycherley comforted himself by saying in private that Pope 'was not able to make a suit of clothes, but could perhaps turn an old coat'. Pope, on his side, bemoaned Wycherley's vanished memory; for anyone, if they were to help Wycherley remake his poems, must follow glints and flying feathers, birds that had flown from distant aviaries down all the avenues of his mind. Pope was embarrassed by the incessant quotations (without the quotation marks), and reminiscences in the old gentleman's works. When these were pointed out: 'Gadzooks', said poor old Mr Wycherley, turning rather red and looking very hard at his young friend for a moment, 'so it is. I am immensely obliged to you. Pray cross it out.' 'A stranger phenomenon', Pope told Spence, 'I never did see!' But the phenomenon grew worse, not better. At last, after Pope had been 'plagued up and down for two years', the blow fell: for the intrepid youth suggested to Wycherley that, with regard to a great many of the pieces, it would be as well to destroy the whole design and fabric, and to print them as single thoughts in prose, in the manner of La Rochefoucauld's *Maxims*! Goliath was stunned by such a suggestion, coming to such a man from such a small and inexperienced youth; and the end of the adventure was a letter from Wycherley recalling his outraged progeny, and a letter from Pope declaring that as merely marking the repetitions on the margin of the pages would not dispose of those repetitions, nor rectify the method, nor correct the matter, nor improve the poetry, he would prefer that the manuscripts should be taken out of his hands. Indeed, all was exactly as shrewd Mr Pope had foreseen it would be. The friendship was broken off, and Wycherley lived for five years after this, with nobody to throw stones at other people's birds floating in and out of his head, and intruding their alien voices into his poems. But at the very end, at the last flicker of his life, the friendship was patched up, and Pope visited him as he lay on his deathbed. There is a description of that closing scene in one of Pope's letters to his friend, Edward Blount:

'I know of nothing that will be so interesting to you at present, as some circumstances of the last act of that eminent comic poet, and our friend, Wycherley. He has often told me, as I doubt not he did all his acquaintance, that he would marry as soon as his life was despaired of. Accordingly, a few days before his death, he underwent the ceremony; and joined together those two sacraments which, wise men say, should be the last we receive; for, if you observe, matrimony is placed after extreme unction in our catechism, as a kind of hint of the order of time in which they are to be taken. The old man then lay down, satisfied in the conscience of having by this one act paid his just debts, obliged a woman, who (he was told) had merit, and shown an heroic resentment of the ill-usage of his next heir. Some hundred pounds which he had with the lady discharged those debts; a jointure of four hundred a year made her a recompense; and the nephew he left to comfort himself as well as he could, with the miserable remains of a mortgaged estate. I saw our friend twice after this was done, less peevish in his sickness than he used to be in his health; neither much afraid of dying nor (which in him had been more likely) much ashamed of marrying. The evening before he expired, he called his young wife to the bedside, and earnestly entreated her not to deny him one request, the last he should make. Upon her assurances of consenting to it, he told her: "My dear, it is only this, that you will never marry an old man again." I cannot help remarking that sickness, which often destroys both wit and wisdom, yet seldom has power to remove that talent which we call humour. Mr Wycherley showed his, even in this last compliment; though I think his request a little hard, for why should he bar her from doubling the jointure on the same easy terms.

'So trivial as these circumstances are, I should not be displeased myself to know such trifles, when they concern or characterize any eminent person. The wisest and wittiest of men are seldom wiser or wittier than others in these sober moments. At least one friend ended much in the character he had lived in; and Horace's rule for a play may as well be applied to him as a playwright.

Servetur ad imum
Qualis ab incepto processerit, et sibi constet.'

It is difficult at this distant date to discover the truth about this, or indeed any of Pope's quarrels–and it is the more difficult because of Pope's habit of falsifying his letters. By the time that his correspondence with Wycherley was published, he was ashamed of his admiration for and adulation of the old and ruined wit. He saw that unhappy and bold-fronted ruin in his true light, and, unwilling that his former admiration should be known, omitted some passages from the letters and added others. He failed to publish a letter in which Wycherley gave a gentle remonstrance against too great flatteries; he did not print the phrases that had called forth the remonstrance, and he actually coined a letter to Wycherley out of a letter which he had once written to his friend Caryll. That letter, when given the false light of having been written by Pope to Wycherley, places the writer in the position of remonstrating with the older man of letters for too excessive a flattery towards him. The positions are reversed. No matter how we look at the story of Pope and Wycherley, it gives us a feeling of sadness.

Before this outrage on Wycherley's feelings and poems had been effected, the old dramatist had shown Pope's Pastorals to Walsh, who is now little remembered, but whom Dryden had considered the first critic of the day, and whose praise was then much to be desired. In fact, his encouragement, and the praise

Pope received from him, had a great effect upon the young poet. Walsh, who was Knight of the Shire in Parliament, and who lived at Abberley, in Worcestershire, admired the Pastorals so greatly that he invited Pope to spend part of the summer at Abberley. But that summer seems very far away, and the memory of this famous critic and man of fashion is a strange and ghostly one, for only one echo floats down to us from this periwigged phantom: 'We had several great poets, but we never had one that was correct'; and he advised the seventeen-year-old poet to make correctness his aim.

Meanwhile, the peaceful life at Binfield was undisturbed by the noise of literary quarrels. The young poet soon became acquainted with all the families in the forest, those 'port-wine-coloured gentry' who must have appeared so strange to him. He became a friend of John Caryll, who was not 'port-wine-coloured', and whose uncle, having been in the service of King James the Second, followed that monarch into exile, received a titular peerage, and held office in that mournful and deserted Court, full of echoes of forgotten laughter, dead pomp, and – still more ghostly – sad tears.

But there were other and less safe friends for the youth. It was about this time that he made the acquaintance of that elderly rake Henry Cromwell, whom Gay called 'honest hatless Cromwell with red breeches,' and of whom Doctor Johnson could learn nothing excepting that he rode a-hunting in a tyewig. I have no idea why he was singled out as peculiarly 'honest', but it is supposed that he was called 'hatless' from his habit of standing, hat in hand, before the ladies. For he was a great lady's man. He was at once pedantic – he wrote tiresome and lifeless verses to Celia, epigrams, etc., - and a persistent and untiring rake. Though he was one of the 'port-wine-coloured gentry' of the country (he possessed the estate of Beesby, in Lincolnshire), he was also a man about town, a man of fashion. He frequented Will's coffee-house, he was on speaking terms with actresses, and stood hatless before the reigning beauties of the day. In fact, he had been everywhere, and had seen everything – perhaps, even, a little too much. He had even exchanged snuff with Dryden. He was a friend of Wycherley, Gay and Dennis. But alas, when he entered into company with the Muses, they, unlike the actresses, and the reigning beauties, fled, as we shall see from this distressing poem, preserved among the Bodleian manuscripts, and quoted in Carruthers' *Life of Pope:*

VENUS AT BATH

BY MR CROMWELL

The sportive mistress of the Paphian Court,
Leaving loved Cyprus, did to Bath resort.
Think not Adonis, to avoid her love,
For Venus has as many shapes as Jove;
At church she takes a *Fowler's* face to charm;
Or walks, salutes in *Wentworth's* graceful form;
Her shape is *Morris*; *Abingdon's* her air,
And then she kills with *Scurlock's* eyes and hair.
She baulks a *Worsley,* raffles a *Fingal*;
She's *Balam* at the bath, and *Greville* at the ball.

This poem, however painful, must have made Mr Cromwell universally popular. In addition to writing this, and other poems of the same kind, Mr Cromwell had translated some of Ovid's elegies for Tonson's *Miscellany,* and he revised Pope's translation of Statius. The young poet was excessively proud of knowing such a man of the world, and the man of the world had a very bad effect on him, but this was only to be expected. Under Cromwell's tuition, Pope developed a very 'knowing' air in his letters to his elderly friend, in fact he became, if the truth were told, not a little silly. He was silly, for instance (after a visit to London which he paid in 1708) about Mrs Sappho Nelson, an exceedingly respectable Roman Catholic lady who wrote a little weak and ladylike verse, anonymously, and who was known to, and corresponded with, many of Pope's friends in the forest, including Teresa Blount.

'Sir', Pope wrote to Cromwell, 'I believe it was with me when I left the town, as it is with a great many honest men when they leave the world, whose loss itself they do not so much regret as that of their friends whom they leave behind in it. For

I do not know one thing for which I can envy London, but for your continuing there. Yet I guess you will expect me to recant this expression, when I tell you that Sappho (by which heathenish name you have christened a very orthodox lady) did not accompany me into the country. Well, you have your lady in the town still, and I have my heart in the country still, which being totally unemployed as yet, has the more room in it for my friends, and does not want a corner at your service', etc. etc.

However, a month later, Mrs Sappho Nelson *did* appear in the country, and Pope, in a letter to Cromwell, says: 'I made no question but the news of Sappho's staying behind me in the town would surprise you. But she has since come into the country, and to surprise you more, I will inform you, that the first person she named, when I waited on her, was one Mr Cromwell. What an ascendant have you over all the sex, who could gain the fair one's heart by appearing before her in a long, black, unpowdered periwig; nay, without so much as the very extremities of clean linen in neckcloth and cuffs. I guess that your friend Vertumnus, among all the forms he assumed to win the good graces of Pomona, never took upon him that of a slovenly beau.' This letter has a youthful silliness about it, but I prefer Pope when he is announcing to Cromwell his resolution to 'drown all high thoughts in the Lethe of cowslip wine'.

On one occasion, Cromwell paid a visit to Binfield, and Pope asked him to 'bring a very considerable number of pint bottles with you', because Cromwell had promised to stay for as many days as he brought bottles. We do not know what Mrs Pope thought of her visitor, but he must, at least, have been a welcome contrast, in some ways, to the kindly, hard-hunting, hard-drinking squires of the neighbourhood, although Pope, with his natural gift for adapting himself to his company, seems to have been liked by them. 'I assure you', he tells Cromwell, 'I am looked upon in the neighbourhood for a very sober, well-disposed person; no great hunter, indeed, but a great esteemer of the noble sport, and only unhappy in my want of a constitution for this and that drinking. They all say, 'tis pity I am so sickly, and I think 'tis pity they are so healthy. But I say nothing that may destroy their good opinion of me: I have not quoted one Latin author since I came down, but have learned without book a song of Mr Thomas Durfey's, who is your only poet of tolerable reputation in this country. He makes all the merriment in an entertainment, and, but for him, there would be so miserable a dearth of catches, that, I fear, they would (*sans cérémonie*) put either the parson or me upon making some of 'em. Any man, of any quality, is heartily welcome to the best toping-table of our gentry, who can roundly hum out some fragments or rhapsodies of his works: so that in the same manner as it was said of Homer to his detractors: What! dares any man speak against him who has given so many men to *eat*? (meaning the rhapsodists who lived by repeating his verses), so may it be said of Mr Durfey to his detractors: Dares any one despise him, who has made so many men *drink*? Alas, sir! this is a glory which neither you nor I must ever pretend to. Neither you with your Ovid, nor I with my Statius, can amuse a board of justices and extraordinary squires, or gain one turn of approbation, or laugh of admiration. These things (they would say) are too studious; they may do well enough with such as love reading, but give us your ancient poet, Mr Durfey!'

From this letter we can see that rustic natures were, in the eighteenth century, much what they are now, although the difficulty of travelling, and the slowness and discomfort of the public conveyances, succeeded in isolating the country gentlemen and imposing on them a more rustic character than they have now. They seemed rooted in the mould like the kind homely red strawberries – each country gentleman grew rooted in his own grove, surrounded by his own leaves.

Pope's friends in the country read but little; they did not even read the fashionable *Spectator*, but they enjoyed Durfey's broad humour and noisy, cheerful catches. And Durfey was in the habit of visiting Wiltshire every summer with a fishing party, so, as Mr Carruthers has pointed out, he would probably 'spend a night by the way with his roystering admirers in the

Forest'. But we do not know if Pope was ever brought face to face with him.

Pope's friendship with Cromwell lasted for about three years, and then Cromwell, offended, as it seems, by Pope's poetical mastery, annoyed and frightened by his jokes, began to let the friendship cool. Who was Pope, that small and sickly youth, a mere boy who knew nothing of London life, that he should possess, unexpectedly, real genius? Such a possession was not to be expected, it was verging on impertinence! The matter was not improved by Pope accusing his elderly friend of being a pedant, and by Cromwell discovering, in Pope's work, a plagiarism from Voiture. Both sides were justifiably annoyed, and Cromwell did not write a single note to Pope for a whole year. In fact, the correspondence was only resumed many years later, and then under most unpleasant circumstances. For in 1726 a very different Sappho from Mrs Sappho Nelson – a rather frayed and shop-soiled Sappho, Mrs Sappho Thomas, the ex-mistress of Cromwell, being in poor circumstances, sold to Edmund Curll, the publisher, Pope's letters to Cromwell, which the latter had given her. Pope, very angry at this, attacked Cromwell, who, whilst making a faint denial of guilt, seems to have been vexed at his own foolishness in giving the poetess these letters!

'The great value she expresses for all you write', he explained to the injured poet, 'and her passion for having them, was what prevailed upon me to let her keep them. By the interval of twelve years at least, from her possession to the time of printing them, 'tis manifest that I had not the least ground to apprehend such a design; but as people in great straits bring forth their hoards of gold and most valued jewels, so Sappho had recourse to her hid treasure of letters, and played off not only yours to me, but all those to herself (as the lady's last stake) unto the press. As for me, I hope, when you shall coolly consider the many instances of our being deluded by the females, since that great original of Adam by Eve, you will have a more favourable thought of the undesigning error of, your faithful friend, etc.'

From this letter we can see that Cromwell had not lost his old courtly habit or faith in the power of flattery; but Pope was unconvinced, and unflattered. And when Cromwell died in the following year (1728), he left his estate at Beesby to a second cousin, the Reverend Henry Greene, forty pounds a year to his 'faithful and ancient servant', Mrs Isabel Perez (the 'Lady Isabella' whom we find mentioned in Pope's letters), and, feeling perhaps that the lady had already made quite enough out of him, nothing whatever to Mrs Sappho Thomas. Mr Cromwell, unexpected in all things, was anxious that his body should be decently interred, with a proper respect for his birth, in the parish church of St Clement Danes, where he had been in the habit of standing hatless, when he could spare time from the ladies.

CHAPTER V

The Pastorals

THERE is some uncertainty as to the year in which the Pastorals, the first poems of Pope which found their way into print, were begun; but according to the poet himself, he wrote them in 1704, when he was sixteen years of age. And if it were not for the perpetual mystification he raised round all the events of his life, and his habit of pretending that his poems were written in earlier boyhood than was the fact, so that he might be admired as a prodigy, there would be no reason to doubt this. If we can believe the evidence of Walsh's letters to Wycherley, the former had seen the Pastorals before the 20th of April, 1705; but in this case as in many others, we can only take Pope's word that the letter was genuine. However this may be, if we read the correspondence of Sir George Granville, who was afterwards Lord Lansdowne, we shall see that in any case some of the Pastorals were written before the poet was eighteen years of age; for Sir George Granville promises some correspondent that Wycherley would bring with him a young poet whom he and Walsh had taken under their wing. 'His name is Pope. He is not above seventeen or eighteen years of age; and promises miracles. If he goes on as he has begun, in the Pastoral way, as Virgil first tried his strength, we may hope to see English poetry vie with the Roman, and the swan of Windsor sing as sweetly as the Mantuan.'

What can have been the excitement of the household at Binfield, when the Swan of Windsor received a letter from the great Jacob Tonson, the famous publisher, asking for permission to publish the Pastorals in one of his *Miscellanies*!

The letter was dated the 20th April, 1706, and said:'I have lately seen a Pastoral of yours in Mr Walsh's and Congreve's hands which is extremely fine, and is generally approved of by the best judges in poetry. I remember I have formerly seen you at my shop, and am sorry I did not improve my acquaintance with you. If you design your poem for the press, no person shall be more careful in printing of it, nor no one can give a greater encouragement of it.'

The encouragement, however great, was particularly slow in coming, for Tonson's *Sixth Miscellany*, containing the Pastorals, waited to make its appearance till the 2nd of May, 1709, and then the Pastorals were printed at the end of the book, in which Ambrose Philips' Pastorals occupied the place of honour. The same *Miscellany* contained Pope's translation of the episode of Sarpedon from the Iliad, and, as well, the young poet's version of Chaucer's 'January and May'; and the unfortunate Wycherley, who was as yet undisturbed by his young friend's bird-clapping, contributed a helpful and adulatory preface in the shape of some complimentary verses entitled 'To my Friend Mr Pope on his Pastorals'. The poor old man was excessively pleased with the compliment he had paid, and told people that it was 'a damned fine' one, but the verses were rather somnolent and wandering in tone; yet, strangely enough, exhibit, from time to time, especially in the last, and excessively complimentary couplet, a curious and alien energy, briskness, and correctness. This has given rise to a suspicion in certain minds that Pope was not an entire stranger to the composition. In all probability his aid had been invoked, as on many other occasions to make poor old Wycherley's Muse more presentable, and to dress her more finely.

Pope's Pastorals were much admired, and Walsh, in a letter to Wycherley, stated that, without flattery, it must be admitted that Virgil had written nothing so good at such an early age.

I shall examine the whole of Pope's poetry in a subsequent chapter, since if we are to realize the beauty and variety of his heroic couplets, we must compare the subtlety, and varying, shifting depth and lightness of the texture in each poem with that of the other poems in which the substance is different. But now we must compare him with the threadbare and incompetent Mr Philips.

The Pastorals of Pope, perfect as they are in form, show the excessively delicate sense of texture which was, in later years, to produce within the unvarying structure of the heroic couplet, a thousand variations in speed, a thousand differences in texture, height and depth – whilst holding these differences, these waves, these glittering airs and cobwebs of the summer dew, these dark and terrible ruins of chaos, these drums and multitudes of doom, within this immutable structure. Yet these Pastorals suffer from an over-delicacy and debility which is the result of the poet's physique.

They should be regarded more as experiments in technique than in any other way; for in the Pastorals we see the beginning of those experiments in the effect that subtly varied alliterations have upon rhythm, the effect that the difference of texture has upon rhythm, and those experiments in the variety of accent – changed so subtly that to an inexperienced ear the change is almost imperceptible – experiments that were to enrich the capabilities of poetry.

Though in all histories of Prosody, the effect of alliteration upon *texture*, and the effect on rhythm of variety and changes of accent have been considered, to my knowledge the effect of texture itself upon *rhythm*, and upon *speed*, have never been considered; and of this I shall speak in a later chapter.

To return to the Pastorals: it is, I think, true, that the last, and most lovely of these, 'Autumn', contains more beauty (though all the Pastorals must please us technically) than these lines from Pope's translation of Statius – a work begun earlier than these, but finished later.

'Twas now the time when Phoebus yields to night,
And rising Cynthia sheds her silver light.
Wide o'er the world in solemn pomp she drew
Her airy chariot, hung with pearly dew;
All birds and beasts lie hushed; sleep steals away
The wild desires of men, and toils of day,
And brings, descending through the silent air,
A sweet forgetfulness of human care.

This has not the variation of effect of the later poems, but it has an exquisite lightness which equals, though it is more air-hung (because of the almost entire absence of heavy consonants), the beauty of

Go, gentle gales, and bear my sighs along!
For her, the feather'd quires neglect their song;
For her, the limes their pleasing shades deny;
For her, the lilies hang their heads and die.
Ye flow'rs that droop, forsaken by the spring,
Ye birds that, left by summer, cease to sing,
Ye trees that fade when autumn-heats remove,
Say, is not absence death to those who love?
Go, gentle gales, and bear my sighs away!
Cursed be the fields that cause my Delia's stay;
Fade ev'ry blossom, wither ev'ry tree,
Die ev'ry flower, and perish all but she.
What have I said? where'er my Delia flies,
Let spring attend, and sudden flow'rs arise;
Let op'ning roses knotted oaks adorn,
And liquid amber drop from ev'ry thorn.

The difference in texture between these two extracts shows the poet's extraordinary genius for fitting the texture to the subject. In the first extract he is writing about a calm moonlight night; and in this, in such places as he uses hard consonants – a T, for example, or the much heavier B – the rest of the word has, nearly though not quite always, light vowels; and in any case, two words with hard consonants are never placed together; the nearest they approach to each other is in 'birds and beasts', where the more vigorous sound seems necessary to the sense, and endows it with a heightened life.

In the second quotation, that from the Pastorals, a sunny daylight scene, the movement (because the poem possesses an added vigour which is produced by the nearer juxtaposition of hard consonants), appears to be quicker.

It has been a complaint on the part of many people that the shepherds in Pope's Pastorals are less shepherds than wits from the coffee-houses. I think that this is a just complaint. But it might be remembered that he was writing in a form which is completely foreign to our language, and which has its roots in a tradition which is very distant from ours. It might be remembered also, that although a poet is born, he is not born readymade. Experience, and only experience, leads the poet to perfection.

At this time Pope had given proof, not only in his poems but also in a letter to Henry Cromwell, of his passionate interest in Prosody. The letter is dated 25th November, 1710.

'(1) As to the hiatus, it is certainly to be avoided as often as possible; but on the other hand, since the reason of it is only for the sake of the numbers, so if, to avoid it, we make another fault against their smoothness, methinks the very end of that nicety is destroy'd; as when we say, for instance,

But th' old have interest ever in their view

to avoid the hiatus,

The old have interest.

Does not the ear in this place tell us that the hiatus is smoother, less constrained, and so preferable to the cæsura? (By which it seems he means elision).

'(2) I would except against the use of all expletives in verse, as *do* before verbs plural, or even the frequent use of *did* or *does* to change the termination of the rhyme; all these bring us against the usual manner of speech, and are fillers-up of unnecessary syllables.

'(3) Monosyllable lines, unless very artfully managed, are stiff, languishing, and hard.

'(4) The repeating of the same rhymes within four or six lines of each other, which tire the ear with too much of the like sound.

'(5) The too frequent use of Alexandrines, which are never graceful, but where there is some majesty added to the verse by them, or when there cannot be found a word in them but what is absolutely needful .

'(6) Every nice ear must, I believe, have observed that in any smooth English verse of ten syllables, there is naturally a pause either at the fourth, fifth, or sixth syllables; as for example, Waller:

'At the fifth:

Where'er thy navy spreads her canvas wings,

'At the fourth:

Honour to thee, and peace to all she brings.

'At the sixth:

Like tracks of leverets in morning snow.

'Now I fancy that, to preserve an exact harmony and variety, none of these pauses should be continued above three lines together, without the interposition of another; else it will be very apt to weary the ear with one continued tone – at least it does mine.'

It may be said at this point, that when Pope published his correspondence, this letter was no longer addressed to his offending old-time friend, Henry Cromwell, but to Walsh, and the date affixed was 22nd October, 1706! But whoever the letter was, or was not, addressed to, he adhered rigidly to the rules laid down in it, both in the translation from Statius and in the Pastorals.

On the appearance of the *Miscellany*, it was natural that Pope's Pastorals should be greatly admired by discriminating critics; but it was equally natural that those by Ambrose Philips should enchant a different, and far wider, public. And this enchantment was due to several reasons. Ambrose Philips' Pastorals were insipid and simpering; they gave the public nothing to think about, and they contained nothing which could hurt even the most wool-gathering head. Moreover, whilst repeating the usual formula of lovers' vows, in bucolic language, they make a pretence of originality through the simple means of substituting the English fairies and the rustics of England, for the gods and shepherds of Greece. There was another reason, also, for this popularity. Philips was a noted and prominent character at the famous coffee-house, 'Button's'. He was a zealous Whig, and a vain man who prided himself, like Malvolio, on his stockings – though in this case they were not cross-gartered. He was a loud and unceasing talker, he knew everybody, and he was exceedingly foppish. An amusing story of his vanity is told in Spence's *Anecdotes*.

'One evening in the coffee-house, the conversation turning upon the personal appearance of Julius Cæsar: "I should take him", said Philips (being under the spell of his own appearance) "to have been of a lean make, pale complexion, extremely neat in his dress, and five feet seven inches high", for he thought a great man must necessarily look thus. Doctor Swift, who was present, was much interested, but did not agree. "And I", said the Dean, concealing his amusement, "should take him to have been a plump man, just five feet five inches, not very neatly dressed, in a black gown with pudding sleeves."'

Pope and Swift, indeed, were not the only writers who laughed at Mr Philips; for Henry Carey, in a parody of one of his most puerile poems, invented for him the name 'Namby Pamby', a term which has become part of the English language. Namby was supposed to come from the childish pronunciation of Ambrose, and Pamby was formed by the first letter of Philip's name, and the habit of reduplicating sounds which is natural to babies who can only lisp their first unformed words. But Mr Philips was too conceited a man, and too favoured by Addison, to notice, or to mind, the concerted efforts of the wits against him. His prominence among the Whigs gained for his very inferior poems a popularity that the young and unpolitically-minded Pope could not hope to gain for his. In addition, Addison, who liked an easy life, and mildness in poetry, was delighted with the 'originality' of Ambrose Philips, and praised him in the highest terms. At first there was no rivalry between the two shepherds and worshippers of Pan, and they met at 'Button's', and were polite to each other; and Pope was generous about his rival, even going so far as to agree with the *Tatler* that 'we have no better Eclogues in our language'.

But the tune changed when, only three years after the publication of the volume, essays upon the *Miscellany* began to appear. Eulogistic as the *Spectator* had been on the subject of Ambrose Philips and his genius, the *Guardian* was far more so, and, not content with reviewing Mr Philips once, reviewed him five times, and at great length each time. It is true that the papers were believed to be written by Tickell, who was a member of Mr Philips' admiring audience at 'Button's', and who was also a staunch Whig, and therefore an adherent of Mr Philips' poetry. But the public could not know this, and Pope became furiously angry. For not only was the flattery of Philips excessive and ridiculous, but Pope's Pastorals, which appeared in the same volume, were ignored altogether. This, very naturally, enraged Pope, and it is only fair to say that his rage came as much from a disinterested love of poetry as from an injured vanity. He found, and took, a very amusing and perfectly justifiable revenge. This revenge has been much rebuked by certain of his critics, who affect to see in it one further proof of his malicious and sly character. But those critics are persons who are only too willing to blame him for every episode of his life, and who are unable, or unwilling, to understand his character. The malice, if it existed, was entirely harmless and childlike; and Pope proved, at least, that he had found a way in which to combat biased and uninstructed criticism. He was too fine and instinctive (as well as learned) a poet, not to perceive the difference in value between his own poetry and that of Philips. Yet the *Guardian* insisted that there had been only four true masters of pastoral poetry in more than two thousand years: 'Theocritus, who left his domain to Virgil; Virgil, who left his to his son Spenser; and Spenser, who was succeeded by his eldest born, Philips.' It is scarcely to be imagined that Pope, who knew poetry when he saw it, should have liked that statement. Nor is it to be imagined that he could endure such depths of unillumined criticism as those to which Addison had fallen in comparing Philips with Spenser, and in adding: 'I dare not say they have excelled Virgil! But I may be allowed, for the honour of our language, to suppose it more capable of that pretty rusticity than Latin.'

For the honour of our language Pope, in his turn, set to work to examine this pretty rusticity. He saw no reason why, if Mr Philips could have five papers devoted to his genius in the *Guardian*, a sixth should not follow them. He wrote, accordingly, a sixth paper on these Pastorals, imitating with extraordinary and particular care, the style of the other five; and in this paper he pretended to clear the writer from any charge of bias in not having mentioned the Pastorals of Pope. There is no difference between the exaggerated and uncritical praise of the sixth paper and that of the other five. But in this, by dint of exposing the ridiculous nature of Philips' simplicity in quotations of the utmost absurdity, and by the use of frequent quotations from his own poetry, which only served to throw the absurdity of the others into greater relief, he disposed of the unhappy Mr Philips once and for all.

'It is a justice I owe to Mr Philips', the critic observes gravely, 'to discover these (parts) in which no man can compare with him. First, that beautiful rusticity, of which I shall only produce two instances out of a hundred not yet quoted:

> O woeful day! O day of woe! quoth he,
> And woeful I, who live the day to see!

The simplicity of diction, the melancholy flowing of the numbers, the solemnity of the sound, and the easy turn of the words in our dirge (to make use of our author's expression) are extremely elegant.

'In another of his Pastorals, a shepherd utters a dirge not much inferior to the former, on the following lines:

> Ah me the while! ah me, the luckless day,
> Ah luckless lad! the rather might I say,
> Ah silly I! more silly than my sheep,
> Which on the flowery plain I once did keep.

How he still charms the ear by this artful repetition of the epithets! and how significant is the last verse. I defy the most common reader to repeat them without feeling some motions of compassion.' In contrast to this, 'Mr Pope', says the author, 'has fallen into the same error as Virgil, for his clowns do not converse with the simplicity proper to the country'. Pope ends his paper by remarking that 'after all that hath been said, I hope none think it any injustice to Mr Pope that I forebore to mention him as a Pastoral writer; since, upon the whole, he is of the same class with Moschus and Bion, whom we have excluded that rank, and of whose Eclogues, as well as some of Virgil's, it may be said that (according to the description we have given of this sort of poetry) they are by no means Pastorals, but something better.'

As soon as the paper was completed, Pope sent it anonymously to the *Guardian*. Apparently Steele did not understand that Philips was shown in a ridiculous light, but was deceived by the eulogistic tone of the essay, and, in a spirit of justice, showed it to Pope, declaring that he would 'never publish any paper where one member of the Club was complimented at the expense of another'. Pope, with great generosity, declared that it was only fair to Mr Philips that a paper containing such a just estimate of his genius should be printed; and it *was* printed, and can be found in the *Guardian*, No. 40.

It caused considerable delight, but not to Mr Philips, who was thrown into such a rage that, forgetting the tiny size and deformity of Pope, he kept a birch at 'Button's', and swore that he would use it upon the poet should he dare to appear there. But Pope had fluttered away, and, save for an occasional appearance in the company of Addison and Steele (the former of whom was by this time his acquaintance, the latter being his friend), he preferred, in future, the company at 'Will's,' the coffee-house which had become famous in the past because it was the haunt of Dryden. Mr Philips, therefore, was left to his own gusts of conversation, and to his Whiggish friends.

But Pope had not finished with this luckless shepherd, who certainly was 'more silly than his sheep'. For when *Martin Scriblerus* was published, years afterwards, we find that Pope had remembered Mr Philips very adequately, in that section of the book which is called 'The Art of Sinking in Poetry'. In this, poor Namby Pamby is held up as the greatest master of the 'Infantine', and of 'Inanity, or Nothingness'. 'How prettily' says Pope, 'he asks the sheep to teach him how to bleat:

> Teach me to grieve with bleating moan, my sheep.'

It seems as if the lesson had succeeded!

CHAPTER VI

The Meeting with Teresa and Martha Blount

AS WE have seen, Pope made the acquaintance of Wycherley in the house of Mr Englefield, at Whiteknights in the forest. And there, two years later, when he was nineteen years old, the poet saw the two sisters whose names will for ever be remembered with his, Teresa Blount, and Martha, that everlastingly young and beautiful ghost.

Teresa and Martha Blount were the granddaughters of Mr Englefield, and the daughters of Mr Lister Blount of Mapledurham, near Reading. They came of an ancient family, and were descended from one of two brothers who came to England with William the Conqueror. The family had a romantic history; Charles Blount, the favourite of Queen Elizabeth, sprang from another branch; and they had an ancestress of Spanish royal blood, for in the reign of Edward III a son of Sir John Blount married Sancha de Ayala, a daughter of the House of Castille. From this ancestress Teresa Blount inherited her slanting dark eyes. The sisters therefore came from a house full of the peaceful moonlight ghosts of old love, and haunted, too, by the ghosts of dead chivalry, so that even the wind blowing among the moon-haunted branches, sounded like the clash of lances and the sound of far-off horns. For the famous Sir Walter Blount was another ancestor of the sisters, and so, in the following century, was Sir Michael Blount, the Lieutenant of the Tower of London. It was he, indeed, who bought the Manor of Mapledurham, on the Oxfordshire side of the Thames, and who built there the beautiful Elizabethan house in which the sisters lived. This house was, during the Civil War, besieged by Cromwell's army, and was defended by the Royalist, Sir Charles Blount; but it remained untouched and unspoiled, with its warm gardens shining among the shades of the forest.

When Pope, at the age of nineteen, met the family at Mapledurham, there were three children of this house – the nineteen-year-old Teresa, the seventeen-year-old Martha, and one son, Michael. Gay has described the sisters as 'the fair-haired Martha and Teresa brown', and there is a portrait of the sisters gathering flowers, in which they appear, with their queer sylvan grace, like delicate gazelles from the wild woods – Teresa with her dark eyes, inherited from that far-away Spanish ghost, and her quick foreign look, and Martha with her wild yet gentle slanting blue eyes, like the early spring skies seen through the branches, and her fair hair like the silvery curls of the earliest leaves upon their boughs. The character of the sisters was different, for Teresa was the more circumspect and cautious, and in an innocent and childlike way, the more worldly, and Martha had a happy nature, and a heart as warm as her own walled gardens.

The friendship between the boy and the two lovely sisters was immediate, and at first Pope seems to have been equally devoted to them both. They walked together in the gardens and in the forest when the bells sounded among the leaves, and later, when they could gather the warm apricots and nectarines from the walls of the enclosed gardens. And when Pope walked with his two friends he was no longer 'the little spider', but believed himself to be tall as the heroes'

armed shades,
Glitt'ring thro' the gloomy glades,

and beautiful as the youths who died for love; nor was there any room in his heart for the darkness and pain of deformity.

In Pope's friendship with Teresa and Martha Blount, as in every other event of Pope's life, the time of the events can only be deduced from internal evidence, and it is certain that they were friends in early youth, though Martha Blount, as an old woman with a failing mind, declared that she had only known the poet since the publication of the *Essay on Criticism,* and that she was then 'a very little girl'. But at the time the *Essay on Criticism* was published she was twenty-one years old; and the fact seems to be that in reality she saw the poet first when she was seventeen years of age, and he was nineteen.

Those young and happy days in the forest were unspoiled as yet by the misery that was heaped on Pope – the blackness that was instilled in his veins by Dennis's cruelty, or by the minor and foolish quarrels with Wycherley and Henry Cromwell; for these quarrels did not take place for two or three years after Pope's meeting with the sisters. The two elderly wits and men about town were much given to visiting Whiteknights, where, indeed, they had first met the young poet; they were at this time full of encouragement for him, and of admiration for themselves for having discovered him. The Pastorals had just been published, and poor old Wycherley was mightily pleased with his own damned fine compliment, and was never tired of praising Pope; and of wandering from wit to wit, showing his young protégé's unpublished verses, and growling out that they were damned fine, and remembering Virgil and forgetting him again.

Meanwhile Pope, pleased with the reception of the Pastorals, began to work upon the *Essay on Criticism.* He has succeeded in involving his biographers in the usual muddle as to the date on which the work was begun, having brought about this happy state of affairs by telling Spence, on one occasion, that the *Essay on Criticism* was written in 1709, and published in 1711; on another occasion that he showed Walsh his *Essay on Criticism* in 1706 (he is supposed to have meant 1707). He continued: 'He (Walsh) died the year after'. Whereas Walsh died on the 15th March, 1708. In different editions of Pope's published correspondence with Walsh, the note at one moment says: 'Mr Walsh died at 49 years of age in the year 1708: the year after Mr Pope wrote the Essay on Criticism'. In others the note says: 'Mr Walsh died in 1708, the year after Mr Pope wrote his Essay on Criticism'. The truth, therefore, can be come at only if we find which punctuation is correct.

We shall never know why Pope thought it necessary to bury the facts in this mysterious fashion; but it was his invariable habit to hide all the facts of his life in much the same way as that in which a squirrel buries nuts – allowing them to be discovered, if at all, in the most secret and unexpected places.

We know, however, in spite of all these mystifications, that the *Essay on Criticism* was published on the 15th May, 1711, when Pope was twenty-three years old; and, according to

Lewis, the Catholic bookseller, it passed unnoticed at first, lying 'many days in my shop unnoticed and unread'. But Pope was not going to allow this. Having found that no attention had been aroused by the Essay, he ordered copies to be sent to various noblemen who were known to be interested in literature – to such men as the Duke of Buckingham and Lord Lansdown. These gentlemen showed it to other wits and men of taste, and the sale of the poem began. But long before this, the *Essay* had come to the notice of a very different reader from these polite and lettered gentlemen.

John Dennis was at this time fifty-four years of age, and had spent those fifty-four years in scholarship and in hopeless poverty and unsuccess. He was bitten to the bone by bleak and comfortless poverty, and for this, and for his unsuccess, we must pity him, since none but his own soul could know how far they were responsible for producing in him the black malignancy which was to kill much of the gentleness in Pope's character. Dennis had been a scholar at Cambridge, and he was by now a famous critic; and although this position as a critic did not help him where his poverty was concerned, it had been a medium whereby he had become acquainted with Dryden, Congreve, and Wycherley. Every poem and every drama which he produced, however, failed with the greatest regularity, and in this failure he found the one regularity of his life. Poverty had induced in him an excessive nervous irritability, which found many eccentric outlets; he had, for instance, an unreasonable detestation of the French, and that nation could scarcely be mentioned in his presence without his giving way to an outburst of violence. He was, however, much respected, and much quoted in the coffee-houses. It is difficult to know how the quarrel between Pope and Dennis began. Messrs Elwin and Courthope believe that Dennis had spoken with disapproval of the Pastorals, and certainly this is borne out by the fact that Pope, in his *Epistle to Dr Arbuthnot,* when speaking of his early work, says: 'Yet then did Dennis rave with furious fret.'

It may have been for this reason, or it may have been from a quite harmless sense of fun, that Pope, remembering the grandiose air and dictatorial voice of Dennis, says:

'Twere well might critics still this freedom take,
But Appius reddens at each word you speak,
And stares tremendous, with a threatening eye,
Like some fierce tyrant in old tapestry.

It is difficult to see how a man of Dennis's age and position could have been made angry by this harmless passage, unless he were utterly corrupted by corroding poverty and by that sad and watchful vanity which comes from poverty. However, the name Appius was taken from one of Dennis's peculiarly unsuccessful Tragedies, *Appius and Virginia,* which was born, and died, in 1709. Moreover, Dennis was in the habit of losing his temper, and he was in the habit of using the word 'tremendous,' in the hope that this word would give breadth and splendour to a poverty-stricken line. Therefore, when he saw the verse in question, he burst into a fury which was to have a terrible result upon the young and at that time quite harmless offender.

On the 20th June, 1711, John Dennis published his *Reflections, Critical, and Satyrical, upon a late Rhapsody called an Essay upon Criticism*. In this, he complained that he had been 'attacked in a clandestine manner, in his person instead of his writings.' How this could be, I do not know, for although the *Essay* had been published anonymously, Pope had not kept his authorship secret; and there is no mention at all of John Dennis's person. Dennis's revenge for that very harmless youthful impertinence – if it can even be called an impertinence – is a lasting disgrace to his name. Some of the pamphlet is too coarse to be quoted, but the following passage, if we are to understand subsequent traits in Pope's character, must be allowed to come within the scope of this book:

'I remember a little gentleman whom Mr Walsh used to take into his company, as a double foil to his person and capacity. Enquire between Sunninghill and Oakingham for a young, short, squab gentleman, the very bow of the god of Love, and tell me whether he be a proper author to make personal reflections? He may extol the ancients but he has reason to thank the gods that he was born a modern; for had he been born of

Grecian parents, and his father consequently had by law the absolute disposal of him, his life had been no longer than that of one of his poems, the life of half a day. Let the person of a gentleman of his parts be ever so contemptible, his inward man is ten times more ridiculous; it being impossible that his outward form, though it be that of downright monkey, should differ so much from human shape as his unthinking immaterial part does from human understanding.'

It is impossible to read the paragraph dealing with Pope's bodily deformity without feeling the deepest anger, compassion for its victim, and a kind of horrified pity towards the man who could write such a passage. Pope was at that time barely twenty-three years of age; he was warm-hearted, and compassionate; his mind and his heart were burningly romanticand chivalrous, he was already half in love with Martha Blount, though he, by now conscious of his cold and grinning, grave-struck fate, did not dare confess that love, even to himself. What blackness of despair, what dripping poison, what chaos of the polar night, can have fallen in his heart, ruined by this foolish malignant cruelty?

The black poison which had been instilled into Pope's system was slow in working into each warm vein of the heart; at first he was stunned and bewildered by the pain, lying quite quietly beneath it as he had lain quietly on the heap of stones with which he had been playing when he was a little child of three years old, and a huge and unreasoning beast had knocked him down and injured him. At moments he seemed half numbed, though he was outwardly the same youth that he had been. Indeed, it was not until he knew beyond any doubt that he loved Martha Blount (though he never, excepting for one tragic moment, spoke to any human being of that love) that he realized to the full what Dennis had done to him. Meanwhile, he gave way to every ephemeral fancy, partly for the purpose of deceiving himself as to what had happened to him. For although Pope's real love was unvaryingly given to Martha Blount, his chivalry was easily aroused, and his fancies enjoyed running from place to place like young hares. So, in the very same month as that in which Pope presented Martha

Blount with a copy of the much-sought-after *Miscellany* containing the poem in her honour, we can deduce from the printed correspondence that Pope was immersed in some chivalrous adventure, that he was, in fact, deeply interested in the fortunes or misfortunes of another beauty, 'Mrs W.', who was at one time supposed to have been the subject of the beautiful 'Elegy to the Memory of an Unfortunate Lady'.

Various legends have gathered round the identity of the subject of this Elegy, as round all the episodes in Pope's life. Warton, for instance, believed that she was a lady of the name of Wainsbury; that she was as deformed as Pope himself, and that this was the reason for the bond of sympathy between them; he adds that she did not die by a sword, but that she hanged herself. Hawkins says that she was named Withinsbury. Bowles, in his turn, revived the story told by Voltaire to Condorcet, that the lady was a remote and swan-like beauty, and that she had loved the young Emmanuel Duc de Berry, whom she had known when she was a young girl, at the French Court. All these stories and variations were, in part, due to Pope's habit of mystification, and the cloud palaces of unreality that he raised in his correspondence. But the fact is now certain that whilst the subject of the Elegy is still unknown, the Unfortunate Lady, the Mrs W. of Pope's letters, was a Mrs Weston, the wife of John Weston, of Sutton in Surrey, and the sister of one of the strangest of all soldiers of fortune, Joseph Gage – the extraordinary man whose fantastic success with money was at one time so great that he offered to buy the Crown of Poland and the Island of Sardinia, and to attach Sardinia to Poland as a kitchen garden. Eventually, he lost his fortune through speculating in the Mississippi scheme, but his life continued to change from one fantastic splendour to another; and this Fortunatus, after leading armies for the Spanish King and being rewarded by the present of a silver-mine, died a first-class grandee of Spain.

His sister Elizabeth does not appear to have shared her brother's extraordinary character. As far as we know, she was unremarkable and unnoteworthy, excepting for the fact that she was unhappy in her married life, and was soon separated from her husband. It may be, of course, that she shared her brother's passion for adventure, but very little record remains of her, excepting that she was the author of one of Pope's debacles. Unfortunately for both sides, she found an immediate adherent in Pope, whose craving for adventure could never be satisfied, and he, with that longing for chivalrous romance to which he owed so many of the misunderstandings in his life, espoused the unhappy lady's cause with fire and fury, and interfered in her destiny. He begged Mr Caryll to intercede for her with her guardian, Sir William Goring, and to write to her husband and to her aunt. He quarrelled, or tried to quarrel, with his sister Mrs Rackett and her husband, because they, being older and more sensible than he, refused to set up a state of warfare with their neighbour Mr Weston. The affair ended, of course, exactly as might have been expected. For when Pope had interfered to his heart's desire, the quarrel between Mrs Weston and her husband was patched up, and she returned home. And, equally naturally, Pope received no praise from anybody. He found himself, instead of a hero, the object of censure and the subject of scandal. For the neighbours in the forest had for some time watched him and listened to him whilst he spread a false air of romantic attachment round himself and Mrs Weston, and they had come to the conclusion, which surprised nobody more than Pope (though he had with some skill brought them to it), that he was in love with the lady. What business, they would like to know, had a young unmarried man to interfere in the destiny of an unhappy matron? His sister, Mrs Rackett and her husband, were merely grieved. But the Englefields of Whiteknights, and Mrs Sappho Nelson, were shocked, and showed it. At last even Mrs Weston turned against him, and disapproved of him for his unnecessary zeal. I wonder if the rumours of the scandal reached Mapledurham, and if so, what the justly irritated Martha Blount may have felt!

After this incident, the poet, slightly abashed and confused, tried to exculpate himself by explaining to John Caryll, his confidant and lifelong friend: 'I wrap myself up in the conscience of my integrity, and sleep upon it as soundly as I can'.

He never, as far as we know, saw the Unfortunate Lady again, although she lived till 1724, but he continued to dislike and avoid her husband, and, years afterwards, made a tactless reference to Mr Weston in a letter to Martha Blount.

There are also, in the printed correspondence, references to another Unhappy Lady, but in this matter Pope's conduct was chivalrous without being silly, and did credit both to his heart and to his commonsense. This unhappy lady was a Mrs Cope, a relation of the Carylls; she was the wife of an officer in the army, a base creature who, after he had caused her great misery, deserted her and left her entirely destitute, and dependent upon the mercy of those few friends who remained to her. In this case, Pope went to work calmly and wisely, instead of flying about wildly, and making the object of his interest ridiculous. He interested Caryll in the lady's fate, and, when she settled in France, he made this unhappy and unfriended creature an allowance of £20 a year – a large sum at that time, and one which came from a modest purse. He had met Mrs Cope for the first time in 1712, which was the year of the disaster with the Unfortunate Lady. She lived until 1728, and after her death Pope paid a further sum of £20, due for the bills to surgeons and for the necessities of her lingering illness, to the Abbé Southcote, friend of his boyhood. Mr Carruthers quotes Pope as saying: 'This sum is all I think myself a loser by, because it does her no good'.

This story is typical of the much-maligned Pope throughout his life. But unhappily, it led to a quarrel and an injustice. For the poet, with his usual hot-headedness, accused Caryll of doing nothing to help his relatives; and Caryll was able to convince Pope of the injustice of this accusation, and prove to him that he, also, had helped Mrs Cope with an allowance of £20 a year. The friends, therefore, were reconciled, and it is sad that Pope, who had determined to print his remonstrance to Caryll, should not, also, have published the letter in which he expressed his joy at learning that Caryll was blameless, and his pleasure at his friend's generosity. At the time of the publication of the remonstrance Caryll, his lifelong friend, was lately dead, and it is difficult to understand how Pope could bear to do him this injustice; it can only be imagined that the fatal vanity which was the one grave fault in his character, prevailed for once over that love which was in him so great a strength and beauty. One supposes he was pleased with the remonstrance, and was unable to resist publishing this proof of his own kindly feeling and benevolence, realizing that if he had published Caryll's reply and vindication he would have appeared only hotheaded and impulsive.

The last part of the story is sad; but even so, the affair of Mrs Cope does the poet credit. He was young, he was not rich, and he was already famous and much sought-after: yet he found both the time and money with which to help a deserted and destitute woman who was scarcely even his friend. This episode is only one of the many existent proofs that the charge brought against him that he was cynical in his attitude towards women is untrue, unfounded on reason, for he was deeply chivalrous in his behaviour and invariably idealistic in his thought (in spite of the lines on Sappho); indeed, at times chivalry got the better of good sense, but nothing could teach him any attitude other than this.

He was unteachable, even by the episode of Mrs Weston, although the scandal which resulted had driven him to London. He complained in a letter that 'It is a common practice now for ladies to contract friendships as the great folks in ancient times entered into leagues. They sacrificed a poor animal between them, and commenced inviolable allies *ipso facto*. So now they pull some harmless little creature into pieces, and worry his character together very comfortably. Mrs Nelson and Mrs Englefield have served me just thus; the former of whom has done me all the ill offices that lay in her way, particularly with Mrs Weston and at Whiteknights.'

The 'harmless little creature', being safely in London, began to take lessons in painting from his friend Jervas, a pupil of Sir Godfrey Kneller, and a kindly, generous, but excessively conceited man. He was at this time a fashionable portrait-painter, busily engaged upon the portraits of many of the beauties of his time; he was the author, indeed, of a kind of Gallery of the Famous, which included portraits of Swift, Arbuthnot, and Newton, as well as of Pope. His vanity was due to the fact that he had married a widow worth £20,000; and amusing stories of his self-esteem are endless. On one occasion, having made a copy of a painting by Titian, he perceived immediately that he had outdone that master, and looking from the copy to the original, exclaimed: 'Poor little Tit, how he would stare!'

For a year and a half Pope, who was an inmate of Jervas' house, received daily lessons in painting. Spence, in his *Anecdotes*, tells us: 'I have seen, of Mr Pope's drawing, a grave old Chaucer, from Occleve; a Betterton; a Lucius Verus, large profile; two Turkish heads; a Janizary from the life; Antinous, and St John praying'. Pope himself told Gay in a letter dated the 23rd August, 1713: 'I have thrown away three Dr Swifts, each of which was once my vanity, two Lady Bridgewaters, a Duchess of Montague, half a dozen earls, and one Knight of the Garter.' Carruthers, in his life of the poet, tells us that these were copies, and that Pope did not throw away a portrait of Betterton the actor, copied from Sir Godfrey Kneller, adding that this portrait was placed in the collection of the poet's friend Murray, Lord Mansfield. At the time Carruthers' *Life of Pope* was published (1855) another original picture by Pope was in existence, in Ketley Parsonage, Wellington, Salop; this picture (the frontispiece of the *Essay on Man*) was the property of the vicar of that time, Mr Thompson Stoneham, and is a rather pessimistic affair, entirely deprived of any vestige of *joie de vivre,* painted in water-colours, and accompanied by such gloomy symbols as a philosopher blowing bubbles in the air, a death's head crowned with laurel, and the broken pillars and the fallen statue which were a necessity to the century.

It is believed by some (I do not know on what grounds) that Pope at this time determined to become a professional painter, since he was under the necessity of earning money; but he was very shortsighted, and suffered from headaches and a lack of talent, so the scheme was soon abandoned.

However, with these second-hand representations of nature, and expressions of repentance conveyed through symbols, as well as with his literary career, Pope managed to pass the time with as good a grace as possible, until the Forest had forgotten the affair.

CHAPTER VII

On 'The Rape of the Lock'

AND ON THE MEETING WITH SOME NEW FRIENDS

BEFORE he succeeded in disposing, for the time being, of the unhappy Ambrose Philips, Pope had, as we have already seen, continued the making of poetry. We have seen, in the last chapter, how the enmity aroused by the *Essay on Criticism* was to destroy the happiness and much of the gentleness which were among the most beautiful traits in Pope's character. The poem, however, had aroused an enormous interest in the most powerful literary circle of the day – that of Addison and Steele.

In that age of the worship of wit, when intellect was valued at a higher rate than at any other time since the Athenian age, Addison was, in some ways, the most popular man in England; and his taste was regarded as flawless. That taste had not included Pope's Pastorals, preferring in their stead the insipid works of Mr Philips; but the *Essay on Criticism* was further from the poet and nearer to the wit, and was understood by Addison. That good-tempered, generous, but rather priggish man, commended the *Essay* as a masterpiece of its kind, but rebuked Pope for 'some strokes which had for their purpose belittling modern genius'. The mind which could prefer the Pastorals of Philips to the Pastorals of Pope was complacent towards modern genius, but even so, it should be remembered that the belittled geniuses who were attacked were, besides Dennis, Milbourne and Blackmore, and that they were belittled because they had attacked Dryden. The review in the *Spectator* was unsigned, but Pope imagined it to have been written either by Addison or by Steele. He therefore, with his usual caution, wrote letters to both these pontiffs, thanking them in the warmest terms. Steele's letter in answer to Pope's denied his authorship of the review, and promised to make Pope acquainted with the real author, who was, as Pope had hoped, Addison.

Pope was, accordingly, introduced to Addison, at Button's

Coffee House, but the acquaintance never became a cordial one. The characters of the men differed too widely. Addison was good-hearted, perhaps a little too consciously so, was kind, but rather too deliberately open and just. He might be described as the first of a long line of literary cricketers, for he was always 'playing the game' or being manly and above guile about one thing or another. Manliness and uprightness were the keynote of that character which had been – as Pope told Spence – destined to adorn the Church. ('Mr Addison originally designed to have taken orders, and was diverted from that design by being sent abroad in so encouraging a manner. It was from thence he began to think of public posts.') It must be admitted that Addison had certain opportunities of exhibiting his gifts in this direction. He had, for instance, a stepson, the young Lord Warwick, who was much addicted to riotous living, who, indeed, in the pursuit of vain and frivolous pleasures, would stick at almost nothing. He had even been known to invite Pope to lobster-parties. This course of conduct led Addison, in the end, to invite his stepson to quite another kind of treat: 'I have sent for you,' he told that unsatisfactory young gentleman, tenderly, 'to show you how a Christian can die' – an invitation that roused Doctor Johnson to a frenzy of enthusiasm. 'What effect', says the Doctor, 'this awful scene had on the Earl, I know not; he likewise died himself in a short time. In Tickell's excellent *Elegy* on his friend are these lines:

> He taught us how to live; and oh! too high
> The price of knowledge, taught us how to die.

He alludes, as he told Dr Young, to this moving interview.'

Pope might be regarded as the antithesis of this character; for although he spent a large part of his life in doing kindnesses, and although he was the truest and loyalest of friends, he had the unfortunate inhibition against speaking the truth to which I have referred; and this did not agree with Addison's cricketing spirit. Again, Addison did not enjoy the presence of an equal, or a master mind; he must be the first of his circle, therefore Pope's acquaintance with the great Addison did not develop into friendship, and even the acquaintanceship was of a cool order. Richard Steele, on the other hand, realized Pope's genius (though not till after poor Mr Philips had been disposed of), and their friendship was warm and continual.

During the stay in London which led to his meeting with Addison and Steele, Pope made another, and a more beloved friend. This was John Gay, and the friendship lasted until Gay's death, and beyond it. The happy, kindly nature of this childlike creature had survived the misery of his childhood, which had been dark with poverty and with a most unchildlike labour; for, his parents dying when he was only ten years old, he had been apprenticed to a silk mercer, and had known long hours of work in stuffy surroundings, and much unfriended wretchedness. He had, however, been able to free himself before his articles were over, and in 1708 produced a poem in blank verse called 'Wine' – a compliment to the then admired Mr John Philips' poem 'Cyder'. How Gay existed at that time, nobody knows, but it is probable that he did hack-work for booksellers, and lived as wretchedly as many another author. He was, however, by the time that Pope met him, more or less famous as a writer, and this fame procured for him, at the age of twenty-four, the place of steward or secretary to the old Duchess of Monmouth. Doctor Johnson rebukes poor Gay for his loss of independence, but the loss does not seem to have spoilt that simple creature in the least. He was one of those characters that are born to be looked after, to be treated like children all through their lives. He had a childlike delight in finery and good food – (alas, how little he can have had of either until that rebuked loss of independence!). He liked plenty of ribbons and a fine wig, and to stay at Bath where he was surrounded by beauties; and these loves and tastes were a constant source of amusement to himself and to his friends, all of whom loved him with great devotion and laughed at him endlessly. He did not mind being laughed at – regarding it as a proof that he was loved. At first his career was not very successful, but *The Beggar's Opera* and *Polly* (the former work having been inspired by Dean Swift's typical request that he should write some Newgate Pastorals) procured for him all the ribbons that he could possibly want, and, as well, a home in the house of the Duke of Queensberry, where he was petted like a child. That fantastic and strange woman, the Duchess, with her odd clothes, her fly-away air, and her disconcerting speeches and brave battles, was devoted to him, and the Duke looked after his money, giving it to him as he needed it; and scolding him affectionately for his extravagance. Pope, on his side, loved Gay with all the tenderness of his nature, and was inconsolable at his death.

On the 26th July, 1711, shortly after the appearance of the *Essay on Criticism,* we find Steele suggesting to Pope that he should write some words for music, though how the *Essay* could have suggested that to him, while the Pastorals failed to do so, we shall never know. Pope wrote, in answer to this request, the 'Ode on Saint Cecilia's Day', a poem which has been unfavourably compared with Dryden's Ode on the same subject, and it must be admitted that Pope's is less splendid, as a whole. But it contains several superb, and many beautiful lines. How superb, for instance, is

> Thy stone, O Sisyphus, stands still,
> Ixion rests upon his wheel.

It is difficult to understand how the poet who could produce these lines could also produce the anti-climax of some of the lines in this poem.

Then again, how beautiful are the couplets:

> By the hero's armed shades,
> Glitt'ring thro' the gloomy glades,
> By the youths that died for love,
> Wand'ring in the myrtle grove,

Followed by the disaster:

> Restore, restore Eurydice to life;
> Oh, take the husband, or return the wife!

Richard Steele was responsible (and this is less to his credit) for *The Messiah,* a pastoral composition, which appeared in the *Spectator* of the 14th May, 1712. It is not one of Pope's successful works, as the very smoothness of the texture, which had formed the beauty of the Pastorals, was completely out of place in this context. He had not yet attained the terrible command over accumulated quantities that he showed in *The Dunciad,* and *The Messiah* therefore is a sacred scene more in the manner of Carlo Dolci than of Michael Angelo.

The first draft of *The Rape of the Lock* appeared later in the same month that had seen the publication of *The Messiah* (the complete, and lovelier version was not, it is believed, finished till December 1715). The first, and very incomplete version of this lovely masterpiece was published in *A Miscellany* by Bernard Lintot, and contained as well, Pope's translation of the first book of the *Thebais* of Statius, the paraphrase of Chaucer's 'The Wife of Bath' and 'The Lines to a Young Lady' – a tribute which is now known as *The Epistle to Martha Blount.* The first version of *The Rape of the Lock* consisted of two cantos only, and the poet declared that the writing of these had taken him only a fortnight. It has been held by some of his biographers that *The Rape of the Lock* was the cause of the coolness with Addison, since Addison advised Pope against lengthening the poem, and it has been imagined that, since the longer version contained some of the greatest perfections to be found in Pope's verse, Pope believed the advice to be due to jealousy. But it is far likelier that Pope was angry with Addison because of his attitude towards John Dennis when Pope undertook Addison's defence against Dennis.

The Rape of the Lock, that miracle of the summer air, airy and glittering as the nets of the summer light and early dew over the strawberry beds – a poem so airy that it might have been woven by the long fingers of the sylphs in their dark and glittering Indian gauzes, floating like a little wind among the jewelled dark dews on the leaves of the fruit-trees – this flawless poem was written as the result of a quarrel between two Roman Catholic families, friends of the Carylls. The young and impetuous Lord Petre, who was twenty-two years old, cut off a lock from the head of Miss Arabella Fermor, the famous beauty. Miss Fermor was exceedingly angry. Her family was, if anything, angrier; the battle grew in size, and Lord Petre's family joined in. At last Caryll, hoping to pacify both sides, suggested that Pope should write a poem on the subject, showing the incident in the airiest light, in the hope that it would restore a sense of perspective to both the enraged families. Pope, accordingly, wrote the first draft of *The Rape of the Lock*, but unfortunately, far from calming the combatants, it added a fresh victim, for Pope had the very slightest acquaintance with the lady, who, instead of being enchanted at being the inspiration of one of the loveliest poems in the English language, became more angry, and more insulted, whilst Sir George Brown of Kiddington, the Sir Plume of the poem, was ruffled as if by a storm of wind, was furious at being made ridiculous, and vowed vengeance. Indeed, he joined forces with the enraged Mr Weston, the husband of the Unfortunate Lady, in his campaign against Pope, and that injured poet, whose reputation in the Forest had not quite recovered, as yet, from his championship of the Lady in question, felt his position to be a little precarious.

Meanwhile, Pope was at work upon the descriptive part of *Windsor Forest*, which was not, however, published till 1713, by which time Lord Lansdowne had suggested that Pope should write the concluding lines, dealing with the Peace of Utrecht. The poem is more polished even than the Pastorals, and it is evident that more experience had gone to it than to the making of these – (the two works were begun at the same time). But though, for the reason of its greater polish and perfection, *Windsor Forest* cannot be regarded as such an early work, it belongs to his imitative period, and must be considered in relation with this. 'The Design', says Doctor Johnson, 'is evidently derived from Cooper's Hill, with some attention to Waller's poem on the Park: but Pope cannot be denied to excel his masters in variety and elegance, and in the art of interchanging description, narrative, and morality.'

Alas, that 'morality' which is so often the downfall of poets, tripped up the poet in *Windsor Forest* more than once, as in these lines:

> Fair Liberty, Britannia's goddess, rears
> Her cheerful head, and leads the golden years.

Patriotism, too, and loyalty to the reigning house, were responsible for a few tumbles. Here is a remarkable instance:

> At length great Anna said – 'Let discord cease!'
> She said, the world obeyed, and all was peace!

Messrs Elwin and Courthope complain that Pope had forced Father Thames to bow low before Queen Anne like a Lord Mayor presenting an address; and I am afraid there is some justice in this complaint, for the passage referred to has a very urban, not to say municipal, note. But the poem contains very great beauties, such as these:

> Ev'n the wild heath displays her purple dyes,
> And 'midst the desert fruitful fields arise,
> That crowned with tufted trees and springing corn,
> Like verdant isles the sable waste adorn.
> Let India boast her plants, nor envy we
> The weeping amber, or the balmy tree.

And these more splendid lines:

> The shady empire shall retain no trace
> Of war or blood, but in the sylvan chace;

A less great technician would have made a complete failure of the last quoted couplet, with its varying A sounds.

It was about this time that Pope met Dean Swift and their lifelong friendship began. At the time of their meeting, Swift was forty-six years of age, and Pope was but twenty-five; the one was a rank and terrible madman of genius, the other a man of genius whose deformity and ill-health made him subject to fits of rage – yet not once in their friendship of thirty-one years was there a quarrel (if we except the unfortunate affair about the Dean's letters – the truth of which it is impossible to find, since each authority and every document contradict all the others). There was no shade of a quarrel, though, years later, Swift was troubled in his deafness because Pope's physical weakness made it impossible for him to shout loudly enough. Pope's admiration for every aspect, even for the physical aspect, of Swift was immense. 'The picture of Dr Swift', he told Spence, 'is very like him; though his face has a look of dullness in it, he has very particular eyes: they are quite azure as the heavens, and there's a very uncommon archness in them.'

How were those eyes changed in Swift's last and appalling illness, after he had seen the being who most loved him and whom he most loved, dead of the long misery caused by that madness in his nature which would not let him acknowledge her, or his love for her! It is impossible to read without suffering that moving funeral oration, written as she lay dead – that belated tribute of love, which breaks off suddenly in the middle, with the words 'my head aches', and is continued only on the next day, like some stony and hopeless route march which had to be accomplished: '*January 29th*: My head aches, and I can write no more.'

'*January 30, Tuesday*:

'This is the night of the funeral, which my sickness will not suffer me to attend. It is now nine at night, and I am removed into another appartment, that I may not see the light in the church, which is just over against the window of my bedchamber. With all the softness of temper that became a lady, she had the personal courage of a hero ...'

In Swift's last illness, the blindness of the mind was equalled by the blindness of the eyes. For one of those eyes which Pope had noticed for 'their look of uncommon archness' was devoured by an inflammation, the size of an egg, so that he was not easily restrained by five attendants from tearing out his eye. The inflammation subsided, but he sank into a lethargy, silent as the darkest grave, and motionless as the dead: there was no Stella to comfort him now. So, after a year of complete silence, broken only by one sentence, uttered when he was told that the usual bonfires were being lit to celebrate his birthday: 'It is all folly, they had better let it alone' – he died.

But this was thirty years before that time, and Swift was unaware of his approaching fate. He had come to England nearly three years before on business in connection with the twentieths which the Irish clergy were obliged to pay to the Crown; and also because he hoped to obtain some good clerical appointment which would enable him to live in the society of his fellow-writers and wits. Only the year before he came to England (in 1709), he had asked for preferment from the Earl of Halifax – for he hoped to obtain the reversion of Dr South's prebend at Westminster. 'Pray, my lord, desire Dr South to die about the fall of the leaf.' This Christian prayer was not answered, for though the leaves fell, Dr South did not, and Swift wrote again to Lord Halifax, entreating that if 'the gentle winter' did not remove the unnecessary Dr South, Swift might instead be appointed Bishop of Cork, since there was some hope that the existent Bishop might die, as he had the spotted fever. This cleric was less persistent than Dr South, and left the Bishopric vacant, but the heartless Lord Halifax conferred it, not upon the Christian Dean, but upon the Provost of Trinity College. This naturally enraged Swift, and the fact that he was a violent Tory and a fiery ally of Harley and Bolingbroke did not improve matters. But the very work which had made his fame, *A Tale of a Tub,* stood in the way of his preferment, and after all his trouble, all his aid in restoring the Tories to power, and all his pious wishes about other clerics, he was, in the end, obliged to return to his exile in Ireland, and to remain, for the rest of his life, the Dean of St Patrick's. To this office he was appointed in 1713. The Tories did not cease to find him useful, and, about three months after the time when he returned to Ireland, he was recalled to London once more, in order to arbitrate between Harley and Bolingbroke, whose open quarrels threatened to break up the Tory Ministry. It was on this occasion that he met Pope, and that their friendship began. Their correspondence began at the end of 1713, and letters were exchanged between them unvaryingly for twenty-six years. The correspondence ceased only with Swift's madness. The friendship began through Swift's admiration of the poem *Windsor Forest*; but though it can be said that whilst this brought him one friend, it must also be acknowledged that it nearly deprived him of another.

It is sad to think that with the publication of *Windsor Forest* Pope succeeded in hurting the feelings of Sir William Trumbull, his earliest and kindest friend. In a letter to another acquaintance, the old diplomat complained, with an evident sense of hurt, that he had suggested the writing of the poem, yet that his name was not so much as mentioned.

In short, the years 1712 and 1713, though they brought

Alexander Pope increasing fame, and a number of new and important acquaintances, cannot be regarded as having been uniformly happy. The families in the forest regarded him askance, because of his interference in Mrs Weston's affairs; he had made fresh enemies in the unreasoning and stupid Fermor, and in Sir George Brown; he had hurt the feelings of Sir William Trumbull, and, finally, he had aroused the public school and cricketing spirit in Addison. It was in 1713, during the more or less enforced visit to London to which I have referred, that Pope had his first taste of Addison's literary cricketing. The young poet had been invited by Addison to write a prologue for the tragedy of *Cato*, and had, therefore, found himself to a certain extent involved in the fate of the play, which was produced on the 14th of April, 1713, amidst violent applause, and, as Pope explains, a great effort on the part of Whigs and Tories to endow it with a political significance. The political excitement was great, and Mr Addison sat in a side box with three or four friends, and two or three flasks of burgundy and champagne. Pope's prologue, which had given him additional fame, appeared on the 18th of April, in the *Guardian*, which had by now succeeded the old *Spectator*. Unluckily, this prologue had been preceded, not very long before, by the appearance of the five papers on Mr Philips' Pastorals, to which I have referred in a previous chapter. Pope was not, therefore, convinced at the moment of the friendliness of Addison, and, as we have seen, he hastened to give Mr Philips a sixth review. This episode, for some reason, aroused Addison's cricketing spirit, and that spirit was awakened still further by Pope's anonymously-published 'Narrative of Dr Robert Norris on the Frenzy of J.D.' This narrative was called forth by Dennis's attack on Addison – for, enraged at seeing the tragedy of *Cato* prefaced by his enemy Pope, Dennis had written a furious and insulting review of the play. This gave Pope an opportunity to revenge himself upon Dennis; and he seized the chance. The narrative in question has been much blamed for its cruelty by such critics as Sir Leslie Stephen (who have thought it unnecessary to blame Dennis for his murder of the heart of Pope), but

I can discover in Pope's 'Narrative' only one cruel remark ('By the fireside lay three pennyworth of coal in a *Spectator*') and one coarse phrase, an allusion to an ordinary medical procedure. But neither the cruelty nor the coarseness enter into comparison with the cruelty and coarseness which Dennis exhibited towards Pope, and which Addison had not thought it necessary to rebuke. Pope, however, he did rebuke, and to this end he induced Sir Richard Steele to write the following letter to Lintot, the publisher of the 'Narrative'. The letter is dated 4th August, 1713.

'Mr Lintot,

'Mr Addison desires me to tell you he wholly disapproves of the manner of treating Mr Dennis in a little pamphlet by way of Dr Norris' account. When he thinks fit to take notice of Mr Dennis' objections to his writings, he will do it in a way Mr Dennis shall have no just reason to complain of; but when the papers above mentioned were offered to be communicated to him, he said he could not, either in honour or in conscience, be privy to such a treatment, and was sorry to hear of it.

'I am, Sir, your very humble servant,

'RICHARD STEELE'

In this manner was the public school spirit vindicated. The letter gave Dennis a further opportunity for attacking Pope, and he seized it, printing the letter in the Preface to his 'Remarks on *The Rape of the Lock*' (1728). Carruthers, in his *Life of Pope,* says of the letter written by Steele at the instigation of Addison, that 'It was at once insulting Pope and affording Dennis a triumph at the expense of a man of genius, who had come forward, if not in defence of Addison, at least in ridicule of Addison's unfair and malignant critic'.

Pope was to have a still further example of the cricketing spirit in Addison's advice to Lady Mary Wortley that she should leave the poet's company, 'he will play you one ill trick or another'.

It must, however, be admitted that Addison could behave with nobility and generosity, and this was shown by his treatment of Pope after that much-irritated man had written the famous satire on Addison, but this was at a later time, and will be dealt with later.

CHAPTER VIII

Minor Episodes

1713-1714

As we saw in a previous chapter, Pope had by this time become acquainted with Dean Swift; and the first memorial of an acquaintance which turned, in later years, to one of the most famous of all literary friendships, was the founding of the Scriblerus Club. The chief members of this society or club, were the Dean, Pope, Gay, and Dr Arbuthnot, the remarkable and kindly Scotsman who had superseded the errant Dr Radcliffe as Physician-Extraordinary to Queen Anne in 1705. Dr Arbuthnot's wit and kindliness were much appreciated by Dean Swift, who believed that, as a wit, he exceeded all his friends. The Doctor wrote *The History of John Bull, The Art of Political Lying,* and several other skits; and he had a hand in the strange papers which were the joint productions of the Club. He was kind and carefree, and he enjoyed fame so little that he was in the habit of allowing his children to make kites of his papers.

Besides these members might be numbered Bishop Atterbury, of whom we shall hear more in later years, and Parnell, the intemperate and unhappy Irish poet, who lived from 1679 to 1718. The Club was not in any real sense a social or party club; it had no club-house, nor were there any regular meetings. It was more in the nature of a society of men of letters, all of whom were intimate friends, and who were in the habit of meeting together with no formality, to discuss plans for literary work, plots for stories, and projects for keeping Grub Street and their other enemies in some kind of order.

The great memorial of the Scriblerus Club is that strange work called *The Life and Writings of Martin Scriblerus,* for which Swift, Pope, and Arbuthnot were responsible. This work included a strange description of a universe ruled over by 'satyrs' – (wise and educated apes), together with the world-history of these – literary criticism, in which poor Namby-

Pamby was once more a principal Aunt Sally, and other, more obscure, papers. It may also have been responsible for the idea of *The Grub Street Journal,* but of this there is no certainty. And we owe at least the foundation of those great works, *Gulliver's Travels* and *The Dunciad,* to the Club. Both of these must have been discussed at the meetings, and we know from many sources that the Dean, whenever he felt in a savage mood, was in the habit of writing to Pope asking when *The Dunciad* would be finished and the downfall of Grub Street completed. The Club lasted until 1714, when political turmoil caused any Tory Society to be looked upon with a not unnatural suspicion.

As we have seen in the previous chapter, Pope, whose misdemeanours were by this time half forgiven, but not entirely forgotten, by the Forest, spent his summer between London and Binfield. Whilst he was in London he worked at painting with Jervas in the mornings, and spent his evenings talking to other men of letters, and men interested in the arts. Unable, throughout his life, to avoid 'showing off', he wrote at about this time a letter calculated to impress the countrified Mr Caryll, though for some inscrutable reason, in the editions of the Correspondence published in 1735, Pope chose to readdress the letter to Addison! 'This minute, perhaps', he assured his friend, 'I am above the stars, with a thousand systems round about me, looking forward into the vast abyss of eternity, and losing my whole comprehension in the boundless spaces of the extended creation, in dialogues with Whiston and the astronomers' – (no wonder that kind old Sir William Trumbull wrote imploring him, at about this time, to beware of tavern company!) – 'the next moment I am below all trifles, even grovelling with T(idcombe) in the very centre of nonsense.'

This unfortunate gentleman, Mr Tidcombe, was a friend of Cromwell's and one of the company at 'Will's, and he appears to have been generally tolerated and despised. Pope, in one letter to Cromwell, remarks: 'I would as soon write like Durfey as live like Tidcombe, whose beastly, laughable life is at once nasty and diverting.' At one time the diversion in question became too much for Will's Coffee House, and he was turned out, but after some time he was allowed to return, to the pleasure at least of one person, Mr Cromwell, the unexpected frequenter of the church of St Clement Danes, who could find nobody but this rather disreputable gentleman with whom to talk about Church history and the Fathers.

At about this time it is evident that Pope realised he would never be a painter, for he told his friend Gay: 'I have rivalled St Luke himself in painting, and, as it is said an angel came and finished his piece so you would swear a devil put the last hand to mine, it is so begrimed and besmutted. However, I comfort myself with a Christian reflection that I have not broken the commandments, for my pictures are not the likeness of anything in heaven above, or in the earth below, or in the waters under the earth. Neither will anybody adore or worship them, except the Indians should have a sight of them, who, they tell us, worship certain pagods or idols purely for their ugliness.'

Meanwhile, Pope wrote more or less regularly for the *Guardian,* and I intend to quote one paper which shows all the insensitiveness and brutality for which he has been so justly blamed. This paper appeared on the 21st May, 1713, and was on the subject of the treatment of animals. The beastly cruelty from which these poor subjects of man could then find no redress, was almost universal in this age, though there were remarkable exceptions from this general cruelty. There was, for instance, Monsieur Saint-Evremond, though his habit of kindliness seems to have been induced as much by slovenliness as by charity. Of this old gentleman, a character who would have interested Edmund Lear, Pope remarked to Spence: 'Monsieur Saint-Evremond would talk for ever. He was a great epicure and as great a sloven. He lived, you know, to a great old age, and in the latter part of his life used to be always feeding his ducks; or the fowls that he kept in his chamber. He had a great variety of them, and other sorts of animals, all over his house. He used always to say, "that when we grow old, and our own spirits decay, it reanimates one to have a number of living creatures about one, and to be much with them."'

These admirable sentiments were shared, though in a less

eccentric way, by Pope, whose tender-heartedness was shown in a thousand ways. When Spence expressed to Pope his pleasure at the prospect of seeing a certain Dr Hales, because 'he is so worthy and good a man.' Pope answered: 'Yes, he is a very good man; only I'm sorry he has his hands so much imbrued in blood.' – 'What, he cuts up rats?' – 'Ay, and dogs too! (with what emphasis and concern he spoke it). Indeed, he commits most of these barbarities, with the thought of being of use to man: but how do we know, that we have a right to kill creatures that we are so little above as dogs, for our curiosity, or even for some use to us.' 'I used to carry it too far', Spence remarked: 'I thought they had reason as well as we.' 'So they have to be sure', was the reply. 'All our disputes about that, are only disputes about words. Man has reason enough only to know what is necessary for him to know; and dogs have just that too.' 'But then they must have souls too; as unperishable in their nature as ours?' 'And what harm would that be to us?', the poet replied.

It was in this spirit, therefore, compassionate of their miseries and unfriended state, that Pope wrote the paper for the *Guardian* which will be found in Appendix A at the end of this book, printed in full.

But another, and infinitely greater project than any article in the *Guardian*, was being formed. This was the plan to translate the Iliad. Translations from the classics were pleasing to the culture of the time; booksellers were eager for them, and now that Chapman was regarded as rough and uncouth, and the translations of Hobbes and Ogilby were found to be, if not uncouth (Ogilby had started life as a dancing master, and a certain smoothness of manners, if not of manner, is discernible in his literary work), at least insufficient, it was clearly indicated that a new translation would be valuable. Isaiah, as we have seen, had been forced into a periwig (not entirely to his advantage), but what did not suit Isaiah, as no original poem evolved from the collaboration between that prophet and Pope, did at least produce the effect of a great new and original work when applied to Homer.

By this time Pope was acquainted with all the more powerful Ministers in the Government, and it was thought, therefore, that publication by subscription was the best way of ensuring a large response. Pope's proposals for this subscription volume of the Iliad, together with an introduction, notes and maps, were brought out in October 1713, and the response was beyond anything that could have been hoped for. Jacob Tonson had been the first publisher to make an offer for the translation, but that cautious business man was easily outdone by Bernard Lintot, who offered to pay £200 for each volume, and to supply sets to the subscribers free of charge. This translation was the foundation of Pope's fortune – apart from the small fortune which had been his father's: for there were six volumes at a guinea each, and the subscribers numbered nearly 600. It is believed, indeed, that Pope received £5,000 or £6,000 from the Iliad alone – an enormous sum in those days. But the work took him six years, and the worry and trouble was immense. All the poet's friends were diligent in finding subscribers; Dean Swift was indefatigable; so was Lord Lansdowne; and even Addison (if it is possible to believe that the letters published under his names in Pope's correspondence were written by that great man) offered to help in producing subscribers. But, as Pope remarked afterwards, Addison found not one.

In December Pope returned to the forest, and continued his work of enlarging *The Rape of the Lock,* which had to be finished before the Iliad was begun. The thought of this immense task hung over him heavily; he began to repent that it had ever been considered, and years afterwards he told Spence that in the beginning of his translation of the Iliad, he would have been grateful to anybody who would be kind enough to hang him. Afterwards, he got into the way of working at it, and did the rest of it with pleasure; but the beginning was hard and uncomfortable to him.

It was from Binfield, on the 8th December, 1713, that Pope's first letter was written to Swift, who had by this time been rewarded (and disappointed) by the Deanery of St Patrick, and who had gone to Dublin in the summer to be instituted Dean.

Except for a short visit to London in March 1714, Pope seems to have spent the first part of this year in the Forest, working at the Iliad. His friend Parnell, who was to write the introduction to the Iliad, paid an immense visit to Binfield in the spring, in order to collaborate with Pope in his study of the classical commentators – since he was a better Greek scholar than the poet. On the 4th May the two friends invited John Gay to join them, and spend a month in the Forest, surrounded by books, and friendship, and the comforts that he loved.

Meanwhile Dean Swift, angry with the political folly of his friends Harley and Bolingbroke, and in a fit of dudgeon because he had failed to obtain the post of historiographer to Queen Anne, had become the paying guest of a country clergyman, thirty miles from Binfield, and there revenged himself on the world in general by boring himself into a state of muleish muteness; since for days together he would refuse to speak. He lived the simple life, and paid the country clergyman (who must have found him an unaccountable guest) a guinea a week for his board. The life at the vicarage does not seem to have held many excitements, apart from the Dean's behaviour, which could not be relied upon, and which contained many possibilities; but Swift seems to have revelled in his self-inflicted boredom, for he told Vanessa in a letter (after explaining that he liked his reverend host very well): 'Mr Geree is such a melancholy, thoughtful man, partly from nature and partly from solitude, that I shall soon catch the spleen from him. His wife has been this month twenty miles off at her father's, and will not return within these ten days, and perhaps the house will be worse when she comes. I read all day, or walk, and do not speak so many words as I have now writ in three days.'

How different was this country life to that of Windsor Park, when the Dean was in favour with the Court and the Court was in favour with him. How much (in spite of his grumbling) he had enjoyed the hunts in the Park, which he had described to Stella, with stout Queen Anne following in 'a chaise with one horse, which she drives herself, and drives furiously, like Jehu, and is a mighty hunter, like Nimrod'. Besides these more savage pleasures, there were the joys of the summer days when the Court went out for a day's picnicking in the Park. All the Maids of Honour and Ladies-in-Waiting were there, with the Countess of Shrewsbury, who seemed very interested in the Dean; she was in a one-horse chaise, but he was on horseback, and wore his coat of bright camlet, faced with red velvet, and with silver buttons. They talked all day beneath the great velvet faunal leaves that cast a shadow like pale green water... But now he was out of favour with the Court, and the Court was out of favour with him, and he dined every day at twelve, supped early 'with a glass of ale', and went to bed at ten o'clock – this being a sure sign that something had vexed the Dean.

Pope and Parnell invaded this hermitage on a Sunday in the first week of July, and spent a few days with the Dean; and it must be admitted that Pope, whose temper was not so curmudgeonly as that of his reverend friend, was more amused than stunned by the boredom, and wrote a less depressed, though equally eloquent description of that Tartarean gloom, to Arbuthnot:

'From Letcombe, near Wantage.
July 4.

'This day, the envoys deputed to Dean Swift arrived here during the time of Divine service. They were received at the back door, and, having paid the usual compliments on their part, and received the usual chidings on that of the dean, were introduced to his landlady and entertained with a pint of the Lord Bolingbroke's Florence. The health of that great minister was drunk in that pint, together with the Lord Treasurer's, whose wine we also wished for; after which were commemorated Dr Arbuthnot and Mr Lewis in a sort of cider, plentiful in these parts, and not altogether unknown in the taverns of London. There was likewise a sideboard of coffee, which the dean roasted with his own hands, his landlady attending all the while that office was performing. He talked of politics over coffee with the air and style of an old statesman, who had known something formerly, but was shamefully ignorant of the last three weeks. When we mentioned the welfare of England he laughed at us, and said Muscovy would become a flourishing empire very shortly. He seems to have wrong notions of the British Court, but gave us a hint as if he had a correspondence with the King of Sweden.'

In the intervals of discussing the possibilities of Muscovy becoming a flourishing empire, it is probable that the three friends talked about politics and books, and about their future plans for work. It may have been at this time, awed by the rather gloomy pastoral atmosphere in this savage retreat, that Pope planned the writing of some American pastorals. He must certainly have discussed these with Swift, and we know that he spoke of them at some other time, to Gay; and he told Spence: 'It might be a very pretty subject for any good genius that way, to write American pastorals; or rather pastorals adapted to the manners of *several of the ruder nations, as well as the Americans*. I once had a thought of writing such, and talked it over with Gay; but other things came in my way and took me off from it.'

The italics are mine. It is sad to think that the pastorals adapted to that rude nation were never written, for the phrase alone gives us some idea of the delight these would have aroused, although it is difficult to imagine how the smoothness of Pope's technique could have been adapted to the *gaucherie* in question.

It may have been at this time, also, that the Dean thought out that suggestion which he, at some later time, made to Gay, on the subject of Pastorals – that suggestion which led to the writing of *The Beggar's Opera*. 'Dr Swift had been observing once to Mr Gay, what an odd pretty sort of thing a Newgate Pastoral might make.' In short, the gloom, at once imprisoning and pastoral, of this clerical retreat might, indeed, suggest Pastorals of any kind, if that kind was sufficiently uncivil.

It may be assumed that the talk on this, as on many other occasions, must have been very largely about books. The Dean's taste differed slightly from that of Pope: he was in the habit of recommending the poet to read Rabelais, scolding him with some impatience for not doing so, but Pope found 'many things in his works, in which he could not see any manner of meaning driven in, that I could never read him with any patience'. Pope's taste in poetry was completely unaffected by the likes and dislikes of the age. He admired and read Chaucer, and knew intimately the work of all the minor Elizabethan and Jacobean and Carolean writers: he found Webster, Marston, Goff, Kyd, and Massinger, 'tolerable' writers of tragedy in the time of Ben Jonson – whom, apparently, he did not admire; he thought Carew 'a bad Waller', Crashaw (strangely enough) 'a worse sort of Cowley'; Herbert 'lower than Crashaw, Sir John Beaumont higher, and Donne a good deal so'. He admired Donne very greatly, and especially for his wit. Indeed, it is probable that no poet of his or any other time, was more learned on the subject of his art.

It was these matters that the friends discussed as they walked among the fields, where the dust was so dry that it might have been the dust of all the dead philosophers in the world – where the Martha-coloured scabious waved aimlessly, and, from time to time, from far beyond the cotton-nightcap trees, there came a sound of crazy hen-coop laughter, cackling at the Dean, and raising the black anger that was lying like some dark well in his heart.

After this visit, Pope returned to Binfield and to Homer. He was in the habit of beginning the translation as the early light clustered like pale flowers round the shutters of his country window, and the first rustic sounds buzzed, like bees, through the great trees that floated on the faunal breeze as though they were magical islands. Then the poet, in his thread satin nightgown, striped red and white and lined with a yellow Persian, and wearing a nightcap of the same, sat up in bed to drink his early dish of chocolate, and fought again the battles of the Greek foam-borne heroes against Troy. Several verses were written each morning, before the poet left his bed. In translating both the Iliad and the Odyssey, his habit was to follow his first inspiration, and then, after he had followed it where it led him, to correct each book; first he compared it with the original, and then with those translations which he found most admirable; then, last of all, he gave great care to the correction of the versification, for he is one of the most corrected, as he is one of the most correct, of poets. There is hardly a line in the manuscript which is not altered; a million words are changed, and the construction is turned a million times. The original copy of the translation became the property of Bolingbroke, and after his death it passed into the hands of Mallet, the mean creature who was willing to betray and blacken Pope, after the poet's death, in order to earn Bolingbroke's favour. Mallet's widow presented it in 1766 to the British Museum; where it lies in a hundred bits and pieces, written on the back of architectural plans for the Tusculum that was so soon to come into being at Twickenham, and on the backs of household bills, and of letters from Steele and Addison; one piece of paper, indeed, was used to enfold the cherries which he sent to Teresa and Martha Blount from Mr Dancastle's garden (the ladies by this time were reconciled to him, and the episode of Mrs Weston was, if not forgotten, at least passed over in silence):

'Dear Ladies', the letter runs, 'You have here all the fruit Mr Dancastle's garden affords, that I could find in any degree of ripeness. They were on the trees at eleven o'clock this morning, and I hope will be with you before night. Pray return, sealed up by the bearer, every single bit of paper that wraps them up; for they are the only copies of this part of Homer. If the fruit is not as good as I wish, let the gallantry of this wrapping paper make up for it: I am yours (no signature).'

CHAPTER IX

The Publication of Homer

THE WORK of translating Homer continued, with Parnell at the poet's elbow, helping him with advice and scholarship; Pope's writing-table was crammed with such translations as the verse translation by Eobanus Hessius, of whom Doctor Johnson said that he was an unwearying writer of Latin verses; and the French translations by La Valerie, and the English translations by Hobbes, Chapman, and Ogilby. In the autumn of 1714 Pope travelled to Oxford; for he had decided to enlarge the scope of his notes to the translation of the Iliad, and his stay in Oxford would give him opportunities of studying otherwise unobtainable books, and also certain maps of ancient Greece. He and his engraver then undertook the work of 'removing mountains' (as he told Edward Blount in a letter); they altered the course of rivers, they abolished towns; finally, their defiance of the work of Providence went so far that they forced the Scamander to flow into the Ægean Sea instead of into the Hellespont.

Meanwhile the rumours of the translation, and the poet's growing and phenomenal fame, brought him new, fashionable, and influential friends; and fresh acquaintances among the Ministers. Lord Halifax was numbered among these, but he could not be regarded as an easy friend, at first sight, for Pope to handle, since his character had to be explained by Dr Garth, who knew him well. Lord Halifax was rather painfully anxious to appear as a man of scholarship and taste, and as both these pretensions were built upon no foundations, and might collapse at any moment, the hours which he spent in upholding them seemed like an eternity both to himself and to his companions. At first, he startled Pope considerably. When the translation of the first two or three books of the Iliad was completed, the man of scholarship and taste, in his character of patron of the arts, expressed his wish to Pope that he should have the pleasure of hearing them read at his house. The poet complied with the request, the other members of the audience being Addison, Congreve, and Garth. What was the poet's astonishment (since he knew that those particular lines could not be bettered as regards versification) when Lord Halifax, who, whilst listening, had, beneath his ivy-bush of a wig, invented and worn an owl-like face expressive of great concentration and learning, stopped him from time to time, with mingled civility and gravity. 'I beg your pardon, Mr Pope', said Lord Halifax, with an evident wish to help; 'but there is something in that passage which does not quite please me. Be so good as to mark the place, and consider it a little more at your leisure. I am sure you can give it a better turn'. Pope returned from this visit in Dr Garth's chariot, and, as they drove along, remarked that Lord Halifax's 'loose and general observations had placed him in a good deal of difficulty, since he could not conceive what his Lordship had found to complain of in any of those verses'. Garth laughed heartily at Pope's embarrassment, and explained that when the poet knew Lord Halifax better, these exhibitions of learning and good taste would puzzle him less. 'You need not look over the places', the Doctor continued: 'all you need to do is to call on him two or three months hence, thank him for his kind observations on those passages, and read them to him as altered'. Pope did as he was advised, and Lord Halifax was enraptured with the result: 'Ay now, Mr Pope', the man of learning exclaimed: 'they are perfectly right; nothing could be better.'

The first volume of Homer, containing the first four books of the Iliad, with a Preface, Essay, and Observations, appeared in June, 1715, and caused, in all probability, the greatest excitement ever aroused by any book of verse. The coffee-houses buzzed like hives of bees, the drawing-rooms were a-flutter with excited ladies. The King subscribed £200 to the undertaking, and the Prince of Wales subscribed £100, while the other subscribers numbered 573, and of these, several had put down their names for more than one copy; never, therefore, had any poet been so highly paid before, nor has any been so highly paid since that time, for when the six volumes of the

Iliad were completed, the entire sum which Pope gained, if we include the £200 a volume which had already been paid to him by the publisher, was £5,320 4*s*. Of this sum, a certain part had to be paid to those who had assisted him in the translation and in preparing the notes. Parnell was the author of the *Life of Homer,* and this was a present from him to Pope – (a present which was not received too generously by the poet, who said that the trouble he had had in correcting this was so great that he could have written it himself with less). Broome, Jortin and a third person whose name we do not know, had been employed in the work of consulting Eustathius, and in compiling the notes. These helpers, according to Sir Leslie Stephen, were none too generously paid in return for their services to Pope. But I find this difficult to believe, since a lack of generosity was never among the poet's faults. It is pleasant to think that Lintot, the publisher (who was usually referred to in Pope's letters as 'that fool', as though there were no other fool) behaved with real courage and generosity in this enterprise. He was at first exposed to a great loss, for some person was mean enough to produce a pirated edition of the first four books (the pirated edition was printed in Holland) and Lintot was obliged, therefore, to withdraw the folio edition he had printed, and to publish it in another format, in duodecimo; but he was brave enough to produce 7,500 copies of that issue. This was a courageous undertaking, but his faith in the poet was justly rewarded, for he made a fortune from the enterprise, and this fortune was on such a scale that he, and his son after him, served as High Sheriffs of Sussex.

Unfortunately, the very same week as that in which Pope's first volume of Homer was published, was chosen by Mr Tickell, the admirer and chosen companion of Namby-Pamby Philips, and the author of the five encomiums on his Pastorals which appeared in the *Guardian,* for the appearance of his own translation of the first book of the Iliad. This started a fresh battle, and Pope admitted that the nation was not more violently divided into the rival camps of Tories and Whigs, than were 'the idle fellows of the feather' about the two translations.

Lintot, on the 10th of June, wrote to Pope saying that 400 copies of his translation had been delivered to the subscribers, and, at the same time, that he had sent the poet Tickell's book to amuse an idle hour. He adds: 'It is already condemned here, and the malice and juggle at Button's is the conversation of those who have spare moments from politics.'

It is instructive to compare the two versions, and, at the same time, to see the alterations Pope has made in his finished copy from the original draft.

Pope's finished version runs thus:

The wrath of Peleus' son, the direful spring
Of all the Grecian woes, O goddess, sing!
That wrath which hurl'd to Pluto's gloomy reign
The souls of mighty chiefs untimely slain;
Whose limbs unbury'd on the naked shore
Devouring dogs and hungry vultures tore.
Since great Achilles and Atrides strove,
Such was the sov'reign doom, and such the will of Jove.
Declare, O Muse! in what ill-fated hour
Sprung the fierce strife, from what offended pow'r?
Latona's son a dire contagion spread,
And heap'd the camp with mountains of the dead;
The King of Men his reverend priest defy'd,
And, for the king's offence, the people dy'd.

The first few lines of this were changed thus, from the unfinished version, or rough draft:

The stern Pelides' rage, O goddess, sing,
wrath
Of all the woes of Greece the fatal spring,
Grecian
That strew'd with warriors dead the Phrygian plain,
heroes
And peopled the dark hell with heroes slain;
fill'd the shady hell with chiefs untimely.

The reason for most of these alterations is obvious. The 'i' sound in Pelides, quickly followed by the 'a' in rage, unhinge the line by giving too violent a lilting movement to the middle of the line. The word 'direful' with its huge fiery smoky sound, is obviously better, in its place in the line, than the smaller and rather tiny sound of 'fatal', which is not heavy enough. The elided sound in 'warriors' with its stressed first syllable, and the two following syllables that are so unweighted they can be regarded, less in the nature of one unstressed syllable and one half-stressed syllable, than in the nature of one quarter-stressed and one half-stressed syllable – this gives a ridiculous head-over-heels effect, which is totally unsuitable, and is, above all, unsuitable to the stateliness of the heroic couplet.

On the other hand, the line

> And peopled the dark hell with heroes slain

and still more, the expression 'the shady hell' are, to my, mind, so beautiful that I regret that (had it been possible technically to make use of these), Pope did not decide upon these or one of these, in preference to the line as it stands in the finished version. But whether we like Pope's finished version or his unfinished version, these beautiful couplets make poor Mr Tickell's translation of the same lines look very strange:

> Achilles' fatal wrath, whence discord rose
> That brought the sons of Greece unmingled woes,
> O goddess sing! Full many a hero's ghost
> Was driven untimely to the infernal coast,
> While in promiscuous heaps their bodies lay,
> A feast for dogs and every bird of prey.
> So did the sire of gods and men fulfil
> His steadfast purpose and almighty will,
> What time the haughty chiefs their jars began,
> Atrides, king of men, and Peleus' godlike son.
> What god in strife the princes did engage?
> Apollo burning with vindictive rage
> Against the scornful king whose impious pride
> His priest dishonour'd and his power defied;
> Hence swift contagion by the gods' commands
> Swept through the camp and thinn'd the Grecian bands.

A wretched affair, in which Mr Tickell presents the lamentable appearance of a dwarfed Laocoon, inextricably interwined in a serpentine entanglement of S's.

Addison, who had preferred Namby-Pamby Philips' Pastorals to those of Pope, naturally preferred Tickell's Homer to that of Pope; and considerable ill-feeling was aroused. Even Gay was unable to resist repeating malicious remarks, and inflaming the naturally irritable character of the poet: 'I am informed', he told Pope, 'that at Button's your character is made very free with as to morals, etc, and Mr Addison says that your translation and Tickell's are both well done, but that the latter has more of Homer'. Pope, who was as touchy as Addison himself on the subject of moral worth, naturally did not forget any aspersions cast upon his own. It should be remembered, however, that Tickell's behaviour in the matter of the translation was very creditable; for he prefixed the book by a few remarks in which he announced that when he began translating Homer he had intended translating the whole of the Iliad, but 'had had the pleasure of being diverted from that design by finding the work had fallen into a much abler hand'. Indeed, his only design in publishing that small fragment from the Iliad was to interest the reading public in a projected translation of the Odyssey.

Pope never questioned the fairness of Tickell, but with Addison it was a very different matter. He could have induced Tickell to withhold the translation, but had not done so, though, on the other hand, it could not be said that he had canvassed for Tickell. But Pope's entire hope in life, as far as money was concerned, was centred on the translation from Homer. By that he must stand or fall. Either he would remain poor throughout his life, or he would earn a sufficient fortune by it; either his career and reputation as a poet would be placed beyond dispute, or it would be ruined, so great was the undertaking. Addison, who could have helped him to the fame and fortune he deserved, did nothing, save to hinder him. He allowed Tickell's translation to be published when, as Mr Carruthers has pointed out, Pope's entire hope in life was placed in jeopardy by this; Addison's praises of Tickell were repeated by all the Whigs at Button's, to the detriment of Pope. And the poet could not forget how Addison had censured the 'strokes of ill-nature' in the *Essay on Criticism* – (strokes so gentle that nobody who did not suffer from megalomania could have resented them). He could not forget, too, the preference Addison had shown for the Pastorals of Philips, nor how he had, as Mr Carruthers pointed out, 'employed Steele to write a gratuitous and insulting letter, condemning the satire on Dennis'.

For these reasons, slowly but surely, Pope's resentment against Addison grew, until it burst into flame. On the 15th of July, in a letter to Craggs, there are remarks about 'the little senate of Cato', and Addison's 'humblest slave, Tickell, whose translation of Homer was undertaken merely to please the Great Turk in poetry, who can never bear a brother on the throne, and who must be surrounded by whisperers, mutes, nodders and winkers, whose duty in life it is to strangle the reputation of all rivals'. This letter was the basis of that great satire, the character of Atticus, or Addison, which was printed first in the *St James Journal* of the 15th December, 1722, and was then printed in *Cythereia* 1723 (April). There is no evidence that it was printed with Pope's knowledge before 1727. Having been revised, it was made part of the *Epistle to Dr. Arbuthnot*.

The couplets, originally, ran thus:

If Dennis writes and rails in furious pet,
I'll answer Dennis when I am in debt;
If meagre Gildon draws his meaner quill,
I wish the man a dinner and sit still;
But should there one whose better stars conspire
To form a Bard, and raise a genius higher;
Blest with each talent, and each art to please,
And born to live, converse, and write with ease;
Should such a *one*, resolved to reign alone,
Bear, like a Turk, no brother near the throne,
View him with jealous, yet with scornful eyes,
Hate him for arts, that caused himself to rise;
Damn with faint praise, assent with civil leer,
And without sneering teach the rest to sneer,
Alike reserved to blame or to commend,
A tim'rous foe and a suspicious friend;
Fearing e'en fools; by flatterers besieged,

And so obliging that he ne'er obliged;
Willing to wound, and yet afraid to strike,
Just hit the fault, and hesitate dislike;
Who when two wits on rival themes contest,
Approves of both but likes the worst the best.
Like Cato, give his little senate laws
And sits attentive to his own applause,
While wits and templars ev'ry sentence raise,
And wonder with a foolish face of praise
Who would not laugh if such a man there be?
Who would not weep if Addison were he?

This was afterwards changed in various ways, before it found a final place in the *Epistle to Dr Arbuthnot* with many altered lines.

The new version of the portrait is to be found in the *Miscellanies* of 1727, and Mr Carruthers believes that until then Pope believed the rival translator of Homer to be Tickell, and not, as he hinted afterwards to Spence, Addison himself.

However, at the time of which I am writing, the Satire was yet, if not unthought of, at least unwritten. The coldness between Pope and Addison had already lasted for a year; but, during that time, Addison had expressed a wish to use his influence in Pope's favour at Court; he had, according to himself, been afraid that Swift might have carried the poet too far into the enemy's camp, politically; this had placed him in a delicate position; but now, he believed that everything was safe, and he would exert himself in Pope's favour. Pope, in his turn, told Jervas that he admired Addison's character, but that he expected nothing but civility from him, however much he wished for Addison's friendship; and he added that Namby-Pamby Philips had, with scandalous meanness, raised suspicions of him in the mind of Addison. He then wrote to Addison, with considerable spirit, saying that all he hoped from the Whigs was that *civility* which he got from the Tories – since he was 'neither so proud as to be insensible of any good office, nor so humble as not to dare heartily to despise any man who does me an injustice'. He could not believe that Addison could speak one thing and think another, and therefore, to show his belief in Addison's sincerity, he would ask him to read over the first two books of the translation of Homer, and, as well, to point out the 'strokes of ill-nature' in the *Essay on Criticism* with which he had found fault in his essay in the *Spectator*. The *Essay* was about to be reprinted, and Pope promised, if these faults were pointed out to him, to erase them. He received, however, no reply in writing; and the verbal reply was that Addison would be glad to be excused from reading the first book of the translation, since his friend Mr Tickell was about to publish his version, undertaken when he was at Oxford; and should Addison read Pope's, it would have the air of double-dealing. Pope understood this, and felt no resentment. But unfortunately the matter did not stop there. Fresh people made mischief; what they heard, they repeated, and what they did not hear, they invented. The young Lord Warwick, whose respect for his prospective stepfather Addison may, or may not, have been tempered by an all too filial lack of affection, told Pope that 'it was in vain for him to endeavour to be well with Mr Addison; that his (Addison's) jealous temper would never admit of a settled friendship between them'. Spence repeats to us Pope's version of the conversation; Pope is reported to have said: 'and to convince me of what he had said, Lord Warwick assured me that Addison had encouraged Gildon to publish those scandals, and had given him ten guineas after they were published. The next day, while I was heated with what I had heard, I wrote a letter to Mr Addison, to let him know that I was not unacquainted with this behaviour of his, that if I was to speak severely of him in return for it, it should not be in such a dirty way; that I should rather tell him fairly of his faults, and allow his good qualities; and that it should be something in the following manner. I then subjoined the first sketch of what has since been called my satire on Addison. He used me very civilly ever after; and never did me any injustice that I know of from that time to his death, which was about three years later.'

Ayre, in his Memoir of Pope, has a much more amusing and characteristic (though I am afraid entirely fictitious) account of a meeting between Pope and Addison, which had been arranged by Steele in order that the quarrel might be made up. I wish it were a true record, for it shows each of the great men in his finest feathers, and riding on the highest hobby-horses of moral worth which even they had succeeded in mounting. 'Mr Pope spoke in such a manner as plainly showed he thought Mr Addison the aggressor, and expected him to condescend and own himself the cause of the breach between them. But he was deceived; for Mr Addison, without appearing to be in anger, though quite overcome with it, began a formal speech, said that he had always wished him well, and often had endeavoured to be his friend, and as such advised him, if his nature was capable of it, to divest himself of part of his vanity, which was too great for his merit; said that he had not arrived yet to that pitch of excellence he might imagine, or think his most partial readers imagined; said when he and Sir Richard Steele corrected his verses they had a different air; he reminded Mr Pope of the amendments of a line in the poem called the Messiah, by Sir Richard Steele. (See note to *The Messiah*.) He proceeded to lay before him all the mistakes and inaccuracies hinted at by the crowd of scribblers and writers, some good, some bad, who had attacked Mr Pope, and added many things which he objected to; speaking of Mr Pope's Homer, he said to be sure he was not to blame to get so large a sum of money, but it was an ill-executed thing, and not equal to Tickell's who had all the spirit of Homer. This afterwards appeared to be wrote by Mr Addison, though Tickell's name was made use of. Mr Addison concluded, still in a low hollow voice of feigned temper, that he was not solicitous about his own fame as a poet, but of truth; that he had quitted the Muses to enter into the business of the public; and all that he spoke was through friendship and a desire that Mr Pope, as he would do if he was much humbler, might look better to the world. Mr Gay spoke a few words in answer before Mr Pope, but his expectations from the Court made him very cautious. It was not so with our poet: he told Mr Addison he appealed from his judgment, did not esteem him able to correct him, and that he had long known him too well to expect any friendship; upbraided him with being a pensioner from his youth, sacrificing the very learning that was purchased with the public money to a mean thirst for power; that he was sent abroad to encourage literature, and had always endeavoured to cuff down new-fledged merit. At last the contest grew so warm, that they parted without any ceremony, and Mr Pope immediately wrote those verses which are not thought by all to be a very false character of Mr Addison.'

A superb scene, and I can hardly forgive those scholars who, in their 'solicitude for truth' have pronounced it to be unfounded on fact. It must be said that Lord Warwick's story about Gildon having been paid ten guineas by Addison in order to publish scandals about Pope in his *Life of Wycherley*, is untrue also. Nothing in Addison's character, which was dignified, upright, and almost devoid of malice, gives the least reason for such a suspicion being entertained against him. The wretched Gildon was a poor hack-writer, and there is no evidence that Addison knew him; Addison was above the publication of scandal, and, in any case, he knew enough of the eighteen-year-old Lord Warwick's character not to trust him with the story of such a mean act, had he committed it. The only blame which could attach to Addison with regard to Pope's translation of Homer, was that in his personal friendship for Tickell, he was too anxious to serve him, and allowed this friendship to undermine his critical sense. But he made a noble reparation for this fault, and under difficult circumstances. Pope's satire on Addison was written early in 1716, and was sent to Addison, if we may believe Spence, almost as soon as it was written. Addison's only reply was to praise Pope's Homer, in the most generous terms, in a paper contained in the *Freeholder* on 7th May. 'The illiterate among our countrymen may learn to judge from Dryden's Virgil of the most perfect epic performance; and those parts of Homer which have already been published by Mr Pope, give us reason to think that the Iliad will appear in English with as little disadvantage to that immortal poem.'

Addison had, in many ways, a generous and wide-minded character, and in this episode he showed it.

CHAPTER X

The Friendship with Teresa and Martha Blount

FORGIVEN by his neighbours of the Forest for the misguided affair of the Unfortunate Lady, Pope was received at Whiteknights, with open arms, as though the indiscretion had never taken place: even Mrs Sappho Nelson was powerless to make any further mischief. Welcomed at Whiteknights Pope was, by now, an even more constant visitor at Mapledurham.

How short were the summer days, when the poet and the two sisters picked the wild strawberries in the woods, and climbed the rocks in search of wilder and more goatish berries; the white mist of the intense heat, hanging among the woods, was more comforting than the thick gold rays of the sun, that had changed the young people till they were dark as negresses, though Martha's gold hair shone wild as the long gold hair of a planet. Their voices fell like waterfalls from the grey rocks, and there was none to answer them but that paler nymph Echo.

When they were separated, they corresponded; when they were near to each other, their young laughter floated through the gardens from the time when the white morning mists died among the fruit-trees, to the time when the young people's shadows lengthened and were like silent birds walking beside them upon the grass.

But then came the darkness of anxiety, clanging through their hearts, for Martha caught the smallpox; and among the Mapledurham MSS there is this letter, written in a youthful hand:

'Madam, the chief cause I have to repent my leaving the town, is the uncertainty I am in every day of your sister's state of health. I really expected by every post to hear of her recovery, but, on the contrary, each letter has been a new awakening to my apprehensions, and I have ever since suffered alarms upon alarms on her account. A month ago I should have laughed at any one who told me that my heart would be perpetually beating for a lady that was thirty miles off from me; and indeed, I never imagined my concern would be half so great for any young woman whom I have been no more obliged to than to so innocent an one as she. But, Madam, it is with the utmost seriousness I assure you, no relation can be more sensibly touched than I, nor any danger, if any I have, could affect me with more uneasiness (though as I never had a sister, I can't be quite so good a judge as you how far human nature would carry me). I have felt some weaknesses of a tender kind, which I would not be free from; and I am glad to find my value for people so rightly placed as to perceive them on this occasion.

'I cannot be so good a Christian as to be willing to resign my own happiness here for hers in another life. I do more than wish for her safety, for every wish I make I find immediately changed into a prayer, and a more fervent one than I had learned to make till now.

'May her life be longer and happier than perhaps herself may desire, that is, as long and as happy as you can wish: may her beauty be as great as possible, that is, as it always was, or as yours is. But whatever ravages a merciless distemper may commit, I dare promise her boldly, what few (if any) of her makers of visits dare to do: she shall have one man as much her admirer as ever. As for your part, madam, you have me so much more than ever since I have been a witness to the generous tenderness you have shown upon this occasion.

'I beg Mrs Blount and Mr Blount to believe me very faithfully their servant, and that your good mother will accept a thousand thanks for her maid's letters, and oblige me with the continuance of them by every post. I entreat her pardon that I did not take my leave of her; but when I parted from you I was under some compulsion, which I believe you might perceive. I thought at that moment to have snatched a minute or two more to have called again that night. But when I know I act uprightly, I depend upon forgiveness from such as I think you

are. I hope you will always be just, and that is, always look upon me as, madam, your most obedient, faithful and humble servant
'A. POPE

'To Mrs Teresa Blount, next door to my Lord Salisburys, in King Street, by St. James Square.'

When, thirty years after the writing of that letter, age had wrought more ravages on Martha Blount's face and form than the changes that had been wrought by the disease, when she was no longer a shy and delicate fawn, and only her blue eyes remained as a memory of her beauty, Pope saw her still as the young and lovely girl who had held his heart in her hands, in that far-off spring.

The difference between the letters written to Teresa and Martha Blount and those inscribed to Lady Mary Montagu, is very marked. In his letters to the sisters, there are no hollow and windy gallantries, no powdered effigies of an unreal passion; we feel in these the calm and the certainty of immortal things. This love, at least, would be untouched by death, or by the trivialities of life. In the case of Martha, this enduring love was hers for ever; in the case of Teresa, the friendship, as beautiful in its different way as his love for Martha, would have lasted into eternity, had it not been that, through some weakness in her character, or through some misguidance within her, she betrayed that friendship – or he believed that she had betrayed it.

It is true that in his letters to Teresa, he was in the habit of paying her compliments, and making love to her; but this lovemaking was made and received in a jocular spirit. Neither the writer nor the recipient of the letters took it seriously.

Teresa, whose worldliness exceeded that of Martha, went to London to witness the Coronation of George the First in 1714, and on her return Pope addressed a poetical epistle to her, but this, we feel, must have been kept a secret from the elder members of the families at Mapledurham and Whiteknights, since, though it was a compliment to Teresa, it was scarcely a compliment to them. The Epistle contrasted the pleasures experienced by Teresa in London with those very different ones which she endured at home:

> She went to plain-work, and to purling brooks,
> Old-fashioned halls, dull aunts, and croaking rooks,
> She went from opera, park, assembly, play,
> To morning walks, and prayers three hours a day.

But the letters to the sisters were, as a rule, more respectful in tone. The respect, indeed, was at moments of an almost exaggerated character. They began, if addressed to one of the sisters, with the word 'Madam'; if addressed to both, with 'Ladies' or 'Dear Ladies' (in moments of expansion). Nothing could have been more sober.

What, therefore, can have been the astonishment of Miss Martha Blount when she received the following letter, written from Bath:

'Most Divine – It is some proof of my sincerity towards you, that I write when I am prepared by drinking to speak the truth, and sure a letter after twelve at night must abound with that noble ingredient. That heart must have abundance of flames, which is at once warmed by wine and you: wine awakens and refreshes the lurking passions of the mind, as varnish does the colours which are sunk in a picture, and brings them out in all their natural glowings. My good qualities have been so frozen and locked up in a dull constitution at all my former sober hours, that it is very astonishing in me, now I am drunk, to find so much virtue in me. In these overflowings of my heart I pay you my thanks for those two obliging letters you favoured me with of the 18th and 24th instant. That which begins "My charming Mr Pope!" was a delight to me beyond all expression. You have at last entirely gained the conquest over your fair sister. It is true you are not handsome, for you are a woman, and think you are not: but this good-humour and tenderness for me has a charm that cannot be resisted. That face must needs be irresistible which was adorned with smiles when it could not see the Coronation (of George I). I do not suppose you will show this letter out of vanity, as I doubt not your sister does all I write to her. Indeed, to correspond with Mr Pope may make anyone proud who lives under a dejection of heart in the country. Everyone values Mr Pope, but everyone for a different reason: one for his adherence to the Catholic faith; another for his neglect of Popish superstition; one for his grave behaviour, another for his whimsicalness; Mr Titcomb, for his grave atheistical jests; Mr Caryll, for his moral and Christian sentences; Mrs Teresa, for his reflections on Mrs Patty (Martha), and Mrs Patty for his reflections on Mrs Teresa, etc.'

Poor little creature!

It must be admitted that this letter is as frank a tribute to Bacchus as anything to be found in literature, if we except certain poems of the Chinese.

We do not know how the lady replied.

In 1715 the brother of the ladies married; and from that time onwards, they lived with their mother in London, first in Bolton Street, and afterwards in Welbeck Street.

From that moment, the poet began to tire of Windsor Forest. And in the following year, his father having sold his estate at Binfield, the family moved to Chiswick, 'under the wing of my Lord Burlington'. The new house was one of a row which went under the name of 'Mawson's New Buildings'. The houses were excessively tall, and looked out over the landing-stage of the river, having, in front, a row of pollard elms.

Pope took leave of his friends in the forest with regret: 'Parting', he said, 'from honest Mr Dancastle with tenderness, and from old Sir William Trumbull as from a venerable prophet, foretelling, with lifted hands, the miseries to come, from which he is fast going to be removed himself.'

From this time onwards, Pope spent his time in a more fashionable society, and Teresa and Martha Blount, those countrified young ladies, enjoyed this society as much as the poet. In a letter to Mrs Patty, the poet speaks of three or four days spent in high luxury with some company at 'my Lord Burlington's: We are to walk, ride, ramble, dine, drink and lie together. His gardens are delightful, his music ravishing.'

Pope's friendship for the sisters took a thousand forms – varying from a present to Mrs Patty of the five volumes of *The Grand Cyrus,* to his care in speculating on her behalf, in the South Sea venture.

'I have lately been told', he wrote, 'my person is in danger, and (in any such case) the sum of £1,121 will be left for you in Mr Gay's hands. I have made that matter secure against accidents.'

Their meetings were continual, their correspondence unending, and Homer himself could not separate the friends for more than a short time, although Pope was working at high pressure on the translation of the Iliad, and complained, from time to time, that it came between them. He was busy, as well, with the preparation of a collected edition of his poems, with the addition of 'The Elegy to the Memory of an Unfortunate Lady', and the Epistle of Eloisa. But his work was soon to be interrupted by a deep and unquenchable sorrow.

Shortly after old Mr Pope, the first and the most loving of all his son's admirers, had the happiness and pride of seeing these beautiful poems in print, he died, to the inexpressible grief of the best and most beloved of sons. His death occurred at Chiswick, on the 23rd of October, 1717, and he was buried at Chiswick. 'He had lived to experience (said Bowles, in his *Life of Pope*) the greatest happiness an aged parent can receive, in witnessing the fame and prosperity of a son, whose natural infirmities had led him to forebode a far different fate.' He died with the feelings so beautifully expressed and pathetically described by Dr Morell:

> Tears, such as tender fathers shed,
> Warm from my aged eyes descend,
> For joy to think when I am dead
> My son shall have mankind his friend.

Pope turned for comfort to Martha Blount, at this moment as at every other time in his life.

'My poor Father died last night. Believe me, since I do not forget you this moment, I never shall.'

To this note, written on a small scrap of paper, his friend replied:

'Sir, my sister and I shall be home all day. If any company comes that you do not like, I'll go up into my room with you. I hope we shall see you.'

Bowles, who could write the tender and moving passage that I have quoted above, then sank to the depths of insinuating that the last sentence in this letter hinted at an intrigue between Pope and Martha Blount. Yet Pope, who was excessively careful of his reputation, regarded that letter as so innocent that he left it with his other papers. Bowles is disgraced eternally by this heartless and unfounded insinuation against a friendship which was beautiful and innocent as youth, deep as the grave, and eternal as the life to come.

* * *

During these years of friendship and of correspondence, the love that Pope felt for Martha Blount, the friendship he gave both the sisters, increased and deepened. The reason for the sad and mortal chill that shadowed the friendship between the poet and Teresa Blount will remain one of the cold secrets of the grave. None of his biographers have discovered the true cause of it; we can only guess at the reason – and that reason, so unutterably sad that it is cold as the grave itself, remained buried in the poet's breast. We know only, that in the same year that his father died (1717) the poet wrote this letter to the sisters he had loved:

'Dear Ladies – I think myself obliged to desire you would not put off any diversion you may find in the prospect of seeing me on Saturday, which is very uncertain. I take this occasion to tell you once for all, that I design no longer to be a constant companion when I have ceased to be an agreeable one. You only have had, as my friends, the privilege of knowing my unhappiness, and are therefore the only people whom my company must necessarily make melancholy. I will not bring myself to you at all hours like a skeleton, to come across your diversions and dash your pleasures. Nothing can be more shocking than to be perpetually meeting the ghost of an old acquaintance, which is all you can ever see of me.

'You must not think this is to proceed from any coldness, or the least decrease of friendship to you. If you had any love for me, I should always be glad to gratify you with an object that you thought agreeable. But as your regard is friendship and esteem, those are things which are well – perhaps better – preserved absent than present. A man who loves you is a joy to your eyes at all times. A man that you esteem is a solemn kind of thing, like a priest, only wanted at a certain hour, to do his office. 'Tis like oil in a salad – necessary, but of no manner of taste.

'And you may depend upon it, I will wait upon you on any occasion at the first summons as long as I live. Let me open my whole heart to you. I have sometimes found myself inclined to be in love with you, and as I have reason to know, from your temper and conduct, how miserably I should be used in the circumstances, it is worth my while to avoid it. It is enough to be disagreeable without adding food to it by constant slavery. I have heard, indeed, of women that have had a kindness for men of my make ...

'I love you so well that I tell you the truth, and that has made me write this letter. I will see you less frequently this winter, as you'll less want company. When the gay part of the world is gone, I'll be ready to stop the gap of a vacant hour whenever you please. Till then I'll converse with those who are more indifferent to me, as you will with those who are more entertaining. I wish you every pleasure God and man can pour upon ye; and I faithfully promise you all the good I can do, which is the service of one who will ever be, ladies, entirely yours.'

(No signature.)

Who can know the true facts of the case, the sequence of events, the conversations that passed between them? We can only guess at these. But the pain and the bewilderment of mind, these live still, though the writer of that letter has been in the grave for nearly two hundred years.

This letter, written a little later (it is dated 21st February, 1717-18, and addressed to Teresa Blount) is equally mysterious:

'Madam, I am too much out of order to trouble you with a long letter. But I desire to know what is your meaning, to resent my complying with your request, and endeavouring to serve you in the way you proposed, as if I had done you some great injury? You told me, if such a thing was the secret of my heart, you should entirely forgive, and think well of me. I told it, and find the contrary. You pretended so much generosity, as to offer your service on my behalf. The minute after, you did me as ill an office as you could, in telling the party concerned, it was all but an amusement, occasioned by my loss of another lady.

'You express yourself desirous of increasing your present income upon life. I proposed the only method I then could find, and you encouraged me to proceed in it. (The bond which Pope executed in her favour is dated March 1717 – *i.e.* 1717-18.) When it was done, you received it as if it were an affront; since, when I find the very thing in the very manner you wished, and mention it to you, you do not think it worth an answer.

'If your meaning be, that the very things you ask and wish, become odious to you, when it is I that comply with them, or bring them about, pray own it, and deceive me no longer with any thought, but that you hate me. My friendship is too warm and sincere to be trifled with: therefore, if you have any meaning, tell it me, or you must allow me to take away that which perhaps you do not care to keep. Your humble servant, etc.'

What treachery, misfortune, or misunderstanding, had wrecked this friendship? We shall never know with any certainty. But from the tone of the letter, and from certain hints, we may guess that the unhappy Pope, in an unguarded moment, had confessed his love for Martha Blount; and that Teresa had, in the first place, encouraged him in his hopes, and had then, urged by who knows what motives, wronged him, deeply and unforgivably, by traducing that love to Martha. We do not know what was her motive, or by what impulse she was led or driven. She may have been actuated by a sense of Pope's deformity, and of his pitiable illness. She may have been led, by her memory of his foolish behaviour in the matter of Mrs Weston, and his exaggerated compliments and expressions of gallantry towards herself, to believe that his love for Martha was unreal. She may have been led by love of her sister, or driven by some mad gust of jealousy, because the light expressions of love for herself were unmeant, and because those same expressions, when addressed to her sister, covered a love that was deep as the grave. Whatever her motives may have been, the friendship lay dead, killed by some act of hers.

He never forgave her, though there was an outward pretence of reconciliation. Yet, in spite of what she had done, he, who was supposed to have known no feeling save resentment and hatred, could yet be so magnanimous as to help her fallen fortunes (for she was not rich) by making her a small annuity.

Who knows what dream he may have nourished, in the belief that his genius, his great qualities of heart, his faithfulness, might somehow, in the hearts of these friends, prevail over the thought of his tiny and deformed body? That dream was broken and murdered now.

From that moment, he was held together only by the coldness of his fate. So are the bones of the dead held together by the chill of death; and so, in later years, did his weakened body rely upon its iron cage to stay it from being scattered. The rest of his life was spent in the eagle-shadow of winter and of his high fate.

Yet he, whose heart was said to have been shrunken and dead before it was born, could yet show such nobility of feeling that, although from this time onwards his heart seemed the suicide that is buried at the cross-roads, for passing feet to beat upon, he could transmute his love for Martha Blount into an even nobler and wider friendship, that lives long after he has been hidden by the grave.

CHAPTER XI

Fashionable Life

If we read any contemporary history of life in the time of Queen Anne and of George I, or if we read the journals and gazettes, with their perpetual cries of 'Lost' and 'Stolen', our first impression is of a huge tropical wind blowing; the wind rushes through the narrow streets, blowing the street cries through all the town, blowing the passengers (on foot and in sedan-chairs) after them, blowing the silks out of the houses, blowing the negro slaves, unweighted even by their silver collars, out of their masters' gardens, away and away, into other steets where the houses are patched and rotten with age and disease (houses that look out over the Docks, where the small-pox-yellow mud cracks and mutters). 'Pretty Maids, Pretty Pins, Pretty Women', shriek the ventriloquist parrot-voices of the street-cries; 'Ripe Strawberries', 'A Bed-Matt or a Door-Matt', 'Old Shoes for some Brooms', 'Maids any Cunny-skins', 'Buy a Rabbit, a Rabbit', 'Chimney Sweep', 'Lilly-white Vinegar, 3*d* a quart', 'Buy my Dutche Biskets', 'Ripe Speregas', 'Maids buy a Mop', 'Buy my Flounders', 'Old Cloaks Suits or Coats', 'Fair Lemons and Oranges', 'Old Chairs to Mend', 'Twelve pence a peck Oysters', 'Troope every one'. 'Old Satten, old Taffety or Velvet', 'Ha, ha, ha, Poor Jack' (and the sun beating him as he lay on the desert isle), 'Buy my dish of Great Eels', 'Buy a True Singing-Bird,' 'Buy any Wax or Wafers', 'A Merry New Song', 'Buy my new Singing Glasses', 'Any work for John Cooper,' 'Sixpence a pound Fair Cherryes', 'Remember the poor Prisoners', 'Delicate Cucumbers'.

Whirled along with these, are sedan-chairs, containing ladies whose little mouths are freckled by the sun with motes like the golden freckles borne by the strawberries in country gardens; their hair, dark as the leaves in those gardens, or like butter-yellow satin ribbons, is hidden beneath their wigs, just as the long gilded hair of the hay will be hidden beneath the snow, delicate and green, veined as the flowers of the wood-strawberries.

Here sits Lady Flutter with the lap-dog Veney on her knee, Veney who is as hairy as the enormous satyr sun that is rolling among his rays as though they were thick haycocks, rolling on the tops of the great trees as though they were velvety lawns.

The streets are narrow, and the huge sun and shadow in them makes a great Roman Colonnade, beneath which the sedan-chairs pass, beneath which the noseless beggars hide: dark as the smaller shades, they creep under these enormous arches. Where will they sleep tonight? In the desert island of Covent Garden, with the moonlight whispering against those shores like a tropical sea? Or will they lie and rot in the houses near the Docks, looking over the mud, that spreads like the smallpox – the mud where no wave ever comes? 'Make way there', says a gouty-legged chairman, pushing those ragged shades away with great disgust, as he carries a person of quality to her morning's exercise.

Some of the streets are narrow as Venetian canals; so green and shady are they, it seems the green and ageless water is flowing through them. But the hot sun, that country giant, that has swallowed all the gold spangles of the dew from the great faunal trees, and has dried all the haycocks until they are dry and rustling as his own rays, will soon conquer these.

Here comes a Bartholomew baby beau, newly launched out of a chocolate-house, with his pocket empty as his brains, swearing, as the beggars pull at his coat-tails, 'Impair my Vigour!' 'Never stir alive', 'Blister me!' then taking off his hat to Mr Froth as he passes by. But Mr Froth is a little drunk and does not observe him. Mr Froth has come from a gaming-house near Covent Garden, where they play Gleek, Primero, In and In, the Ace of Hearts, Pharaoh, Basset and Hazard, Rolly-Polly, Marlborough's Battles and particularly the Eo.

Here comes Lady Hectick in her sedan-chair, going to enquire about the play-bills, and old Lady Spiteley with her black monkey beside her, like a shadow of Death, and, outside the sedan, the delicate fawning dust is mimicking her, mopping and mowing, like a pale ghost of the monkey that sits beside her.

Oh, what is it that is being blown out of the windows of the mercers' houses? 'Stolen by the Tropical Wind', the bills will say, 'Stolen out of the house of Mr Peter Paggen of Love Lane near Eastcheap', and chased by the naked satyr sun (who will mistake them for those last gold spangles of the dew he has drunk from the trees), 'one Isabella colour kincock gown flowered with green and gold, one yellow Atlas petticoat, edged with silver, one yellow chintz gown and petticoat, Silver Tishea, Shaggs, Tabbey (for country lawns), Mowhairs (for satyr forests), Grazets (for smooth lawns again), Flowered Damasks (for moonlight), Sarsnets, Italian mantuas, Spanish and English druggets, Calamancoes (for the canal-like streets), Russels, Shalloons, Rateens, and Salapeens, and those Indian stuffs for wearing when the moonlight sighs like a sea among the great colonnades – Bafts, Baguzees, Ponabaguzees, Chelloes, Chints. Mamoodies, Oringal, Doreas, Gorgorians, Mahmudhiatees, Guinea Stuffs, Nicanees, Pallampores, Sallampores, Soverguzees, Cutanees, Doorguzies, Millaes, Gurracs, Humhums, Bulshauls, Izarees, Coffees, Allejars, Atlasses, Pelongs, Paunches, Soosies, Buffraes, Doodanies, and Succutums', stuffs that all seem woven by the long and air-thin fingers of Alexander Pope's sylphs Zephyretta, Brillante and Momentilla – hovering above the little silken waves:

He summons straight his denizens of air;
The lucid squadrons round the sails repair:
Soft o'er the shrouds aërial whispers breathe,
That seemed but zephyrs to the train beneath.
Some to the sun their insect-wings unfold,
Waft on the breeze, or sink in clouds of gold;
Transparent forms, too fine for mortal sight,
Their fluid bodies half dissolved in light.
Loose to the wind their airy garments flew
Thin glitt'ring textures of the filmy dew,
Dipped in the richest tincture of the skies,
Where light disports in ever-mingling dyes;
While ev'ry beam new transient colours flings,
Colours that change whene'er they wave their wings.

Those thin glittering textures are blowing far away; they will be caught among the shining branches of the fruit-trees in the great gardens; and next morning, when the sunburnt gardener and the great rough and hairy satyr sun climb together through those huge branches, and shake down the laughing fruit from between the sharp and glittering leaves, they will believe those thin textures are the lost beliefs of the night cobwebs and of the dew.

But some of those textures are blowing here, blowing along the street, and the East India young man named Cæsar, who ran away from his master, the negro maid, much pitted with smallpox, who speaks English well, and who had a piece of her left ear bitten off by a dog – (she has on a striped waistcoat and petticoat) – the tall young negro fellow commonly known as Jack Chelsea, whose collar has been filed off, and the blackamoor boy called Pompey who bears a silver collar engraved: 'Captain Thomas Mitchell's Negro, living in Griffith Street in Shadwell', these are running away. They must find the smallpox-yellow huts near the Docks as soon as possible, for there they will not be afraid any longer, even though the small waves bark at them like dogs. They will be safe and quiet, in the huts, when the moonlight shines on the otherwise empty floor like a bouquet of pale flowers.

But it was in the fashionable neighbourhoods, far from the mud houses and the mud of the Docks, that Alexander Pope spent his time. For since the publication of the Iliad, the fashionable world was incomplete without him.

'Sir', one invitation runs, 'my lady Duchess being drunk at this moment, so not able to write herself, has commanded me to acquaint you, that there is to be music on the water on Thursday next; therefore desires you to be that evening at her house in Bond Street by six o'clock at farthest, and her Grace will call of you there to take you to her barge, which she ordered to be ready at that time at Whitehall, with provisions, and shall land you on the wished-for shore. I am, sir,

Your humble servant 'MADDISON'

[This is believed to have been an invitation from the famous beauty Isabella Bentinck, who had married, a short time before, the Duke of Kingston, Lady Mary Wortley's father.]

For by this time, not only the wits and the patrons of the arts, but the beauties and the ladies of fashion, felt the necessity of Pope's companionship. The maids of honour in the court of the inexpensive Princess Caroline – Mary Bellenden, Mary Lepell, Mrs Howard (with whom Dean Swift quarrelled because she was ungrateful in the matter of a plaid nightgown) – these ladies walked with the poet at Richmond Lodge, talked with him at Hámpton Court, in the great summer days, when the few and heavy raindrops fell on the hot sward like the cards in *The Rape of the Lock*;

> And parti-coloured troops, a shining train,
> Draw forth to combat on the velvet plain.

So the heavy raindrops fall and race together. The lives of ladies-in-waiting, these complained to him, were very hard: 'To eat Westphalia ham in a morning, ride over hedges and ditches (this refers to the hunting in Windsor Park), come home in the heat of the day with a fever and a red mark on the forehead from a beaver hat; simper an hour and catch cold in the Princess's apartments, thence to dinner with what appetite they may; and after that, till midnight, walk, work, or think, which way they please.' 'Mrs Lepell', he told Teresa Blount, 'walked with me three hours or more by moonlight, and we met no creature of any quality save the King, who gave audience to the Lord Chamberlain.'

The Royal Family were well-disposed towards Alexander Pope: for the King and the Prince of Wales were proud of being among the chief patrons of literature – as we have seen from their subscriptions towards the Iliad. Later, when the full glories of the Grotto had been revealed, Pope was invited to assist the Prince of Wales in designing part of the garden at Kew; and several other, and later, incidents of the poet's relations with the Royal Family have been revealed. Chief among these is the painful incident of the Royal Monument at Bath, and in this, Alexander Pope, the Prince of Wales, and Beau Nash were the principal actors.

Pope had met Beau Nash for the first time, as far as we know, when he travelled to Bath in company with Jervas, Dr Arbuthnot, and Colonel Henry Disney, who was always known as 'Duke Disney' from his habit of using the word 'Duke' as an exclamation, or an expletive. Swift said of him that he was 'a fellow of abundance of good humour, an old battered rake, but very honest; not an old man, but an old rake. It was he that said of Jenny Kingdom, the maid of honour, who is a little old, that "since she could not get a husband, the Queen should give her a brevet to act as a married woman".' I cannot help feeling that Dean Swift's appreciation of this joke with its fine barrack-room roll, and tanned and seasoned old-soldier-like character, does more credit to his heart than his head; but it is undoubted that he did appreciate it, and a great many others of the same kind. Pope, Dr Arbuthnot, Jervas, and Duke Disney were, therefore, happy companions; they attended the routs and balls which were ruled over by Beau Nash, and so the poet's acquaintance with this good-natured and tragic adventurer began. The acquaintance bore a strange and an unexpected fruit.

It seems that in the year 1738, the Prince of Wales, who was staying in Bath, did Beau Nash the signal honour of presenting him with a large gold-enamelled snuff-box. Alas, this snuff-box, with others which he received, were sold that he might procure food and a fire, when he, who had done a thousand recorded and unrecorded generosities to others, was eighty years old, and nothing remained to the former Beau and uncrowned King of Bath but a few long winding stories (all illustrating his former grandeur), fewer and fewer and still more inattentive listeners, many memories of those powerful people whom, before their fortune came, he had saved from ruin (and who, now that they were safe, could not be troubled to save the tedious old man), a rickety attic, and a miserable and insufficient pension. But in 1738 there was no question of selling his records of grandeurs to procure food; the Beau was at the height of fashion, he was able to help those who in after years would not help him, people were eager to listen to his stories, and he himself took a pride in his tall white hat, his cane, and his coach and-four.

Delighted with such a signal mark of the royal favour as the gold snuff-box, Beau Nash was seized with the idea of erecting an obelisk in honour of the Prince. The obelisk was erected, and filled, not only Beau Nash, but also Oliver Goldsmith, with an awed admiration. I cannot do better than to quote Goldsmith, in order to do justice both to the memorial and to the very unworthy backslidings of genius which were connected with it. 'This handsome memorial in honour of the good-natured Prince is erected (said Goldsmith in his Life of Nash) in Queen Square. It is enclosed with a stone balustrade, and in the middle of every side there are large iron gates. In the centre is the obelisk, seventy feet high, and terminating in a point. The expenses of this were eighty pounds, and Mr Nash was determined that the inscription should answer the magnificence of the pile. With this view, he wrote to Mr Pope at London requesting an inscription.' The poet, to Mr Nash's (and Mr Goldsmith's) surprise and indignation, wriggled violently, and tried to escape. He owned himself unequal to the task 'even granting it possible to express an inexpressible idea', and he actually ended the letter by suggesting, firmly enough, that the Beau should write the inscription himself! But Mr Nash was nothing if not tenacious; he pinned the poet down, and the end of the affair was that Pope wrote an inscription that rendered Goldsmith almost, but not quite, speechless with disappointment.

The inscription ran thus:

> In memory of honours bestow'd
> And in gratitude for benefits conferr'd on this city
> By His Royal Highness
> Frederick Prince of Wales
> And his Royal Consort
> In the year 1738,
> This obelisk is erected by
> Richard Nash Esqre.

'Nothing can be more frigid', as Goldsmith very rightly observes: 'though the subject was worthy of the utmost exertions of genius.'

But this disappointment, although it must have lessened Beau Nash's opinion of the poet, seems in no way to have disappointed His Royal Highness. Or perhaps he regarded the subject as so 'inexpressible', and so undoubtedly worthy of the utmost exertions of genius that he believed those exertions had been made.

At any rate, two years after this time, a letter from George Lyttelton to Pope, conveyed His Royal Highness's message that he had a mind to present the poet with some urns or vases for the garden at Twickenham; it conveyed also the Prince's command that Pope should inform Lyttelton as soon as possible what number and size would suit him best (for the number was to depend upon the size). 'You can have', said Lyttelton with a touch of caution, 'six small ones for your Laurel Circus, or two large ones to terminate points as you like best.' Indeed, the Prince's generosity did not stop there, for he presented Pope with busts of philosophers for his library. And he visited Twickenham and dined with the poet, carrying his kindness so far that during dinner he gave his opinions very freely and weightily on the subject of Poetry.

In the midst of this monologue, it was observed that the poet was asleep – a phenomenon that was recorded, but otherwise passed over in dignified silence by Doctor Johnson in his *Life of Pope*.

But all this took place years after the night when Pope walked in the gardens of Hampton Court with Mary Lepell, and watched the King giving audience to the Lord Chamberlain.

In the year or two years which followed the publication of the first book of the Iliad, he spent his nights – and the earliest hours of the morning – in drinking burgundy and champagne with Lord Warwick and listening to his stories of his stepfather Addison, or in the October Club, with the wits and the rakes. He spent his mornings in the Library of Lord Oxford, which, in after times he used much as a tiny cuckoo would use a giant wren's nest – implanting in it the (slightly altered) letters from old Mr Wycherley to himself, and from himself to old Mr Wycherley – in order, he explained, that they would be safe from those villainous persons who would like to injure the reputation of both authors by publishing the papers. They would be safe, he explained, because Lord Oxford was a man of honour. Unhappily Lord Oxford *was* a man of honour, and they *were* safe, and when Pope understood, at last, that there was not the slightest chance of these manuscripts being stolen (as he assumed they would be) – and published, he had very considerable difficulty in getting them away from Lord Oxford, who was determined to keep his word and protect his friend at all costs. The matter was a very difficult one, and needing much diplomacy. In short, the whole of Pope's carefully built-up fabric had to be undone, and a fresh one started, and in the commencement of the new one the poet, no doubt, found his consolation.

With the patrons of the arts he spent his time, or a large part of it. But most of all was spent in the company of that unexplainable woman, Lady Mary Wortley Montagu.

CHAPTER XII

Lady Mary Wortley

IT WAS in the year 1715 that Pope met, and was dazzled by, Lady Mary Wortley Montagu, a woman of fashion with a reputation for beauty and a reputation for wit. The first was gained for her when she was eight years old by the social position and care of her father, the Duke of Kingston. This indefatigable nobleman sent for her to the Kit-Cat Club, where she was nominated as a toast, her health was drunk, and her name was engraved upon a drinking-glass; and she was 'passed from the lap of one poet or patriot or statesman to the arms of another'. We do not know what gave rise to her reputation for wit, unless it was gained under the same auspices and on the same occasion; according to her own account, her gifts were so great that she 'picked up a knowledge of Latin' for herself; other and more sober admirers, however, state that she shared a classical education with her brother.

On the accession of George I, her husband, Edward Wortley, received, through the efforts of his cousin Charles Montagu, Earl of Halifax, an appointment as one of the Commissioners of the Treasury; and Lady Mary proceeded to dazzle London, and, in attaching Pope to her train, to present the world with the curious spectacle of a comet attached to the stick of a damp but noisy rocket. The stick, however held for some time.

It may not be out of place to examine Lady Mary's character at this moment. No instance of her wit remains, unless her letters may be regarded as such, or the remark quoted by Spence: 'Sure there cannot be a more detestable set of beings upon the earth, than those anti-knight errants, who run about only to ruin as many ladies as they can.' In spite of this instance of her wit, Lady Mary was, however, not averse to ruining ladies in another, and more cold-blooded way. Very properly delicate as were her ideas of decency when she fancied that any attack was made upon herself, she yet considered that she was too much a woman of the world, too emancipated a wit, to allow these foolish ideas of decency to interfere if there was an opportunity of wounding another person. Why, for instance, should it matter, if such an inferior mind (when compared to hers) as that of Grizel Baillie, daughter of Baillie of Jerviswood, and afterwards the wife of Sir Alexander Murray of Stanhope, was given an incurable wound? The person who caused the wound was Lady Mary Wortley, and she, who must be protected at all costs from the results of her own indiscretion, was given the right, by her wit, to injure those who had never done her any harm. The unfortunate Grizel Baillie was praised by Lady Harvey as the kindest, best, and most valued friend she ever had. She harmed no one, nor did she slander any. But she was involved, as a girl, in a very painful incident. Arthur Grey, one of her father's footmen, forced his way into her room at midnight, with a pistol in his hand, and declared his passion for her. She escaped; Grey was tried and transported for the offence, and the affair might have been forgotten; but this was an admirable opportunity for an exercise of Lady Mary Wortley's wit, and she, who so resented the attack which Pope made upon an unknown Sappho, yet thought it right and proper to make this incident, so painful to the victim, the subject of one of her own boring and incompetent 'poetical epistles', written in the character of the footman, Arthur Grey.

Many other instances of her delicacy and kindness are recorded. The aunt of Walpole, as a young girl of seventeen, was decoyed into the house of a certain nobleman whose reputation was evil. She went to the house innocently, at the invitation of the man's wife, but, though she stayed there for but a day and a night, her reputation, through no fault of her own, was ruined. What misery this caused her, she, alone, could tell. Years afterwards, she was married to a gentleman who was absent from England at the time this incident occurred, and her past guiltless history was forgotten – by all but Lady Mary Wortley, who thought fit to resuscitate the story, as an opportunity for exercising her own wit. The husband of the unhappy girl – (she does not call her an unhappy girl, nor does she seem to realize any possibility of mental suffering) – was a victim, according to Lady Mary, who had been the girl's friend, and he, who was absent from London at the time of the girl's ruin, married her all unknowing of her history.

Nobody seems to have cut Lady Mary Wortley. Horace Walpole, according to Pinkerton, after explaining that he had known Lady Mary as a child, said: 'She was always a dirty little thing. This habit continued with her.' Pinkerton must have been mistaken in the earlier part of the statement, since Lady Mary was twenty-seven years older than Horace Walpole; but the last part of the statement, that relating to 'a dirty little thing', holds. She was that, if she was nothing else.

She is reported to have had calm good sense; and she may have had this necessary, and rather pedestrian, quality. But such of her 'wit' as remains to us is intolerably obvious; and she was incapable of seeing the behaviour of others as actuated by any but the basest motives.

Pope, for instance, whose reverence for other great men has never been doubted by any but this small mind, was accused by her of remaining friends with Swift and with Sir Godfrey Kneller, only with a view to obtaining legacies from them. In her letter to the Countess of Bute on the subject of Lord Orrery's *Remarks on the Life and Writings of Swift*, she says: 'There can be no worse picture made of the Doctor's morals than he has given us himself in the letters printed by Pope. We see him vain, trifling, ungrateful to his patron, the Earl of Oxford, making a servile court where he had any interested views, and meanly abusive when they were disappointed, and, as he says (in his own phrase) flying in the face of mankind, in company with his adorer Pope. It is pleasant to consider that, had it not been for the good-nature of these very mortals they contemn, these two superior beings were entitled, by their birth and hereditary fortune, to be only a couple of link boys. I am of opinion their friendship would have continued, though they had remained in the same kingdom; it had a very strong foundation, the love of flattery on the one side, and the love of flattery on the other. Pope courted, with the utmost assiduity, all the old men from whom he could hope a legacy, the D. of

Buckingham, Lord Peterborough, Sir G. Kneller, Lord Bolingbroke, Mr Wycherley, Mr Congreve, Lord Harcourt, etc, and I do not doubt, projected to sweep the Dean's whole inheritance if he could have persuaded him to throw up his deanery, and come to die in his house; and his general preaching against money was meant to induce people to throw it away, that he might pick it up.'

A figure is certainly reflected in this tarnished mirror of Lady Mary Wortley's wit – but it is the figure, not of an unhappy madman of genius, or of a cripple of genius; it is the low and creeping figure of 'a dirty little thing', who is now only remembered because of the fame of one man's poetry and of another man's invention – the figure reflected is that of Lady Mary Wortley.

The man whose 'general preaching against money was meant to induce people to throw it away, that he might pick it up' – loved it so much that, as a young man of twenty-three (before he made his fortune from the translation of Homer, and whilst he was still unable to buy books without practising economies), he could yet make an allowance to a deserted and friendless woman whom he knew to be dying, and who was almost a stranger to him; he relieved the poverty of many destitute creatures with the utmost generosity; he saved Richard Savage from starvation. Martha Blount said of him: 'He did not know anything of the value of money; and his greatest delight was in doing good offices for his friends. I used to know, by his particular vivacity, and the pleasure that appeared in his face, when he came to town on such errands, or when he was employed on them, which was very often.' Indeed, the record of Pope's benevolence and kindness is unending, and would be recognized were it not that those unhappy beings who are deformed physically have the added burden of a totally imaginary malice and wickedness imputed to them. I do not, however, know one instance of kindness or generosity of the straight-backed Lady Mary Wortley. This lady of quality, when her face is unlit by the deathless flares of the link-boy Pope, remains to us in the character of a dilapidated macaw, with a hard piercing laugh, mirthless and joyless, with a few undescriptive, unimaginative phrases, with a parrot's powers of observation, and a parrot's hard and poisonous bite.

Lady Mary Wortley rushed, like an unexploded rocket, into the poet's life at exactly the right (or the wrong) moment. For, intoxicated by his success with the translation of the Iliad, and with the fame that it had brought him, and in defiance, perhaps, of Dennis's insults about his deformity, Pope wished to appear as a man of fashion. He would show creatures of that kind, how little deformity matters, when it is allied to genius! Though Dennis could notice his deformity, the fashionable beauties about the Court did not; they were proud to be seen with Mr Pope the great poet – (Alexander Pope, the crippled hunchback). So he could be seen, fluttering like a tiny moth, among their great gardens. But Lady Mary Wortley was, to him, the crowning proof of his achievement. She was his answer to John Dennis; she, who can never have knowingly administered comfort to any living creature, was yet a salve for the wounds he had received.

In 1716 Mr Wortley resigned the office of a Commissioner at the Treasury, and became the Ambassador at the Porte; Lady Mary accompanied him, and was thus, at last, able to bore members of her own sex, since the Turkish women, being confined in harems, were unable to get away from her. Pope was disconsolate at her absence from England, and wrote her many letters in which the gallantry was more obvious than the sense. The letters appear hard and hollow, for all their expression of devotion; but no doubt Pope, with his extraordinary and sensitive genius, was unable, in this as in all else, to resist fitting the style to the theme. He wished to appear disconsolate, but in all probability Lady Mary, who did not lack shrewdness, no matter how deficient she was in other and more generous qualities, knew that he was not quite so disconsolate as he seemed – knew at any rate that he enjoyed being disconsolate. When the collected edition of his works was published, in 1717, and a third volume of the Iliad was issued, he sent these to Lady Mary at Constantinople. 'There are few things in them', the accompanying letter says, 'but what you have already seen, except the Epistle of Eloisa to Abelard, in which you will find one passage that I cannot tell whether to wish you should understand or not'. The passage referred to is probably the conclusion of the poem:

> And sure if fate some future bard should join
> In sad similitude of griefs to mine,
> Condemned whole years in absence to deplore,
> And image charms he must behold no more;
> Such if there be, who loves so long, so well;
> Let him our sad, our tender story tell;
> The well-sung woes will soothe my pensive ghost;
> He best can paint them who shall feel them most.

These are not among Pope's most successful couplets; but, even so, it is a soothing reflection that the very same lines had been copied out and sent, with the very same implication (though a different application) to Martha Blount before the volume appeared:

'The Epistle of Eloise', he told Miss Blount, 'grows warm, and begins to have some breathings of the heart in it, which may make posterity think I was in love. I can scarce find it in my heart to leave out the conclusion I once intended for it.'

At last, when it was felt that the Turks had suffered enough, Lady Mary Wortley's husband was recalled from the Porte, and the couple started for England, the journey from Constantinople being undertaken in June 1718. Pope was in a seventh heaven of delight at the prospect of seeing Lady Mary again, and, forgetting his horror of a sea-journey, became almost, but not quite, determined to meet her in Italy, his reason being that he wished to see her on the very spot where Curtius sacrificed himself for his country. 'I would fain', he proclaimed, 'behold the best and brightest thing I know in the scene of ancient virtue and glory.' The journey was ponderous and slow as the lady's wit; indeed, she and the sober Mr Wortley (who seems, during all his life, to have neither received nor given so much as one single idea) did not arrive at Dover until the 1st November 1718. By this time the poet, far from beholding the best and brightest thing he knew in the scene of ancient virtue and glory was, instead, in the country, working at his translation from Homer. He wrote, however, a letter to the best and brightest thing, and this contains a passage congratulating her on her return; but the rest of the letter is an enthusiastic description of an ancient Gothic house, Stanton Harcourt, which was the scene of his labours. Unfortunately the description bears little or no resemblance to the original; and the letter itself was eventually to undergo the same singular change, since, when it was printed, it was readdressed (with a few deletions) to Sheffield Duke of Buckingham!

However, the letters continued, though from this time they were less concerned with the anguish of parted lovers than with Gothic ruins, and with society.

Lady Mary and Mr Wortley decided to live in London, and, as they were in need of a house for the summer of the following year, Pope bargained with Sir Godfrey Kneller for a house at Twickenham. On this occasion Sir Godfrey appeared in the light, almost, of a financial magnate with a genius for vested interests; but Lady Mary got the house, and saw the poet continually. The next step was to induce Sir Godfrey to paint a portrait of the lady, and this was done, and was the reason for some extempore lines extolling Lady Mary's unearthly beauty and 'the equal lustre of the heavenly mind'.

But the heavenly mind had, even at this time, begun to weary the poet. Perhaps the first feeling of weariness was the result of a letter written by Pope to Lady Mary (some time before her return), on the subject of the death of two rustic lovers. Pope, with his usual romantic enthusiasm, wrote as follows:

'I have a mind to fill the rest of this paper with an accident that happened just under my eyes, and has made a great impression upon me. I have just passed part of this summer at an old romantic seat of Lord Harcourt's, which he lent me. It overlooks a common field, where, under the shade of a haycock, sat two lovers, as constant as ever were found in romance, beneath a spreading beech. The name of the one (let it sound as it will) was John Hewet; of the other Sarah Drew. John was a well-set man, about five-and-twenty, Sarah a brown woman of eighteen. John had for several months borne the labour of the day in the same field with Sarah; when she milked, it was his morning and evening charge to bring the cows to her pail. Their love was the talk, but not the scandal of the whole neighbourhood; for all they aimed at was the blameless possession of each other in marriage. It was but this very morning that he had obtained her father's consent, and it was but till the next week that they were to wait to be happy. Perhaps this very day, in the intervals of their work, they were talking of their wedding clothes; and John was now matching several kinds of poppies and field-flowers to her complexion, to make her a present of knots for the day. While they were thus employed (it was the last of July) a terrible storm of thunder and lightning arose, that drove the labourers to what shelter the trees or hedges afforded. Sarah, frighted and out of breath, sank on a haycock, and John (who never separated from her) sat by her side, having raked two or three heaps together to secure her. Immediately there was heard so loud a crack as if heaven had burst asunder. The labourers, all solicitous for each other's safety, called to one another: those that were nearest our lovers, hearing no answer, crept to the place where they lay; they first saw a little smoke, and after, this faithful pair – John, with one arm about his Sarah's neck, and the other held over her face, as if to screen her from the lightning. They were struck dead, and already grown stiff and cold in this tender posture. There was no mark or discolouring on their bodies, only that Sarah's eyebrow was a little singed, and a small spot between her breasts. They were buried the next day, in one grave, in the parish of Stanton Harcourt, in Oxfordshire; where my lord Harcourt, at my request, has erected a monument over them. Of the following epitaphs which I made, the critics have chosen the godly one: I like neither, but wish you had been in England to have done this office better; I think 'twas what you could not have refused me on so moving an occasion:

I

'When Eastern lovers feed the fun'ral fire,
On the same pile their faithful fair expire;
Here pitying Heav'n that virtue mutual found,
And blasted both, that it might neither wound.
Hearts so sincere th' Almighty saw well pleas'd,
Sent his own lightning, and the victims seiz'd.

II

'Think not, by rig'rous judgment seiz'd,
A pair so faithful could expire;
Victims so pure Heav'n saw well pleas'd
And snatch'd them in celestial fire.

III

'Live well, and fear no sudden fate;
When God calls virtue to the grave,
Alike 'tis justice, soon or late,
Mercy alike to kill or save.
Virtue unmov'd can hear the call,
And face the flash that melts the ball.

'Upon the whole, I can't think these people unhappy. The greatest happiness, next to living as they would have done, was to die as they did. The greatest honour people of this low degree could have, was to be remembered on a little monument; unless you will give them another – that of being honoured with a tear from the finest eyes in the world. I know you have tenderness; you must have it; it is the very emanation of good sense and virtue; the finest minds, like the finest metals, dissolve the easiest.'

A letter describing this incident had been sent to Miss Martha Blount, three weeks before. For Pope, economical in all things (excepting in generosity towards the destitute), allowed this quality to extend even to his letters. But when the letter to Lady Mary Wortley was published, it appeared under the heading: 'From Mr Gay to Mr F ...', for Lady Mary, having quarrelled with the poet, was to be deprived of the honour of having her name associated with his correspondence.

Lady Mary's answer to this letter was characteristic of her at her best; and I must admit that in it she shows very considerable sense and vigour, though the letter exhibits also her usual cynicism.

'I must applaud your good-nature, in supposing that your pastoral lovers (vulgarly called haymakers) would have lived in everlasting joy and harmony, if the lightning had not interrupted their scheme of happiness. I see no reason to imagine, that John Hughes and Sarah Drew were either wiser or more virtuous than their neighbours. That a well-set man of twenty-five should have a fancy to marry a brown maid of eighteen, is nothing marvellous; and I cannot help thinking that, had they married, their lives would have passed in the common track with their fellow-parishioners. His endeavouring to shield her from a storm was a natural action, and what he would certainly have done for his horse, if he had been in the same situation. Neither am I of opinion that their sudden death was the reward of their mutual virtue. You know the Jews were reproved for thinking a village destroyed by fire more wicked than those that had escaped the thunder. Time and chance happen to all men. Since you desire me to try my skill in an epitaph, I think the following lines, perhaps more just, though not so poetical, as yours:

'Here lies John Hughes and Sarah Drew;
Perhaps you'll say, what's that to you?
Believe me friend, much may be said
On this poor couple that are dead.
On Sunday next they should have married;
But see how oddly things are carried!
On Thursday last it rained and lightn'd;
These tender lovers, sadly frightened,
Shelter'd beneath the cocking hay,
In hopes to pass the time away;
But the bold thunder found them out
(Commission'd for that end no doubt);
And seizing on their trembling breath
Consign'd them to the shades of death.
Who knows if 'twas not kindly done?
For had they seen the next year's sun,

A beaten wife and cuckold swain
Had jointly curs'd the marriage chain;
Now they are happy in their doom,
For Pope has writ upon their tomb.

'I confess these sentiments are not altogether so heroic as yours; but I hope you will forgive them in favour of the last two lines. You see how much I esteem the honour you have done them; though I am not very impatient to have the same, and had rather continue to be your stupid *living* humble servant, than be celebrated by all the pens in Europe.'

Nothing could exhibit the difference between the two characters in a clearer light than do these two letters. The *naïveté* and fundamental simplicity of Pope, his craving for romance, his warm heart, his genuine response to and understanding of the affection of others; these qualities are seen, side by side with a good deal of perfectly genuine silliness, a certain amount of artifice, and an intent and strained gaze fixed upon the verdict of posterity. In Lady Mary Wortley's letter we see a fund of common sense, a good deal of natural cynicism, and a certain coarse good humour. Later, the good humour was whittled away, and only the coarseness remained, as far as Pope was concerned.

As we have seen, the lady returned to England, and the friendship was resumed, but, even if we remember the proposed portrait of Sir Godfrey Kneller, it was yet evident that some shadow, some essence of decay, clung about 'the brightest thing'. Time drifted on, and the poet drifted away, slowly, half imperceptibly. In an undated letter, which is ascribed to the year 1720-21 (since it speaks of the death of a 'great Minister' – and both Lord Stanhope and Craggs died in February of that year), Lady Mary tells her sister, Lady Mar: 'I see sometimes Mr Congreve, and very seldom Mr Pope, who continues to embellish his house at Twickenham. He has made a subterranean grotto, which he has furnished with looking-glasses, and *they tell me* it has a very good effect. I here send you some verses addressed to Mr Gay, who wrote him a congratulatory letter on the finishing his house. I stifled them here; and I beg they may die the same death at Paris, and never go further than your closet:

> 'Ah, friend! 'tis true – this truth you lovers know –
> In vain my structures rise, my gardens grow;
> In vain fair Thames reflects the double scenes
> Of hanging mountains and of sloping greens;
> Joy lives not here – to happier seats it flies,
> And only dwells where W——casts her eyes.
> 'What is the gay parterre, the chequer'd shade,
>
> The morning bower, the ev'ning colonnade,
> But soft recesses of uneasy minds,
> To sigh unheard in, to the passing winds?
> So the struck deer in some sequestrate part
> Lies down to die, the arrow at his heart;
> There stretch'd unseen in coverts hid from day,
> Bleeds drop by drop, and pants his life away.'

There is a sign of wounded vanity about this letter; who was this cripple, this hunchback, this poet of genius, that he dared avoid the company of Lady Mary Wortley? who indeed! By the middle of September 1721 the friendship had ceased completely; following a letter in Lady Mary's handwriting. The poet was, at that moment, visiting Lord Bathurst at Cirencester, and Lady Mary's letter was on the subject of a harpsichord which he seems to have hired, or borrowed, and which he had promised to lend (and had been unable to lend) Lady Mary Wortley for one of her evening parties – for the lady was of too economical a nature to pay for anything, either materially or spiritually, if she could avoid it. With that letter the correspondence ended. Lady Mary's revenge for the slight was worthy of her; though the first explanation she gave of the rupture – (her explanation was to Spence) – was harmless: 'I got a common friend to ask Mr Pope why he had left off visiting me? He answered, negligently, that he went as often as he used to do. I then got Dr Arbuthnot to ask him what Lady M. had done to him? He said that Lady M. and Lord Hervey had pressed him once together (and I don't remember that we were ever together with him in all our lives) to write a satire on some certain persons; that he refused it; and that this had occasioned the breach between us.' But there were other versions of the reason for this quarrel, versions spread by Lady Mary: one (given, this time, to Lady Pomfret) was that 'when she became much acquainted with the Duke of Wharton, Pope grew jealous, and that occasioned a breach between them.' The third version is that 'at some ill-chosen time, when she least expected what romances call *a declaration,* he made such passionate love to her, as, in spite of her utmost endeavours to be angry and look grave, produced an immoderate fit of laughter; from which moment he became her implacable enemy.'

In this way, and by the propagation of this story, fluttering down on him from the tops of the vast and sleepy trees, floating along the galleries of the great houses frequented by this tiny and crippled being ('the little Alexander that the women laugh at') – in this way, and by these means, did Lady Mary Wortley avenge her wounded vanity, and finish the work that John Dennis had begun.

It has been the fashion, among those people who wish to decry Pope because he was at once a man of genius and a cripple (and neither abnormality could be forgiven him), to present Lady Mary Wortley in the character of a martyr to the monster Pope; but I have yet to learn in what her martyrdom consisted. It is evident that at one time Pope had some kind of innocent infatuation for her, due, probably, to the fact that he found in her some temporary drug against his misery, some balm for his hopeless longing for the beloved Martha Blount. It is regarded as creditable to Lady Mary that she answered his letters in a cool style, but this must be ascribed to the fact that she wished to appear in the eyes of the world as the object of so great a poet's adoration, whilst giving that poet (and hunchback) nothing in return. In the end, one of two things happened; either he became bored with her unceasing rattle, and her cynicism, which was unvarying – since her 'wit' forbade her to see any virtue in any human being, or, having seen it, to allow its existence without attempting to show in it some form of corruption – or her story is true – that he made her a declaration of love, and that she, overcome with the humour of this sentiment being entertained towards Lady Mary Wortley by a soul inhabiting so contemptible a body, laughed at him.

Pope's detractors, in their wish to deform his character, have shown no distaste for this mean and pygmy vanity, this final murderous injury to a man who had already been sufficiently injured by the cruelty of Dennis. Yet they are willing to bolster up her hysterical claim to be the victim of the two coarse lines about a modern Sappho, in the Epistles. Pope, himself, denied that she was the person meant, and indeed, there seems no reason to suppose that she was.

Lady Mary Wortley's stories about the reason for her estrangement from Pope floated round and round the fashionable part of the city, and the country places that knew her; but the poet made no reply, nor did he ever give any reason for that coolness, save that he had withdrawn from her society because she had too much wit for him. But the often-repeated story of her laughter gave his mind an irreparable injury. In *The Dunciad* he published two lines which for many years seemed inexplicable:

> Whence hapless Monsieur much complains at Paris
> Of wrongs from Duchesses and Lady Maries;

and the note to this passage says ('The Dunciad', *Works,* vol. 2, published in 1735): 'This passage was thought to allude to a famous lady, who cheated a French wit of £5,000 in the South Sea year. But the author meant it in general of all bragging travellers, and of all w—— and cheats under the name of ladies.'

At last the mystery was solved, by the publication of a letter from Lady Mary Wortley to her sister, the Countess of Mar: the passage in *The Dunciad* refers to Lady Mary's unfortunate adventure with a certain unpleasant Frenchman, a Monseiur Ruremonde. This gentleman had pursued Lady Mary with his attentions for almost a year, personally, and by letter, and he came at last, to Paris to pay her a visit. Lady Mary, whose vanity was only equalled by her cynicism, but who had, also, a certain streak of honesty in her, was unaware of, or perhaps preferred to be blind to, this person's character. She advised him to sell his shares in the South Sea Fund, and he, in his turn, placed the money he received from these in her hands, asking her to invest it for him. According to her story, it was at his urgent entreaty that she laid out the money for him; but unfortunately, no sooner had he left Paris, than the shares fell more than a half. Several letters passed between them, and then Lady Mary's admirer wrote to her, saying that he was fully aware of the part she had played; she had his money, of that he was convinced, and unless she paid him £2,000, he would print her letters to him. Lady Mary asked him to appoint persons who would examine her accounts; but the Frenchman still bullied, blustered and blackmailed her. Finally he wrote to her husband (but she intercepted the letter); and his threats to publish the correspondence were unceasing. On this occasion, it is impossible not to feel sorry for her, so great and so obvious was her fright, which showed itself in her imploring letters to her sister, calling for help, and even in her threats to have Monsieur Ruremonde soundly thrashed. But still the blustering continued. By the time the matter ended, Lady Mary must have been heartily sick of both vanity and money. At last the affair did come to an ending, and we presume it was a peaceable ending, since there is no reference to it in the papers of that time; but Pope had come to hear of it in some manner; and he determined that Lady Mary should know that the affair was not so hidden from the world as she had hoped. Not satisfied with this, he produced another, and more obscure allusion to her in the *Epilogue to the Satires*:

> Who starves a sister or forswears a debt.

This line, like the couplet in *The Dunciad,* was for some time not understood; but it is now supposed to refer to the insanity of Lady Mar. There is a blank, as Mr Carruthers has pointed out, in the printed correspondence between Lady Mary and Lady Mar – a blank stretching over twelve years, and during a great part of this time, Lady Mar was insane, and in the care of Lady Mary Wortley. Lord Grange, Lady Mar's brother-in-law, whose reputation was none of the best, owing to his treatment of Lady Grange, accused Lady Mary, to members of his family, of detaining Lady Mar as a lunatic when she was in perfect possession of her senses, so that she herself might benefit by the annual £500 which she received for Lady Mar's keep. He accused her, too, of vexing, teasing and plaguing Lady Mar, in order that she might remain mad. Indeed, we are presented with the pleasing spectacle of a distraught lady being tweaked from the hands of a sister into the hands of a brother-in-law, and back again – snatched from coach to coach, whisked, in a nightgown, from country house to country house. Each of the combatants was, according to himself and herself, actuated by the highest principles; each of the combatants was accused by the other of mercenary motives.

Lady Mary may not have liked these references to unfortunate episodes in her life; but she had no right to complain, since she herself was in the habit, as we have seen, of lampooning her acquaintances, and even those friends who might have supposed they were dear to her.

Fresh causes of annoyance were given to the poet. Lady Mary was supposed by Pope to be, with her friend Lord Hervey, the joint-author of a coarse and witless pamphlet, called 'A Pop upon Pope; or a True and Faithful Account of a late horrid and barbarous whipping committed on the body of Sawney Pope, a Poet, as he was innocently walking in Ham Walks, near the River of Thames, meditating Verses for the Good of the Publick. Supposed to have been done by two evil-disposed Persons, out of Spite and Revenge for a harmless Lampoon which the said Poet had writ upon them'. This odious narrative relates how that two gentlemen advanced upon the poet, and 'knowing him perfectly well, *partly by his back*' (the italics are mine) 'and partly by his face ... did, with a long rod, with great violence and unmerciful hand, strike Master Pope'. As soon as the whipping was accomplished, the two heroes retreated, 'when good Mrs B. (Martha Blount) a good charitable woman, and near neighbour of Master Pope's, at Twickenham, chancing to come by, took him up in her apron, and carried him to the water-side, where she got a boat to convey him home'. The pamphlet then describes Pope as rendered insane from the whipping. But the persecution did not stop there. A forged advertisement was afterwards added to the pamphlet – an advertisement purporting to be taken from *The Daily Post* of Friday, 14th June, 1728, bearing the signature of Pope, and denying that any physical attack had been made upon him. No such advertisement can be traced, and it arose from the malice of the original perpetrators of the attack.

At last, in 1733, the hatred between these former friends rose to its height with the famous couplet about a modern Sappho, in the *Imitation of the First Satire of The Second Book of Horace*. At the time when Pope wrote the *Imitation,* he was prostrated with grief over the death of John Gay, his friend for twenty years, whose easy, sweet and childlike disposition had made him so dearly loved by both Swift and Pope. Indeed, Pope's grief was so great that he fell into a fever. When he was convalescent from this, Lord Bolingbroke happened to visit him one day, and, picking up a book of Horace, read the First Satire of the Second Book, pointing out to Pope how exactly applicable it was to himself. Pope read it again, and in two mornings produced an imitation, which was so greatly appreciated by his circle that he sent it to press within a week. It appeared on 14th February, 1733, and contained the lines:

> Slander or poison dread from Delia's rage,
> Hard words or hanging, if your judge be Page.
> From furious Sappho scarce a milder fate,
> Poxed by her love, or libelled by her hate.

The original of Delia is supposed to be Mary Howard, Countess of Deloraine, the mistress of George II, whom popular imagination believed to have been responsible for the death of a Miss Mackenzie, a beautiful young girl of whom she was jealous. But, as far as we know, the only reason for connecting furious Sappho with Lady Mary Wortley lies in that lady's not otherwise very active imagination. The reason for her belief that she was the original of those lines must remain the only mysterious thing about her. A thousand bedraggled ladies, and especially those who indulged in a little verse-making, were named Sappho by their admirers and enemies; and seven years before this time, another Sappho, Mrs Sappho

Thomas, had incurred Pope's lasting displeasure by selling his boyish letters to Cromwell. This Sappho, at least, was not a lady of an immaculate life, and it is, to my mind, possible that she was the person meant. It is foolish to pretend that because this Sappho figures within four lines of Lady Deloraine, that she must be held to be a woman of high degree; since Grub Street is lashed in the Satire, as well as the fashionable world. However this may be, Lady Mary behaved with her usual indelicacy, complaining to all manner of persons that she was the original of the lines, and finally going so far as to ask Lord Peterborough (who was much shocked by her lack of reticence) to attack Pope on the subject. That brave and sensible man at first refused to mix himself up in so unsavoury a matter; but, after thinking it over, administered to the lady this very well-deserved rebuke:

'Madam – I was very unwilling to have my name made use of in an affair in which I have no concern, and therefore would not engage myself to speak to Mr Pope; but he, coming to my house the moment you went away, I gave him as exact an account as I could of our conversation. He said to me, what I had said to you, that he wondered how the town would apply these lines to any but some noted common woman; that he should be yet more surprised if you should take them to yourself. He named to me four remarkable poetesses and scribblers, Mrs Centlivre, Mrs Haywood, Mrs Manly and Mrs Behn, ladies famous indeed in their generation, and some of them esteemed to have given very unfortunate favours to their friends, assuring me that such only were the objects of his satire. I hope this assurance will prevent your further mistake, and any consequences upon so odd a subject. I have nothing more to add.

'Your ladyship's most humble and obedient servant

'PETERBOROUGH'

Strange as it may seem, even this appalling snub did not cool the lady, and she continued to grumble to everybody, and to exhibit herself in the worst possible light. The more she talked, the more she became persuaded that she was the subject of this couplet, and at last, not only all reason, but all prudence, forsook her. She collaborated with Lord Hervey in some 'Verses addressed to the Imitator of Horace. By a Lady. Printed by A. Dodd, without Temple Bar'. These verses were surrounded by the usual mystification, and Mr Croker was led by this to believe that the verses were the work of Lord Hervey alone. But the Bodleian Library contains a copy of the original edition, inscribed by Lord Oxford: 'The authors of this poem are Lady Mary Wortley, Lord Hervey, and Mr Windham, under Tutor to the Duke of Cumberland, and married to my Lady Deloraine.' Pope certainly believed them to be the authors of this delicate-minded and spirited piece of work, which, after piling insult upon insult, concludes thus:

> Like the first bold assassin be thy lot;
> Ne'er be thy guilt forgiven or forgot;
> But as thou hat'st, be hated by mankind,
> And with the emblem of thy crooked mind
> Marked on thy back, like Cain, by God's own hand,
> Wander like him accursed through the land.

Not content with this, one of the gifted authors returned to the attack in 'A Letter from a Nobleman at Hampton Court to a Doctor of Divinity' – a wandering, weak and watery affair, yet infused with venom. Lord Hervey was the author of this. He was, as far as such a weak person could be determined, the determined ally of Lady Mary Wortley at the time of her breach with Pope; but, although this fact did not endear him to the poet, the latter made no attack upon him until he inserted these two lines in *The First Satire of The Second Book of Horace*:

> The lines are weak, another's pleased to say,
> Lord Fanny spins a thousand such a day.

This was known to refer to Lord Hervey; but although the lines were certainly contemptuous, they were not such as to excuse the attack made upon Pope.

The poet saw that it was now time to teach Lady Mary Wortley and Lord Hervey a severe lesson. The lesson began with the following advertisement, which appeared in the newspapers in November 1733:

'Whereas a great demand hath been made for an answer to a certain scurrilous Epistle from a Nobleman to Dr Sh-r-n; this is to acquaint the public that it hath been hitherto hindered by what seemed a denial of that Epistle by the Noble Lord in the Daily Courant of Nov. 22, affirming that no such Epistle was written by him. But whereas that declaration hath been since undeclared by the Courant, this is to certify, that unless the said Noble Lord shall this week in a manner as public as the injury, deny the said poem to be his, or contradict the aspersions therein contained, there will with all speed be published a most proper reply to the same. 1733.'

A strange advertisement, coming from the pen of the man who has been accused of showing bravery only towards the ragged and unprotected inhabitants of Grub Street!

The proper reply is contained in 'A Letter to a Noble Lord' dated 30th November, 1733. It is not believed that Lord Hervey made the required apology and retraction, yet Pope's answer to him was not published; and Horace Walpole says that it remained unpublished at the request of his uncle, to whom Pope was grateful since he had procured the Abbacy for his old friend Southcote. Pope told Swift in a letter: 'There is a woman's war declared against me by a certain Lord. His weapons are the same which women and children use: a pin to scratch, and a squirt to bespatter. I writ a sort of answer, but was ashamed to enter the lists with him, and after showing it to some people, suppressed it; otherwise it was such as was worthy of him and worthy of me.' The superb letter is so revealing of the nature of Pope, and of the nature of the wounds he received, that it shall form an appendix to this book.

When that letter is read, Lady Mary Whortley may beallowed to rest – not on her own, but on Pope's laurels. She sinks into oblivion, only to rise again, for a moment, when we see her, as Walpole saw her, in an unwary moment of her exile at Rome. 'Her dress" said Walpole, 'her avarice and her impudence must amaze anyone that never heard her name. She wears a foul mob that does not cover her greasy black locks, that hang loose, never combed or curled, an old mazarine blue wrapper, that gapes open and discovers a canvas petticoat. Her face swelled violently on one side, partly covered with a plaster, and partly with white paint, which for cheapness she has bought coarse.' – A homely picture, and with this in our minds we may leave Lady Mary Wortley.

Lord Hervey was destined to a greater fate. He is impaled for ever in the *Epistle to Dr Arbuthnot* by the name of Sporus, in one of the most tremendous passages in all Pope's poetry:

> Let Sporus tremble – A. What? that thing of silk,
> Sporus, that mere white curd of ass's milk?
> Satire or sense, alas! can Sporus feel,
> Who breaks a butterfly upon a wheel?
> P. Yet let me flap this bug with gilded wings,
> This painted child of dirt, that stinks and stings;
> Whose buzz the witty and the fair annoys,
> Yet wit ne'er tastes, and beauty ne'er enjoys:
> So well-bred spaniels civilly delight
> In mumbling of the game they dare not bite.
> Eternal smiles his emptiness betray,
> As shallow streams run dimpling all the way,
> Whether in florid impudence he speaks,
> And, as the prompter breathes, the puppet squeaks;
> Or at the ear of Eve, familiar toad,
> Half froth, half venom, spits himself abroad,
> In puns, or politics, or tales, or lies,
> Or spite, or smut, or rhymes, or blasphemies.
> His wit all see-saw, between that and this,
> Now high, now low, now master up, now miss,
> And he himself one vile antithesis.
> Amphibious thing! that acting either part,
> The trifling head, or the corrupted heart;
> Fop at the toilet, flatterer at the board,
> Now trips a lady, and now struts a lord.
> Eve's tempter thus the rabbins have expressed,
> A cherub's face, a reptile all the rest.
> Beauty that shocks you, parts that none will trust,
> Wit that can creep, and pride that licks the dust.

His enemy has given him, not death, but immortality.

CHAPTER XIII

Twickenham

In the year 1719, two years after the death of his father, Pope removed from Chiswick to a more imposing house, with a garden, at Twickenham – or Twitnam as he preferred to call it. This house and garden, with the celebrated grotto, which was his work, became to him the symbol of the romance which was denied to him in every other part of life excepting his poetry. The house itself was not impressive; it was small, and did not offer any particular opportunities for investing it with romance – but the garden was a different matter – and as for the grotto, the possibilities contained in this were endless. In the garden and the grotto, the poet, as he talked to his illustrious friends, could imagine that he was anyone from Horace to Nero – he could be, in turn, every classical poet of the past, and every philosopher, and every hero of romance – in short, he was every famous person excepting Alexander Pope, the famous poet, Alexander Pope, the crippled hunchback. He enjoyed *receiving* his distinguished guests, the great and terrible Sarah Duchess of Marlborough, Bishop Atterbury, Lord Peterborough, Lord Bolingbroke, etc., in the character of Mr Alexander Pope, the famous poet, knowing that they were drawn to the grotto by the fame of Mr Pope; but once they were seated there, and immersed in conversation, Mr Pope floated away, and Horace or Virgil, or one of the more respected Roman Emperors took his place. The neighbourhood was rich in beauty, great parks with trees flashing like icebergs, small and romantic paths 'twisted and rhymed', great fields with flowering trees, all these were ready for his delight, but all these pleasures were eclipsed and over-shadowed by the glory of the grotto.

A pamphlet was published in 1745 giving 'A Plan of Mr Pope's Garden, as it was left at the time of his death, with a Plan and Perspective View of the Grotto. All taken by J. Searle, his gardener. With an account of all the Gems, Minerals, Spars, and Ores of which it is composed, and from whom they are sent. To which is added a Character of his writings. London. R. Dodsley. Price 1/6*d.*'

There were, it seems, among other rustic pleasures, a Shell Temple, a Vineyard, an Obelisk in Memory of his Mother, a Bowling green, a Grove, an Orangery, a Kitchen Garden. And then we come to details of the grotto, and I cannot resist quoting the whole of the passages dealing with this. The inventory is very conscientious, which is natural considering it is the work of that 'good John' who protected the poet for so many years against the poetesses and poetasters who wished to

rave, recite, and madden round the land.

'AN ACCOUNT OF THE MATERIALS WHICH COMPOSE THE GROTTO

Over the Entrance from the Garden:

Secretum iter et fallentis semita vitae. – HOR.

1 At the entrance of the Grotto next the Garden are various sorts of stones, thrown promiscuously together, in imitation of an Old Ruin; some full of holes, others like honeycombs, which came from Ralph Allen's, Esq., at Widcombe, near Bath. Several fine fossil and snake stones, with petrified wood and moss in various shapes, from the petrifying spring at Nasborough (Knaresborough), in Yorkshire, by the Rev. D. Key. Fine verd-antique from Egypt, with several sorts of Italian sparry marble of divers colours. Amethysts; several clumps of different forms, with some fine pieces of white spar, from her Grace the Duchess of Cleveland, at Raby Castle, in Westmoreland (Durham). Some fine pieces of German spar, intermixed with yellow mundic, with moss and some English pebbles. In the centre is a fine spring.

2 Flints, moss of many sorts, many pieces of Plymouth marble of different colours, from Mr Cooper of that place. Several pieces of well-chosen things from the Glass-house.

Several fine flakes of gold clift from Mr Cambridge, with several fine pieces of white spar from the Duchess of Cleveland.

3 Many small dice of mundic and tin ore. Two sorts of yellow-flaky copper; one showing, by the different strata of metal, that different masses of copper will, though concreted at different times, unite close into one globe or lump. Several groups of Cornish diamonds incrusted, semi-pellucid, and shot round a globe of yellow copper. Many thick incrustations of shot-spar of a yellowish cast, sprinkled with small cubes of mundic, lead ore, kallan, or wild iron. Many fine pieces of yellow mundic, several small Cornish diamonds, tinged with a blackish water, and others with a green water. Several large groups of Cornish diamonds, very transparent, from the Rev. Dr William Borlase, of Ludgvan, in Cornwall. Many fine large pieces of red spar, out of Colonel Stapleton's lead mine, from George Lyttelton, Esq. Fine petrifactions from Gilbert West, Esq., at West Wickham, in Kent. Fine incrustations from Mr Allen's quarries; and several pieces of sparry marble, of different colours, from Plymouth; with many large Cornish diamonds, and other petrifactions which form two fine rocks, with water distilling from them.

4 Fine sparry marble, from Lord Edgecombe's quarry, with different sorts of moss. Several fine pieces of the eruption from Mount Vesuvius, and a fine piece of marble from the Grotto of Egeria, near Rome; from the Rev. Mr Spence. With several fine petrifactions and Plymouth marble, from Mr Cooper. Gold clift from Mr Cambridge, Gloucestershire; and several fine brain-stones from Mr Miller, of Chelsea.

5 Many fine pieces of sparry marble, of divers colours, and between each course of marble many kinds of ores – such as tin ore, copper ore, lead ore, soapy rock, kallan and wild lead intermixed; with large clumps of Cornish diamonds, and several small ores of different degrees of transparency. The several sorts of figured stones are rich white spars, interlaced with black cockle, or spars shot into prisms of different degrees of waters. Some very particular sorts of fossils, of different sizes

and colours; copper ore of a fine purple colour; several fine pieces of granated white mundic, intermixed with plain spar in a copper bed. Several thin crusts or films of bright spar, formed on a surface before shot into protuberances; a lump of yellow copper that has a very singular crust of spar, some grains of mundic interspersed of different colours – some yellow, some purple, and others of a deep blue, inclining to black; all from the Rev. Dr William Borlase. Several fine Bristol stones of different colours, some of a dark brown, others of a yellow cast, etc, from Mrs Broxholme; and several fine incrustations from Mr Allen.

6 Several large pieces of fine crystal, intermixed with yellow mundic. A fine piece of spar, interwoven like many oyster shells, and intermixed with white mundic. A fine piece of spar, with a mixture of copper interwoven like a fine lace. Several pieces of crystal with a brown incrustation, and a mixture of mundic from the Hartz mines, in Germany. A fine piece of gold ore from the Peruvian mines. Silver ore from the mines of Mexico. Several pieces of silver ore from Old Spain. Some large pieces of gold clift from Mr Cambridge, in Gloucestershire. Load ore, copper ore, white spar, petrified wood, Brazil pebbles, Egyptian pebbles, and blood stones, from Mr Brinsden. Some large clumps of amethyst, and several pieces of white spar, from the Duchess of Cleveland. Some fine pieces of red spar, several fine icicles, and several sorts of fossils from George Lyttelton, Esq. Many pieces of coral and petrified moss, and many other curious stones, from the island of St Christopher, in the West Indies; with several humming-birds and their nests, from Antony Brown, Esq., of Abbs Court, in Surrey. Plymouth marble of different colours, one fine Cornish diamond from the Prince's Mine, in Cornwall. Near a hundred-weight from the Rev. Dr Askew. Several fine pieces of yellow mundic. Some purple copper stained by mineral water. Two stones from the Giant's Causeway, in Ireland, from Sir Hans Sloane. Some pieces of petrified wood, with coral and petrified moss round a basin of water.

7 Different kinds of Italian marble. Many fine Kerry stones

of different waters, with several fine fossils from Ireland, from the Earl of Orrery. Many flakes of white spar and mother-amethyst from the Duchess of Cleveland. The roof of small stones, incrusted over, out of the river Thames. Some square dice of mundic. Several pieces of silver ore from old Spain; with several sorts of moss.

8 Different sorts of sparry marble from Italy. Several large stones interwoven like honeycombs; and others like old broken pillars. Many large pieces of Plymouth marble, German spar, and spar from Norway, by Mr Afterloney. The roof of purple spar, and some yellow spar; and several fine square dice of mundic from Mr Ord's mine in Yorkshire. And round a piece of water are fixed different plants, such as maiden-hair, hart's tongue, fern, and several other plants; intermixed with many petrifactions, and some uncommon Cornish diamonds, from Lord Godolphin's great copper works, in Ludgvan.

9 Some very natural rock work, compiled of flints and cinders from the glass-houses, furnaces, etc.; with some grains of mundic artfully mixed with white spar.

10 A fine and very uncommon petrifaction from Okey Hole, in Somersetshire, from Mr Bruce.'

(Curll, in 1735, said: 'He [Pope] has been annually improving the gardens to the amount of £5,000, as Mr Searle, his gardener, assured us. He has lived with Mr Pope above eleven years; and, in the hortulan dialect, told us that there were not ten sticks in the ground when his master took the house.')

The grotto was unfortunate enough to excite (if so volatile a word may be used in connection with so dignified a man) the strong condemnation of Doctor Johnson, who saw in it a proof of the want of seriousness of its owner. His reproof, though awful in its majestic dignity, was restrained; it obliterated the grotto, whilst leaving the owner of the grotto standing upon his Roman pedestal, uninjured among the ruins:

'Being under the necessity', said Doctor Johnson, 'of making a subterranean passage to a garden on the other side of the road, he adorned it with fossil bodies, and dignified it with the title of a grotto; a place of silence and retreat, from which he endeavoured to persuade his friends and himself that cares and passions could be excluded.

'A grotto is not often the wish or pleasure of an Englishman, who has more frequent need to solicit than to exclude the sun; but Pope's excavation was requisite as an entrance to his garden, and, as some men try to be proud of their defects, he extracted an ornament from an inconvenience, and vanity produced a grotto where necessity enforced a passage. It may be frequently remarked of the studious and speculative, that they are proud of trifles, and that their amusements seem frivolous and childish; whether it be that men conscious of great reputation think themselves above the reach of censure, and safe in the admission of negligent indulgences, or that mankind expect from elevated genius an uniformity of greatness, and watch its degradation with malicious wonder; like him who having followed with his eye an eagle into the clouds should lament that she ever descended to a perch.'

I think it cannot be denied that but little of the grotto was left, at the end of this rebuke; but it must be remembered, also, that Doctor Johnson disapproved, invariably, of the softer passions when indulged in by great men. Nothing, for instance, could show this disapproval more strongly than his rebuke to Thomas Gray, over the matter of Mr Walpole's cat: 'In this retirement', said Doctor Johnson, with commendable restraint, 'he wrote (1747) an ode on the Death of Mr Walpole's Cat; and the year after attempted a poem *of more importance, on Government and Education,* of which the fragments which remain have many excellent lines.' The italics are mine.

But though Doctor Johnson, after the poet's death, expressed disapproval of the Grotto, nothing, in the poet's lifetime, could spoil his pleasure, either in the Grotto, or in the garden. He was never tired of planning improvements, or of completing these. He found in this retreat, a refuge from his misery, from his thwarted romanticism, from his deformity, from his illness.

It is true that the garden was not large, but it was larger than the garden of Alcinous, which was the subject of his dreams, and which comprised only four acres. The poet's touching and childlike enthusiasm for these rustic beauties was unending; he played with them as a child plays with the sand castles on the borders of an eternal sea. For in his garden, change meant not decay and sorrow, but the building of fresh and everlasting beauties. Nor was he ever tired of writing descriptions of these to his friends, such descriptions as this, taken from a letter to Edward Blount:

'*Twick'nam. June* 2, 1725.

'Let the young ladies be assured I make nothing new in my gardens without wishing to see the print of their fairy steps in every part of them. I have put the last hand to my works of this kind, in happily finishing the subterraneous way and grotto. I there found a spring of the clearest water, which falls in a perpetual rill, that echoes thro' the cavern day and night. From the river Thames, you can see thro' my arch up a walk of the wilderness, to a kind of open temple, wholly composed of shells in the rustic manner, and from the distance under the temple you look thro' a sloping arcade of trees, and see the sails on the river passing suddenly and vanishing, as thro' a perspective glass. When you shut the doors of this grotto, it becomes on the instant, from a luminous room, a camera obscura; on the walls of which all objects of the river, hills, woods and boats, are forming a moving picture in their visible radiations; and when you have a mind to light it up, it affords you a very different scene. It is finished with shells interspersed with pieces of looking glass in angular forms; and in the ceiling is a star of the same material, at which, when a lamp (of orbicular figure of thin alabaster) is hung in the middle, a thousand pointed rays glitter, and are reflected over the place.

'There are connected to this grotto, by a narrower passage, two porches: one towards the river, of smooth stones full of light, and open; the other toward the garden, shadowed with trees, rough with shells, flints, and iron ore. The bottom is paved with simple pebble, as is also the adjoining walk up the wilderness to the temple, in the natural taste, agreeing not ill with the little dripping murmur, and the aquatic idea of the whole place. It wants nothing to complete it but a good statue, with an inscription, like that beautiful antique one which you know I am so fond of:

> 'Hujus Nympha loci, sacri custodia fontis
> Dormio, dum blandae sentio murmur aquae.
> Parce meum, quisquis tangis cava marmora, somnum
> Rumpere, sive bibas, sive lavare, tace.
>
> 'Nymph of the grot, these sacred springs I keep,
> And to the murmur of these waters sleep;
> Ah, spare my slumbers, gently tread the cave!
> And drink in silence, or in silence lave!

'You'll think I have been very poetical in this description, but it's pretty near the truth. I wish you were to bear testimony how little it owes to art, either the place itself, or the image I give of it.'

Who could avoid loving the poet when he was in this mood?

The house was not large; we are told it consisted of a small hall, paved with stone, and on either side of this, two small parlours, with a corresponding upper story. Pope did not add to the house, although he was never tired of making plans for altering it. But it was large enough for his needs and those of his friends, so the plans were never completed.

Lord Peterborough was a constant (and useful) visitor to Pope's Tusculum. This indomitable nobleman, whose bravery had been shown, not only in his battles, but in daring to shock Bath by wearing boots (which at that time were never worn excepting when travelling) and by doing his own marketing, was often to be seen, by the astonished and fashionable invalids, with his blue ribbon and star pinned to his breast, yet with a cabbage under each arm, or a chicken in his hand. He moved, with such encumbrances, among the elegant ghosts as if these had not been there. They were shocked, and showed it. Handkerchiefs were raised in fluttering hands; eyebrows, delicately painted as the wings of butterflies, were raised also. But in after years the fashionable world had its revenge; for Lord Peterborough was far more shocked by the indelicacy of Lady Mary Wortley in supposing the couplet about Sappho to have been inspired by her, than Bath had been shocked by either boots or chicken.

But now, in a more rustic retreat than Bath, and in surroundings more pleasing to his simple tastes, the great general might often be seen, red-faced and stooping, and with a spade in his hand, digging and digging in his friends' garden.

Another constant visitor to Pope's Tusculum was a very different character (though this character also was capable of bravery) – the cautious, the urbane, the watchful Francis Atterbury, Bishop of Rochester. His portrait shows us a clocklike disc of a face – a face that registered the time, yet was, also, capable of defying it – with a round and inexpressive, yet watchful eye, a plump shaven clerical chin, and the nostrils of a rocking-horse – one might almost imagine that the insides of those nostrils were touched with meat-red paint. Indeed, he *was* a rocking-horse, in many ways, though not as regards politics; for in his political life he was, though a plotter, sincere; and for these ideals he risked death, and suffered banishment.

The Bishop's first cautious appearance in this book is with his letter of condolence about the death of Pope's father, a singularly tactless letter for so eminently careful a divine, since it scarcely mentions the bereavement, but uses it only as an excuse for worrying the poet to change his religion. Pope returned a polite and rather evasive reply, and this was followed by an interchange of letters, which grew more and more affectionate in tone. Indeed, it is probable that Pope had a real regard for the Bishop, although his taste in literature must have been a source of bewilderment to the poet. But on the 2nd of August, 1721, the Bishop on his side showed signs of bewilderment. He writes:

'I have found time to read some parts of Shakespeare which I was least acquainted with. I protest to you in a hundred places I cannot construe him: I do not understand him. The hardest part of Chaucer is more intelligible to me than some of those scenes, not merely through the fault of his edition, but the obscurity of the writer, for obscure he is, and a little (not a little) inclined now and then to bombast, whatever apology you may have contrived on that head for him. There are allusions in him to an hundred things, of which I know nothing and can guess nothing. And yet without some competent knowledge of these matters there is no understanding him.' (These modernist poets!)

Pope's answer to this letter is not recorded; perhaps it was spoken, and not written; in any case, it must have offered some difficulties.

But the Bishop's busy enquiry into the nature of poetry did not end there. For, in spite of the fact that in 1717 the good Bishop had admired Milton, at the request of Pope, five years later (on the 15th June, 1722) we find him urging Pope to polish *Samson Agonistes*! 'I hope', says he, 'you will not utterly forget what passed in the coach about *Samson Agonistes*. I shall not press you as to time, but some time or other, I wish you would review and polish that piece. If, upon a new perusal of it (which I desire you to make) you think as I do, that it is written in the very spirit of the ancients, it deserves your care, and is capable of being improved, with little trouble, into a perfect model and standard of tragic poetry – always allowing for its being a story taken from the Bible; which is an objection that at this time of day is not to be got over.'

It is unnecessary to say that Pope was in no way involved in such a fantastic suggestion; yet the detestable Bowles seized on it as another means of belittling him. 'Pope, however (he says) did not presume to touch it; but the request of Atterbury must ever remain a monument, I will not say of his *want* of *taste* (for no one seems more pleased with Milton) but of the *submission* of his taste and almost faculties where Pope is concerned' – as though Pope had belittled Milton.

Alas, the peaceful visits of the Bishop, his plans for the reformation of Milton's poems, were soon to be disturbed. For on the 24th of August, 1722 he was arrested and charged with having written letters no more destructive than that in which he made an attempt against *Samson Agonistes*, but of a kind prohibited by the law. He had, it seems, plotted treason. He was committed to the Tower, and on the 8th of May, 1723 was brought before the House of Lords to answer the charges against him. Some time before this, he had asked Pope to give evidence that his occupations at the Deanery were peaceable, and the poet, with some courage, agreed to do so. For weeks before the event, he indulged in day-dreams – imagining his own fiery and impassioned speech in defence of the Bishop, the scene in the House of Lords, the astonishment, changing into enthusiasm, of the Peers – imagining, too, the Bishop saved from banishment by the eloquence of his friend, Mr Pope the famous poet, the cheers of the audience, himself enthroned with the Bishop, as the two heroes of the hour.

Alas, none of these things happened. Pope was called to give evidence, but from the moment he began to speak, the day-dream collapsed like a house of cards. He was confused, he was nervous, his memory deserted him, and, as he told Spence, 'though I had but ten words to say, and that on a plain point, how the Bishop spent his time while I was with him at Bromley, I made two or three blunders in it, and that, notwithstanding the first row of lords, which was all I could see, were mostly of my acquaintance'.

The Bishop's defence, though more eloquent than that of Pope, failed; and he was banished to France, where he entered into the service of the Chevalier, and tried, but failed, to raise military expeditions in aid of his master. Before he left England, he presented Pope with his Bible, a sequel to an occasion when he had urged the poet to study the Scriptures. Pope had replied, with his usual pleasing evasiveness: 'I ought first to prepare my mind for a better knowledge even of good profane writers, especially the moralists, etc., before I can be worthy of tasting that supreme of books and sublime of all writings.'

But although Bishop Atterbury had gone, there were many other great personages and some cultivated persons, to take his place. Bolingbroke, who had been exiled from England, was allowed to return at the time of the Bishop's banishment (this roused in Atterbury's mind the suspicion that they had been actually exchanged) and he occupied the place in Pope's life which the Bishop had filled. He proved, indeed, a less dangerous companion for the poet, since from him, as Carruthers has pointed out, no 'chilling religious counsels or grave lectures on Protestantism were to be feared', nor any plans for the reformation of Milton, nor, indeed, any doubts as to the worth of Shakespeare. Pope spent much of his time sitting among haycocks at Battersea or at Dawley, a property which had been bought by Bolingbroke and heightened into such rusticity that even the walls were not spared, but were painted with 'the insignia and even the implements of husbandry' (again I quote from Carruthers).

Rusticity, together with wit, death-bed scenes, and the theatre, were the favourite amusements of the time, and Lord Bolingbroke determined that Dawley should be as rustic as possible. It was. Pope describes the effect of this rusticity in a letter: 'I now hold the pen for my Lord Bolingbroke, who is reading your letter between two haycocks, but his attention is somewhat diverted by casting his eyes on the clouds, not in admiration of what you say, but in fear of a shower ... As to the return of his health and vigour, were you here, you might enquire of his haymakers; but as to his temperance, I can answer that (for one whole day) we have had nothing for dinner but mutton broth, beans, and bacon, and a barn-door fowl. Now his lordship is run after his cart, I have a moment left to myself to tell you that I overheard him yesterday agree with a painter for £200 to paint his country hall with trophies of rakes, spades, prongs, etc. and other ornaments, merely to countenance his calling this place a farm.'

Alas, a certain amount of political plotting, as well as haymaking, was carried out among the haycocks.

Bolingbroke was a constant visitor at Twickenham, and there was obliged, among less strenuous occupations, to read Mr Aaron Hill's *Tragedy of Athelwolde* (that spectre dogging the footsteps of Pope) four times, with the poet as witness and fellow-sufferer.

The visitors to Twickenham were so many and so varied that the different hues of their minds reflected the shining spars, corals, and humming-birds' feathers of the grotto. Voltaire, with his hard wide mind and inspiration, the ancient, the swash-buckling and military-minded Sarah Duchess of Marlborough, over whom the poet sighed, when she failed to keep an appointment: 'Oh, what a girl you are!' these differed widely, though both were equally awe-inspiring. As we have seen in a previous chapter, the Prince of Wales was a visitor, and Pope was believed to have declined the honour of a visit from Queen Caroline – but this story must be apocryphal. It was based on the fact that while the Queen was in residence at Richmond Lodge, in the summer of 1729, she became, suddenly, addicted to a wider social life than had been habitual with her. She dined with Walpole at Windsor and Chelsea; she hunted with him at Windsor. Then she descended upon Twickenham, at the invitation of the Scottish Secretary Johnston, who provided her with entertainment. At this point Pope left Twickenham, for fear that it should be believed that he courted an honour of this kind.

Pope was to be seen every day, or at all times when the entertainment of his friends did not make this impossible, floating down the river in his barge, into which his weakness made it necessary that he should be lifted by the waterman. He was by this time so weakened by his pain that he must be encased in iron; and the waterman said that as he lifted the poet, he could feel that iron structure, but felt hardly at all the tiny body that it held together, as the cold may hold together the bones of the dead.

Sometimes, but very rarely, the poet sat alone among the glittering stones of his grotto. What was he thinking about, sitting there, so quietly? Of that heap of stones into which he was thrown by the wild cow, when she attacked him so wantonly? Of John Dennis? Of the ever-beloved Martha Blount and of Teresa, whom he had loved and trusted, and who had betrayed that trust? Or of that summer day when a shopman and his young son, walking among the leafy mazes of Twickenham, saw a thin little man, in a suit of rusty black and with a cocked hat, who walked with difficulty. The little man, as he passed, heard the boy exclaim, overcome with pity, 'Poor man!' 'Poor man!' said his father: 'that is no poor man. It is the great Mr Alexander Pope!'

CHAPTER XIV

Dean Swift and Pope

In the summer of 1727 Dean Swift paid a visit to Pope at Twickenham; but the visit does not seem to have been an undiluted success. The Dean was suffering once more from the terrible giddiness and deafness which were, in his last years, to imprison him, now in the maelstrom whirl and beat of hell, now in the silence of the polar wastes.

At this time, by an effort of will, the magnitude of which can be gauged only by the power and blackness of his subsequent madness, he was still a visitor in our human world; but he knew that one swirl of the giddiness might hurl him into the other, over that red brink, into something that he could not see clearly; and he needed to avoid that brink by the effort of a terrible caution, which could only be exerted in silence. This was not possible at Twickenham. The house was invaded by so many of Pope's and the Dean's acquaintance, chattering like monkeys, talking like philosophers, that he was drawn nearer and nearer to the maelstrom, hearing in the innocent voices which penetrated that thick mist of his growing deafness, some hint of the appalling roar of the world which so soon would claim him as an inhabitant.

There were other and slight troubles, but all of these increased his uneasiness. Pope, in his kindness and solicitude, fluttered like a little white moth round and round the Dean, increasing his giddiness, while the poet's voice penetrated that black fog like an insect's voice, so tiny and so warning did it sound. Swift, in those hours when he was not half in communication with the other, waiting, watching world into which the madman crashes, tried to keep a hold upon himself. In a letter to Sheridan, dated the 12th August, 1727, he complained of this giddiness and deafness, as though they were not a preparation for that other world which would so soon envelop him, but only the symptoms of an ordinary illness; and he said that he was resolved that if they continued he must leave Twickenham and remove to Greenwich, or somewhere near London, for 'Mr Pope is too sickly and complaisant', and the acquaintances were too many. He complained also in some verses that he was too deaf to hear the weak voice of Pope, and that after looking at each other for a while, they had to return to their several occupations.

During these attacks of giddiness and deafness, Swift was worried almost beyond endurance by the 'elaborate civilities' of Pope, whom, nevertheless, he loved. He therefore left Twickenham, and Pope, who thought the Dean was afraid, not of being bothered, but of bothering Pope, wrote to his friend: 'the best way of convincing you of my indulgence will be, if I live, to visit you in Ireland, and act there as much in my own way as you did here in yours. I will not leave your roof if I am ill ...'

This happy state of affairs was the last thing the Dean wanted; but affection for Pope prevailed over his other feelings; and it may be, too, that he knew that his friend's sickly state of health would make him unwilling to face the Irish Sea when the moment came; so he replied amiably, if gloomily, that Pope was the best and kindest friend in the world, and that he knew nobody alive or dead to whom he was so much obliged, and that if he (the Dean) was angry it was because his friend took too much care of him. (This was true). At the same time, he pointed out that Pope was too ill to be mortified with the care of a sick friend whose giddiness was enough to make any friend uneasy, 'without that unsociable, comfortless deafness'. The case, he pointed out, would have been quite different had Pope been in Swift's house, since 'you could refuse to see anybody, and here is a large house where we need not hear each other if we were both sick. I have a race of orderly, elderly persons of both sexes at command, who are of no consequence, and have gifts proper for attending us, who can bawl when I am deaf, and tread softly when I am only giddy and would sleep'.

In short, each friend enjoyed the thought of the companionship of the other when that other was absent, and each was afraid that his friend might learn how troublesome his company seemed on those occasions when they were together. What would have been the fate of the orderly, elderly persons of no consequence, had the two friends shared a house, it is impossible to conjecture. Some years later, after the death of Stella and of Mrs Pope, the poet begged Dean Swift to give all his money to the poor of Ireland, and to spend the rest of his life in the household at Twickenham, 'since', said Pope, 'I have enough for two'. His letter to Swift (dated the 25th March, 1736) says: 'I find myself little disposed to buy a new house. I have nothing left but to gather up the reliques of a wreck, and look about me to see how few friends I have left ... I am a man of desperate fortunes, that is, a man whose friends are dead: for I never aimed at any other fortune than friends.

'I could keep you, for I am rich, that is, I have more than I want. I can afford room for yourself and two servants; I have indeed room enough, nothing but myself at home. The kind and hearty housewife (his mother) is dead. The agreeable and instructive neighbour (Lord Bolingbroke) is gone. Yet my house is enlarged, and the gardens extend and flourish, as knowing nothing of the guests I have lost. I have more fruit trees and kitchen gardens than you have any thought of: nay, I have good melons and pineapples of my own growth ... For God's sake, why should not you ... e'en give all you have to the poor of Ireland (for whom you have already done everything else) so quit the place, and live and die with me?'

The biographers have brought the usual charge of insincerity against Pope in this, as in every other case of his protestations of friendship. 'He knew', they exclaimed, 'that this was a safe proposal, since the Dean could not leave Ireland.' I do not understand the mentality of the people who bring this charge against Pope, nor why they protest that he could not have wished for the presence of his old and valued friend, his preferred intellectual companion, even if that presence brought various discomforts in its train. Pope's dearly loved father and mother and the old nurse who had been his earliest friend, had been taken from him by death. He was alone, and it was surely natural that he, with his deeply affectionate nature, and his pain and illness, should suffer more from his isolated position than most men. Yet so deep is the prejudice in his disfavour that he cannot be allowed even the possession of those friendships which were rooted the most deeply in his heart, without the imputation of insincerity towards Dean Swift, and of a vulgar intrigue with the beloved and reverenced Martha Blount being brought against him.

It is as well, however, that the two friends did not share a household.

Dean Swift, as we know, was in the habit of walking up and down his room, like a caged beast, for hours at a stretch. He loved disorder and strange tramp-like habits. For instance, during the time when he lived in the Temple and was in the habit of paying a yearly visit to his mother at Leicester, he, drawn by his love of pedestrianism and his love of disorder (and by avarice) would insist on travelling on foot, unless the weather was so bad that he must take refuge in a wagon, when, like Lear, he would appear with straws in his hair. His nightly shelter was a penny lodging, although he allowed himself the luxury of having clean sheets for sixpence. His brotherhood with vagabondage was such that he tried to organize the tattered, maimed, and blinded beggars of Dublin into a sort of army, by making them wear a badge. He had a thousand strange habits which grew odder as his years increased. For instance, when his friends visited him, the Dean had been known to add up the cost of their entertainment, in a loud and rather grumbling voice, but with no real appearance of regret – for he was anxious to be generous with his friends in this respect, and wished to show them that he did not grudge them the sums of money that were spent on offering them hospitality. Pope described to Spence one occasion when he and Gay paid an unexpected visit to the Dean. 'On our coming in: "Hey-day, gentlemen", says the Doctor, "what's the meaning of this visit? How came you to leave all the great lords that you are so fond of, to come hither to see a poor Dean?" "Because we would rather see you than any of them." "Ay, ay, one that did not know you so well as I do might believe you. But since you are come, I must get some supper for you, I suppose." "No, Doctor, we have supped already." "Supped already? that's impossible: why, 'tis not eight o'clock yet." "Indeed we have." "That's very strange. But if you had not supped, I must have got something for you. Let me see, what should I have had! A couple of lobsters? Ay, that would have done very well: two shillings: tarts, a shilling. But you will drink a glass of wine with me, though you supped so much before your usual time, only to spare my pocket?" "No, we had rather talk with you than drink with you." "But if you had supped with me, as in all reason you ought to have done, you must have drunk with me – a bottle of wine, two shillings – two and two is four; and one is five; just two and sixpence a piece. There, Pope, there's half-a-crown for you; and there's another for you, sir; for I won't save anything from you, I'm determined." This was all said and done with his usual seriousness on such occasions; and in spite of everything we could say to the contrary, he actually obliged us to take the money.'

By the time that Pope invited Swift to live at Twickenham the Dean's deafness, always troublesome to himself and to the outside world, had grown almost, if not quite, impenetrable. This disorder was ascribed by the Dean, and by Doctor Johnson, to an immoderate indulgence in fruit – a singularly suitable appetite for one whose immeasurably black and deep eyebrows gave his gravity such an exact resemblance to the gravity of a raven, that one might expect a black and rusty caw, instead of a human voice, to issue from his lips. By now, this thick fog of deafness had increased to such a pitch that conversation was impossible. He was surrounded by a thick black half-mad silence, like the plumage of the raven that he resembled. Doctor Johnson tells us that 'Having thus excluded conversation and desisted from study, he had neither business nor amusement, for having, by some ridiculous resolution or mad vow, determined never to wear spectacles, he could make less use of books in his later years; his ideas, therefore, being neither renovated nor increased by reading, wore gradually away, and left his mind vacant for the vexations of the hour, till at last his anger was heightened into madness'. Nothing remained, therefore, of what had made that great and awe-inspiring figure, but this terrible pedestrianism, which, after his madness had increased into the black smoky Tartarean fire wherein the last dust of his mind was consumed, kept him on his feet for ten hours a day; so that, when his meat was brought to him, cut into mouthfuls as though he were a wild beast, he, having left it till it had stood for an hour, would eat it walking.

Pope, on the other hand, was meticulous and fidgety, flitting like a moth, and as frail as a moth. He was watchful of the moments that flew with such invisible wings, for he knew that but little of that precious and holy time was left to him in which he might bring the poetry which hid in his tortured and deformed body, into the light. It must have been exceedingly difficult for anyone in the household of which he was an inmate, to obtain either rest or peace. Even his friends' households were not spared, for Lord Oxford's maid-servant complained that in the blue cold winter of Forty, she was called from her bed by him five times in one night, to supply him with paper, lest he should lose a thought. And he was in the habit of summoning his and other people's servants to send them on messages, some important, others entirely trivial. He would demand coffee in the middle of the night, not once, but several times. The unhappy little creature had to be dressed and undressed like a child, such was his weakness; it was necessary, too, that he should have his way in everything, or he became fretful and unhappy like a sick child. When he stayed in a friend's house, the whole household was obliged to devote itself to his wants, and even so it could scarcely keep pace with them. We may imagine, from this, what may have been the extent of his demands upon his own household; and yet, in spite of all this, the inmates of his house were devoted to him.

It cannot be denied, therefore, that, with the Dean walking up and down his room all day, and Pope ringing his bell for coffee or for writing-paper all night; with the Dean's penny-house habits, and Pope's habits of the great houses; with the Dean marshalling the beggars, and Pope collecting the Peers;

with the Dean's occasional neglect of food (coupled with a tendency to grumble when there was anything wrong with it), and Pope's almost inordinate love of it; with the Dean's deafness and Pope's love of conversation, life in the household at Twickenham might have been difficult, had not Providence intervened. Providence did intervene, and Swift remained in the Deanery, which was inured to his behaviour.

We may gain some idea of the sufferings to which Twickenham would have been exposed, from the sufferings endured by Watt (Swift's servant) on the journey home from the unlucky visit to which I have referred. It cannot be denied that neither the Dean's visit to England nor his journey home could be counted as a success. The Dean kept a journal recording his travels home to Ireland, and, his gloom and dudgeon having increased during that time, he left the journal behind in an inn, quite by mistake, no doubt, and it was sent to Pope and Gay by the housemaid, which surprised the author of the journal immensely, although it was exactly what he had foreseen would happen.

It throws a strange light on Swift's character that these minor grumblings were meant to disguise from others – and perhaps from himself – the unutterable misery that was eating him away because he knew by now, beyond any doubt, that Stella must soon leave him; for he could never, either in his healthy moments, or in those moments of madness which had the grandeur and the vastness of years, or in those years in which he lay buried in a huge and polar silence, acknowledge the cracks and fissures which foreran the breaking of his heart.

The Journal starts thus: 'September the 22nd, 1727. Friday at 11 in the morning, left Chester'; and from that moment the record was one of almost unmitigated gloom. It was true that the Dean saw some interesting sights, including the tomb of Mr Hook, who was the forty-first child of his mother, but who was, himself, only endowed with twenty-seven children, and who died about 1639. But, to set against the pleasure and interest of this sight, there was the trouble with Inns: at some Inns the Dean found a very good loin of mutton, but the worst ale in the world, and no wine, because only the day before 'a vast number went to Ireld after having drunk out all the wine'. The beer was sour, and the Dean tried a receipt of oyster shells, which he got powdered on purpose, but the receipt did not work, so the Dean walked on the rocks in the evening and looked at nothing in particular, and then went home and put himself to bed, and dreamt that he had got twenty falls from his horse. In other Inns the trouble about food was reversed, and the Dean was able to procure brandy and water for his dinner, but was rewarded for this comfort by a raw chicken.

Then again, there was the dilemma about how to spend the evenings, coupled with the trouble about reading: for the Dean could not read by candlelight (because he refused to wear spectacles), and sleeping made him sick. Yet he must needs spend five hours by himself at night, and retire to his chamber 'and scribble or sit humdrum'. For to whom could he speak? The Dean did not dare talk to anybody, for fear of getting acquaintance with the Irish, and 'the dog is better company than the Vicar, for I remember him of old'.

How then was the Dean to occupy his time? He walked a good way among the rocks, and to a hole in one of them from whence at certain periods the water spouted up several feet high. But even this phenomenon could not interest him for long. At last the Dean took Watt, his servant (whom he called, at varying intervals, dunce, puppy, and liar, and to whom he did not dare talk for fear that Watt should respond in a friendly manner) to see the Wicklow hills; and to see the Wicklow hills they had to climb up 'a monstrous mountain'. But when they had climbed up the monstrous mountain they could not see the Wicklow hills because the day was cloudy. Then it came on to rain, and the Dean and Watt took refuge in a Welsh cabin, where a boy 'fell aroaring' for fear of the Dean. (But this, though it annoyed, did not surprise the Dean, for he had not been courteously treated by a Mr Jones, who was the master of a pacquet boat, and this in spite of the fact that his hat had been positively worn to pieces by taking it off because passers-by insisted on doffing their hats to him). So the boy roared, and

Watt was sent home in the rain to fetch the Dean's coat, but he was so long in doing so that the Dean set out in worse rain than ever to find him, and reached the Inn just as Watt left it, carrying the key of the Dean's room with him, so that the Dean could not get into his room, nor warm himself by his fire. Watt, by this time, was not popular. 'His blunders', the Dean said, 'would bear a history'. But Watt had really excelled himself in the matter of the Dean's washing. Some of his shirts had been put in the great box of goods which went by the carrier to Chester, and all the Dean's cravats had been left behind because Watt thought they could not be washed by the way. The Dean did not dare send anything to the laundress, for who could tell if he might not be called away at a moment's notice, and then the laundress might be left in possession of the washing.

Then there was the trouble with the elements: the fire in his room smoked, but the weather was too cold and damp to allow him to sit without a fire. Then the Dean, who had waited for days for a wind so that he might sail to Ireland, *heard* a wind and opened a window to let the wind in to blow out the smoke; and when the wind came in, the Dean did not like the wind after all, but said it was cross. Then the wind went away, and refused to come back when the Dean wanted it.

The Dean announced suddenly: ' 'Tis allowed that we learn patience by suffering. I have not spirit enough left me to fret. I was so cunning these three days, that whenever I began to rage and storm at the weather I took especial care to turn my face towards Ireland, in hopes by my breath to push the wind forward.' But at last even that forlorn hope had to be given up.

Finally, when the irresponsible wind *did* return, Dean Swift's horse would not gallop, and the pacquet was gone by the time the Dean arrived, simply because he could not ride seventy miles a day!

The Dean, as we have seen, left this Journal behind in the Inn, and it was sent by the maid (who had been struck dumb with astonishment by the unrivalled blunders of Watt) to Pope and Gay. The author of the Journal was astonished beyond all measure that Pope and Gay knew of his sufferings, and exclaimed that nobody but the devil could have informed his friends. But Gay, who understood him very well, spoilt all his fun by writing (in quite a different spirit from that which he had intended to inspire) that Dean Swift's friends would bless little smoky rooms for evermore 'considering it was there you lost your deafness'.

Meanwhile the Dean, who was by this time in Ireland, retired into seclusion because he was angry with the Queen and with Mrs Howard over the matter of the nightgown of Irish plaid: 'they have neither memory nor manners', he complained. So he gave the Vicar a supper, and his wife a shilling to play backgammon with him once a fortnight, and as for people of quality, if they called, the Dean pretended to be deaf.

And all this time, beneath the moth-like frettings of such trivialities, his heart was corroded by the knowledge that Stella must die. There was no hope for it; there was no help for it. The cawing bell of the Deanery swung its pendulum into empty space, like a brain swinging backwards and forwards out of the sunlight into madness. Sometimes that bell had a human tongue: it said 'too late'... Where had he heard those words before?

The last death the woman who had loved him was called upon to endure was borne, like the others, without him.

The earthly end to her faithful love came at six o'clock on the evening of Sunday, 17th January, 1728, when she was alone. She was surrounded by her friends, yet she was alone, since he was not by her side; but to this she had been inured by the other deaths she had passed through. She was his unacknowledged wife: such had been her self-abnegation that she never saw him without the presence of a third person. And there were many persons and things to hide him from her. There was Vanessa – who died (but her presence would be with Stella till the last); her face would come between them, her form would separate them, till the grave and beyond it. And there were minor things: there was fame, there was ambition. And now, as the last beat fluttered away from her heart, if she spoke his name it could not be answered; she lay in her house without him – she who, in answer to his creaking, hesitating offer to acknowledge her as his wife, had whispered 'Too late' ... but she was patient in her aloneness, even now. Swift was surrounded by company at dinner, as was the usual Sunday custom at the Deanery. The paper he began to write that night tells us that at eight o'clock a note was brought to him, with an account of her death ... 'and as soon as I am left alone, which is about eleven at night, I resolve, for my own satisfaction, to say something of her life and character'.

At eleven o'clock that night, he was alone.

From that moment the humanity of Swift ceased; his bones were already the possession of death, although they had an appalling mechanism of movement, yet his flesh changed gradually into stone. He became like the eyeless stone statue of a giant in an immense and tropical forest. Every foolish and volatile moth might brush against him, every songless bird might build among his ruins – he heeded them not. The years passed like water dropping, bringing a little and a gradual change.

The years passed, and the stone grew more and more forest-aged. The statue knew by this time that it was stone, though it was made in the likeness of a giant. In December 1732 Swift's beloved friend Gay died of a fever, in great agony. Pope and Arbuthnot sent the news of their loss to Swift, but as far as his life was concerned (although his work continued still) he was sunk in a huge and stupendous silence; he refused to express his grief. 'Upon (this) event I shall say nothing', he wrote to Pope. Yet Swift had been unable to bring himself to open the letter for five days, for though nothing spoke to him from a human world, yet some insect voice of warning had whispered to him that it contained something evil, something that plotted against the eternal stone. But he said nothing that might tell if any part of the stone could remember still the warmth and the sunlight. Meanwhile, Pope had determined that, Swift being in this strange statue-like sleep, the letters that had passed between them should be published. To bring about this desirable state of affairs, he built up the most airy structures of fabrications and half-lies. First, he caused editions of the letters to be concocted; then he disavowed the letters with the utmost indignation, and at last brought forward the idea that the only way in which matters could be set right, and Swift and himself vindicated, would be that the *true* versions of the letters should be re-published for their own defence. He connived at the publication of this correspondence in England, and by means of a great many subterfuges managed to get a copy sent to Ireland. This gave him his excuse. He became exceedingly indignant; spoke with anger and dignity about the wrong that had been done him already, the greater wrong that would ensue if the correspondence should be published in Ireland. The Dean, he said, was unable to protect himself; he was sunk in apathy, he was unaware of what was going on, and had been made the figure-head behind which the treachery of others lay hidden. Swift was being forced to allow what would injure both himself and those of his friends whom he had trusted most, and who had most trusted him. This then was Pope's excuse for gaining the possession of all the letters, and correcting them as he wished, so that the publication might be complete. Meanwhile, his very indignation brought fresh trouble upon his head, and he was obliged to invent fresh stratagems. For the proposed publisher, Faulkner, deceived by the indignation, agreed (to Pope's great embarrassment), to abide by his decision, and he saw himself faced with the possibility of the letters remaining unpublished. What could Pope do to avert this misfortune? He wrote to Faulkner saying that he realized now that it was too late to suppress the letters. The unhappy state of the Dean, and the intrigues of the Dean's friends, had made it necessary that Pope should protect himself by the publication of the entire correspondence. He forgave the Dean readily, and could not blame him; at the same time, since the letters must be reissued, they had better publish as well, those letters that were in the possession of the Dean; and that would be difficult, owing to the treacherous behaviour of the Dean's friends. Lord Orrery by this time had entered into the fray, and the battle continued for months, with Orrery and Pope alternately bullying and wheedling Mrs Whiteway, Swift's friend, to allow them to have the letters.

Pope had not always been so fortunate with his plans for the publication of his letters; for years before this, he had asked his friend Mr Caryll for the loan of the letters that had passed between them (with the unexpressed design of correcting and publishing them). He was never, alas, able to understand the dangers that lay in the simple minds of men of honour. Caryll complied with his friend's request, but in his innocence kept copies of the letters, and these leapt up, like a jack-in-the-box, when their tidied and edited offspring appeared. That other man of honour, Lord Oxford, nearly defeated him by a simple faith in his protestations. But in this case he was more successful. It must be said at this point, that though Pope has been much blamed for his conduct (and I admit it was tortuous), on the other hand he designed to do nobody any harm; he did not wish to exhibit Swift in an evil light; all he wished to do was to make certain that he himself had not, in an unguarded moment, exposed himself to misunderstanding.

The quarrel of the letters went on; but by this time Swift was beyond understanding it. The noise of quarrelling was to him only like the noise of the summer insects, borne by their light and gauzy wings so near to him, as he crumbled in the forest, that those wings almost brushed his stone.

But the state of being a statue alternated with that of being an appalling machine, galvanized into a violent and mechanical movement, by madness. Increasing in power during the years 1738 and 1739, this madness had conquered his world in 1740, so that it must be left in possession of that world, without interruption from outside. He must not be seen by strange eyes. In July 1740 Mrs Whiteway received this letter from Swift:

'I have been very miserable all night, and today extremely deaf and full of pain. I am so stupid and confounded that I cannot express the mortification I am under both in body and mind. All I can say is that I am not in torture; but I daily and hourly expect it. Pray let me know how your health is, and your family. I hardly understand one word I write. I am sure my days will be very few: few and miserable they must be:

'I am, for those few days, yours entirely

'JON SWIFT.

'If I do not blunder, it is Saturday, July 26, 1740.'

But that unutterable misery, as of the eternal bone when deserted by the flesh, and crying only to the unhearing grave, was soon to be changed again. He could cry now for the solitude and silence of the grave; for the appalling lion claws of his anguish tore him from that grave, and he was exposed to the empty grinning day. The maelstrom waiting below him, watching for his downfall, sometimes rising like immense swollen black seas, sometimes whispering and clattering like a world peopled by apes, sometimes seething and boiling like a hell of lava-pouring volcanoes, sometimes lying silent in a tropical and mirage sunlight (silent for ever, if Stella's voice did not come to make this sunlight real to him and warm) this maelstrom at length burst his roaring cracking world of a brain, that unavailing hell that had been his heart.

In March 1741-42 guardians were appointed for him in the Court of Chancery, since he might commit murder upon himself. He had been found threatening his own image in a mirror.

Sometimes he fell upon his knees and tried to pray, but the Lord's Prayer was all that he could remember. When his cousin, Deane Swift, came to the house and entered the room of this inhabitant of Death, he was met by a terrible sound like the clapping of a bell, issuing from that swollen and blackened tongue, that could utter only the words 'Go ... Go ...' And this sound was succeeded by a silence like that of the deepest forest, broken only by the sound of footsteps walking backwards and forwards – the sound of Swift trying to outstrip his madness.

CHAPTER XV

Troubles and Tombs

EVEN in these degenerate days, it is universally recognized that the poet has nothing whatsoever to do. He writes his verse, we gather, in a fit of desperate and inspired frenzy, and no work is involved, nor is there the need for peace and patience. The affair is perfectly easy, though impressive to the onlooker; nor does the effort last for more than two minutes, since poetry does not have to be kneaded by the poet, as clay must be kneaded by the sculptor. When those two minutes which must be devoted daily to his art have elapsed, the poet can lead a happy *dolce far niente* life for the rest of the twenty-four hours, spending his time in answering letters from persistent correspondents, and in reading and criticizing their verses. I must confess that until I read Pope's correspondence, I had felt that the modern poet's life was delightfully full of these pleasures. Indeed, only a natural moroseness and selfishness saves the modern poet from having even the two minutes allowed to all poets taken away from him. But now that I have read Pope's correspondence, I can see that the life of a poet in the eighteenth century (or at any rate, of so kind a man as Alexander Pope) was even more strenuous. It has always been part of the poet's duty to read all the verses of every incompetent person who is conceited enough to send them to him. But whereas the modern poet is bombarded for the most part with lyrics, the unhappy Pope was bombarded with poetic dramas of an intolerable length and dreariness. And not only was he bombarded with them; he was expected to place them with manager and publishers, to worry influential friends, to interview the Lord Chamberlain, to help in the dramas' production, and when they were produced, to sit through them, and, more difficult still, to force his influential friends to sit through them. And how was the kindness rewarded? In many cases by the most odious treachery. There was, for instance, the case of Mallet, the mean creature who, though he had received this kindness from Pope, and had witnessed his increasing goodness to Savage, yet undertook, after Pope's death, to blast his character, in order to earn the favour of Bolingbroke, with whom he had only the slightest acquaintance.

It is evident from a letter written by Pope to Mallet on 1st November, 1729, that the latter had asked for his help, for the poet says: 'To answer you fairly in a word: if any person of distinction that is in the compass of my acquaintance, or that I can come at by any other man's influence, can be pitched upon by you to do that service, I will do my utmost to have him engaged upon it.' And from a subsequent letter we see that Pope, although he was suffering from one of those violent headaches which martyrized his later life 'which perhaps you will see from the very blind hand that I write in', had yet the kindness to 'have the Lord Chamberlain spoken to by Lord Burlington'. He continues: 'Your play is delivered into my Lord Burlington's hands to give to the Duke (of Grafton). I liked that way best, and will wait on him afterwards or not as may be necessary.' This was, surely, an act of great kindness from a very famous man to a quite obscure one, of no talent. We know how Mallet showed his gratitude, when he was safe from any rebuke which Pope could have offered.

But alas, the bombardment with poetic dramas was not the poet's only trouble; his sufferings did not end there. He was expected also, to choose monuments, as we shall see from the tragi-comedy of Aaron Hill, and from the incident of Sir Godfrey Kneller and the great Tomb-Trouble.

Aaron Hill was an uncourtly but unctuous Polonius of a man, a windy, changeable creature running like a hare from hair-brained scheme to feather-witted scheme. Sir Leslie Stephen has given us a delightful study of him in his *Life of Pope*. Hill was, it seems, 'a prosy and ambitious person, full of literary and other schemes, devising a scheme for extracting oil from beech-nuts, and writing a Pindaric ode on the occasion; felling forests in the Highlands to provide timber for the Navy, and, as might be inferred, spending instead of making a fortune'. Remarkably unsuccessful with his own poetic dramas (although he had written the libretto for Handel's opera, *Rinaldo*) he insisted on corresponding with the famous literary men of his day; and, sooner or later, in this way, and by these means, he would force such a poet as Pope to become acquainted with those otherwise unheeded masterpieces. He was determined that Pope should read them, if everybody else in the world remained ignorant of them; and he succeeded in this, if in nothing else.

The tragi-comedy of Pope and Aaron Hill started in this way. Lintot, on some occasion, showed Pope one of the interminable poems I have mentioned, and afterwards repeated to Hill a nonsensical remark which he imputed to Pope, and which Pope denied ever having made. And indeed, I see no reason to doubt Pope's truthfulness in denying this, since no man in possession of his wits would have troubled to speak such a farrago of nonsense. But Hill flew into a passion, and wrote, for a new edition of his poems, a preface in which Pope was treated with as great insolence as was possible, coming from such threadbare wits. He had asked Pope's advice, we are told, since, in the *Essay on Criticism*, Pope had said that to learn our defects, we should make use of both friends and foes. Pope could not be regarded as a friend, since he was not so much as an acquaintance, but Hill presumed he might treat him as a foe, 'since Mr Dennis has assured us that you are as a kind of foe to everybody but yourself, and on that foundation supports his rough attempt to pull the lion's skin from a certain little ass, and I fear he means you, Sir'.

Pope's criticism, he assures us, was dictated by envy; and amidst this stream of noisy abuse, a figure emerges which, though no name was given, was meant, without any doubt, for Pope: 'A mere poet, that is to say, a wretch who has nothing but the jingle in his brain to ring chimes to his vanity, and whose whole trade is rhyme-jobbing – such a creature is certainly the most worthless encumbrance of his country. His arrogance is the only thing more remarkable than his ignorance.' There is a strangely modern flavour about this tirade. It might, indeed, be one of the outbursts of fury on the part of the unlettered against the lettered, which figure in the correspondence columns of certain morning newspapers of our time. Yet three years after the publication of this abuse, in about the year 1720, we find Hill writing Pope a series of painfully complimentary, not to say servile, letters, one of which was rebuked by Pope gently, but with some dignity: 'I am sincerely so far from resenting this mistake, that I am more displeased at your thinking it necessary to treat me so much in a style of compliment, as you do in your letter.' And indeed I believe that Pope was speaking the truth. At those times when his nerves, and the persistent demands upon him, had not driven him into a passion he had a kindly patience for the conceit, arising from thwarted ambition, of people like Hill. The rebuke, however, only resulted in the compliments becoming still more fulsome. It is, at this point, only fair to say that Hill did 'atone for his guilt' in a Preface to Pope affixed to a poem called 'The Creation', which appeared in 1720. On the appearance of this Preface, Pope, in his turn, became excessively complimentary to Hill, and letters in which the writers praise their own and their correspondents' virtues and gifts, were exchanged at various intervals for some years. Alas, the complimentary style in which Pope attempted to disguise his boredom, was his own undoing. He found himself obliged by Hill to read every poem that the latter had written, and those poems were many. Yet the torments of *ennui* which were forced upon Pope were not always, I may say at this juncture, unavenged, though they were avenged in a manner imperceptible to the victim. A fine example of this painless execution is to be found in the following letter from Pope to Hill, written in 1726:

'Dear Sir. The little thing which you take so kindly, is but a very small part of what I owe you; and whatever my studies, or, to use a proper word, idleness, are capable of producing, ought to be returned you in mere gratitude for the pleasure I have received from your writings; in which, give me leave to say, your goodwill to me in particular is as distinguishable, as the obligation you lay on the public in general. I am very happy in the envy and silly attacks of such people as have awakened the generosity of so powerful a defender. Nor am I ashamed of those weaknesses of mine which they have exposed in print* (the greatest of which was my thinking too candidly of them, to whom I wrote my letters with so much unguarded friendliness and freedom) since you have found a way to turn those weaknesses into virtues, by your partial regard of them. The eye of candour, like the sun, makes all the beauties which it sees; it gives colour and brightness to the meanest objects purely by looking on them ... I shall, indeed, and so will all mankind, be highly pleased to see the great Czar of Muscovy in this light, drawn by himself, like an ancient master, in rough strokes, without heightening or shadowing. What a satisfaction to behold that perfect likeness, without art, affectation, or even the gloss of colouring, with a noble neglect of all that finishing and smoothing, which any other hand would have been obliged to bestow upon so principal a figure! ... There will be no danger of your dressing this Mars too finely, whose armour is not gold but adamant, and whose style in all probability is much more strong than it is polished. I congratulate you that this great treasure is fallen into your hands; and I congratulate all Europe, that it is to be delivered to them through the hands of one, who will think it sacrilege to touch upon, much less to alter, any great lines of such an original.

'I can make you no better return for your great compliment upon me (which it would be arrogance in me to show to any other, and dangerous even to remember myself) but by telling you that it is honour enough to reward all my studies, to find my character and reputation is part of the care of that person to whom the fame and glory of Peter Alexiowitz was committed.'

We can only hope, on reading this letter, that 'the eye of Candour' had moments of unwatchfulness; if it had not, it must have looked with some suspicion on the sincerity of such sentiments, expressed, as they were, by the apostle of perfection. The story which followed is typical of every venture, hope

*(He refers to his letters to Cromwell, which had recently been printed, without his permission, by Curll.)

and aspiration of poor Hill's life. It was rumoured that Peter the Great, on his death-bed in January 1725, ordered a gold medal to be sent to Hill, who was the author of a poetic drama called *The Northern Star*; the Empress, it was asserted, had promised to send him her husband's papers in order to assist him in compiling a life of the dead Emperor. But the medal never reached him, nor did more than a few of the papers – perhaps in consequence of the Empress's death in 1727.

In spite of disappointments, and fluctuations in fortune, the correspondence continued. But alas, in a letter dated 18th January, 1731, we find Hill complaining, gently at first, that he had been made a victim in *The Dunciad,* though he figured in this under his initials only. On 26th January Pope denied that anything of the sort had occurred. Not only was Hill not the person meant, but he, Pope, had had nothing to do with the writing of the notes: 'I should imagine that Dunciad meant you a real compliment, and so it has been thought of many who have asked to whom that passage made that oblique panegyric. As to the notes, I am weary of telling a great truth, which is, I am not the author of them, though I love truth so well as fairly to tell you, Sir, I think even that note a commendation, and should think myself not ill-used to have the same words used of me, therefore, believe me, I was never other than friendly to you in my own mind.'

Though Pope 'loved truth so well', he had borne with some equanimity the separation from her on this occasion, since the notes were undoubtedly supplied by him; but even so, it is difficult to see what Hill found uncomplimentary in the passage complained of:

> Then – essay'd; scarce vanish'd out of sight,
> He buoys up instant, and returns to light:
> He bears no token of the sabler streams,
> And mounts far off among the swans of Thames.

It is difficult too, for any ordinary mind, to understand why Pope should have troubled to be evasive about that verse. I can only imagine that, Hill having been so stupid as to resent it, Pope thought he did not deserve immortality at his hands, and therefore denied that Hill was the person meant. However this may be, I must say that Hill's reply to Pope's shilly-shallying letter was a manly and upright one, reflecting credit on his frankness, and that Pope's subsequent letter was not quite so creditable. Indeed, his divorce from his beloved truth, though temporary, was complete while it lasted: and shocked Doctor Johnson. Yet Doctor Johnson surely thundered at him from too Olympian a height; the thunderbolt was out of all proportion to the offence: 'He was reduced to sneak and shuffle, sometimes to deny, and sometimes to apologize; he first endeavours to wound, and then is afraid to own that he meant a wound.' I cannot see any evidence of a wish to wound, in this case; the compliment, I should have thought, might please a better poet than Hill.

The quarrel, at last, was smoothed over, and a lengthy correspondence begun. The letters on both sides are packed with moral reflections and platitudes; the writers vied with each other in protesting that moral worth is a treasure above riches, that goodness is a greater prize than genius, and so forth. Occasionally Pope, who was sensitive about these matters, received a nasty knock over his moral worth, or reproached Hill with not appreciating it. I think it cannot be denied that Hill was the victor in this affair, not by force of wits, but by sheer force of persistence, for the unhappy Pope was obliged, not only to read Hill's unceasing poetic dramas, but also the verses of Miss Urania Hill, who was then eleven years of age, in return for which pleasure he sent her (we dare not guess in what spirit) his translation of the Odyssey. Mr Hill produced one poetic drama a week, and that, in Pope's opinion, was quite enough for any household. Imagine then, his alarm at this fresh menace in the shape of the budding poetic powers of Miss Urania Hill. It is true that Miss Minerva Hill and her sister Astræa had, so far, shown no sign of inheriting their father's inspiration and industry; but it was too much to hope that, coming from such a family, Pope would be spared this also. He foresaw that in future, the weekly output of the household would be, not *one*, but *four* poetic dramas.

Pope had suffered a good deal from the attentions of learned ladies, since only three years before Miss Urania Hill exhibited the first signs of her inherited talent, he had been endowed by Dean Swift, who had retired to Ireland, with three indomitable authoresses, all of whom swept down on London and the poet without delay. There was Mrs Sykins who had 'a very good taste in poetry', and who, the Dean understood, had gained great applause by her 'one or two' poems; but the Dean had read none of these, excepting six lines which had been sent to him, with a piece of sturgeon, on his birthday, some years before. There was also Mrs Grierson, who was not only proficient in Greek, Latin, midwifery, Hebrew, and French, but who was well-read also in history, mathematics, and philosophy. But worst of all, there was Mrs Barber, who was Ireland's chief poetess, and the wife of a woollen draper. The Dean pointed out to Pope that he could scarcely refuse to see the ladies, because 'if a Christian will be an Estrich, and the only Estrich in a kingdom, he must suffer himself to be seen, and what is worse, without money'. The Estrich, in a letter written in answer to this, oddly enough, made no reference to the ladies, though in a later letter he announced the strange fact that by some unaccountable misfortune he had failed to see Mrs Sykins. But he was not to escape Mrs Barber. (Swift had told Lord Orrery that the poems of this strong-minded woman 'generally contain something new and *useful*, tending to the reproof of vice and folly, and recommending some virtue.') The unhappy Estrich was at this time so ill that he whispered, 'I am but a scrap of myself' – (think how weak and how little that original self had been) – the doctor was obliged to order him baths of asses' milk, and he could neither study nor take exercise, for he was too ill. But in the midst of this illness, Mrs Barber descended upon him, and anxious, no doubt, to recommend the virtue of unselfishness (whilst not reproving the vices of folly and conceit), plagued the poet to correct her pedestrian verses. For once, he was able to resist such an imposition: 'Truly', he told the Dean, 'I should do it very ill; for I can give no attention to anything. Whatever service I can give her, by speaking well, etc. I will. Whatever friends I can get to subscribe to her, I will.'

In the end Pope was able to secure (with a certain amount of pleasure, no doubt) a forged letter, supposed to have been written by Swift to the Queen, pronouncing Mrs Barber to be the 'best female poet of this or any other age – a woman whose genius is honoured by every man of genius in this kingdom, and either honoured or envied by every man of genius in England'. The scandal caused by this letter was tremendous; and it transpired at last, that Mrs Barber was no affair of the Dean's, that he had never visited her house in his life, excepting on one occasion when he happened to be passing her shop, and was invited to come in, and went no further, nor, he explained, stayed for more than three minutes. Dr Delaney was responsible for her; it was he who brought her to the Deanery, several times; it was he who insisted upon the Dean inflicting the lady upon the unhappy Estrich. Could it be conceived, the Dean enquired, that he would write to someone who had used him so ill as the Queen? This referred to the time when Dean Swift had sent Mrs Howard some Irish plaid for a nightgown (the plaid being a present from the Irish weavers), and had offered to supply the Queen with plaid of the same pattern at eight shillings a yard. The Queen had ordered some, but then, instead of thanking the Dean for the present she had behaved as if she had bought it – this being exactly what she *had* done. The Dean, naturally, never forgave her.

By the time all the trouble arising from Dean Swift's literary ladies had abated, Pope felt he had seen quite enough of the race. He was, therefore, nervous of the powers of the eleven-year-old Miss Urania Hill. He was plagued by Hill until he read the manuscript of the *Tragedy of Athelwolde,* not once, but four times, and until he suggested reconstructions and alterations, this being, perhaps, demanded as a proof that he *had* read it. On those suggestions being followed, Hill hinted, at considerable length, and in such a way that the hint could not be ignored, that he would like Pope (and Pope's guest, Lord Bolingbroke) to read it yet again. Pope replied that they should count themselves unhappy if they did not read the *Tragedy of Athelwolde* once or twice again!

Pope was forced to find managers for Hill's plays, and not only he, but his influential friends, were forced to sit through those interminable plays, when they were performed. In fact, to such a pitch was he driven by the determined Mr Hill, that not even the King and the Queen were spared: 'If you think it of any consequence', he wrote to Hill, 'that the King should see it (the Tragedy of Athelwold) in manuscript, I think nothing more easy.' Indeed, the King and Queen would both have been brought face to face with *Athelwolde*, had it not been that, most unfortunately and unaccountably, they were too busy to undertake such an encounter. If we consider that the writing of the *Tragedy of Athelwolde* took the industrious Mr Hill little more than a week, we shall understand the menace under which Pope cowered.

Athelwolde was produced in 1731 – and we find Pope writing to Hill, a little wearily, it must be confessed, to order tickets, and, if possible, ward off a visit.

'Dear Sir, I shall have the pleasure (sick or well) to be at the first representation of your play tomorrow, with Lord Burlington and Lord Bathurst, and one or two more. Another noble Lord, who understands you best, must be contented to read the last two acts in his study; but Sir William Wyndham, with Mr Gay, and some others, will be there also, in another place, in his stead. I write this that I may not take up a minute of your time in calling on me tomorrow; but if you will send to the office tonight for places for four people, we will order a man or two to go to keep them for us. Lord Burlington comes on purpose to town. I am, with great truth, yours, etc. I have yet heard no account from court.'

Nor did Pope's duties cease there. Mrs Hill died, and the widower consulted the owner of the grotto on the choice of a monument: 'Give me leave to hope the benefit of your advice on this mournful occasion ... There is a low and unmeaning lumpishness in the vulgar style of monuments which disgust me as often as I look upon them; and because I would avoid the censure I am giving, let me beg to say whether there is significance in a draught, of which I enclose you an awkward scratch, not a copy. The flat table behind you is black; the figures are white marble. The whole of what you see here is but part of the monument, and will be surrounded by pilasters, arising from a pediment of white marble, having its foundation on a black marble mountain, and supporting a cornice and dome, that will ascend to the point of the cloister-arch. About half way up a craggy path, on the black mountain below, will be the figure of Time in white marble, in an attitude of climbing, obstructed by little Cupids of the same colour; some rolling rocks into his path, from above; some throwing nets at his feet and arms, from below; others in ambuscade, shooting arrows at him from both sides; while Death you see in the draught will seem from an opening between the hills in relievo, to have found admission by a shorter way, and prevented Time, at a distance.'

An elegant affair, and comforting to the feelings of a widower; but history does not relate what the owner of the grotto thought of it.

Time passed, and brought fresh terrors, fresh poetic dramas, in its train. But after some years, Pope succeeded in escaping from the correspondence, though the breach was not open, and he remained on friendly terms with Hill, enquiring after him, from time to time, and sending him affectionate messages.

During Pope's lifetime, Hill begged him (it is only one of many such flattering letters) to 'live – (would you could!) just as long till the virtues your spirit would propagate, became as general as the esteem of your genius'. It is not, perhaps, surprising (since it is typical of the treatment Pope received from those he benefited) to find Hill telling Richardson, after the death of the propagator of virtues, that Pope's fame was due to a 'bladdery swell of management'. 'But', he continues, 'rest his memory in peace! It will very rarely be disturbed by that time he himself is ashes.' For Mr Hill had found it convenient to forget how much, and how often, that 'bladdery swell of management' had assisted him. Alas, how often Pope, in his wish to comfort and assist, brought trouble upon himself.

Another striking instance was the case of Sir Godfrey Kneller and the Great Tomb Trouble. This alarming episode was the result of Sir Godfrey's sense of his own importance, coupled with his extreme reluctance (which must have seemed lamentable to his audience, in that century of theatrical and admired death-beds) to leave this world. In addition, he was inordinately vain. Pope, to whom Sir Godfrey was a constant source of amusement, wished, at one moment, to test how far that vanity would go, and exclaimed to the painter: 'Sir Godfrey, I believe if God Almighty had had your assistance, the world would have been formed more perfect.' 'Fore God, Sir, I believe so too'. was the answer. But now Sir Godfrey had a more important subject for thought than the ill-formation of the world; he was faced with the necessity of leaving it, imperfect as it was. And he was not entirely pacified by his recent dream of the future state, in which, after he had been told to rank himself, as a Roman Catholic, on the right side of God, St Luke, advancing, asked him his name. 'Kneller', was his reply. 'Not the famous Sir Godfrey Kneller of England?' enquired the Saint, excitedly. St Luke was unable to moderate his transports of joy, or to moderate his compliments, when he was told that it was indeed the famous Sir Godfrey Kneller of England, and the two painters discussed, for some time, the technique of their art. But although those transports of joy on the part of St Luke gratified Sir Godfrey for the moment, they could not make him forget the pleasures that he must forego in the future state: indeed, when Pope, who was sitting at the old painter's bedside, and who had noticed very distinct signs of his impatience at the thought of leaving the world, tried to comfort him by telling him he had been a very good man, and no doubt would go to a better place, Sir Godfrey replied: 'Ah, my good friend Mr Pope, I wish God would let me stay at Chilton.'

The Tomb Trouble in itself began with Sir Godfrey's actual

death-bed scene, when he protested, with firmness, and for unassailable reasons, against being buried in Westminster Abbey. It led to a law-suit, and ended with an epitaph which drew down a reproof from Doctor Johnson. A letter from Pope to the Earl of Strafford, dated 6th July, 1725, explains the affair: 'Sir Godfrey sent to me just before he dy'd. He began by telling me he was now convinc'd he could not live, and fell into a passion of tears. I said I hoped he might, but yet if not, he knew it was ye will of God, and therefore would do his best to resign himself to it. He answered with great emotion: "*No, no, no, it is the evil spirit.*" The next word he said was this: "*By God, I will not be buried in Westminster.*" I asked him why not? He answered: "*They do bury fools there.*" Then he said to me: "My good friend, where will you be buried?" I said, "wherever I drop; very likely in Twitnam". He replied: "So will I"; then proceeded to desire I would write his epitaph w'ch I promised him. It would be endless to tell your lordship the strange things he suggested on that head: It must be in Latin, that all foreigners may read it; it must be in English too, etc. I desired him to be easy in all that matter, I w'd certainly do the best that I c'd. Then he desir'd me that I would take down my father's monument. – For it was ye *best place in ye church to be seen at a distance.* This (as y'r l'dship may well imagine), surprised me quite. I hesitated and s'd I fear'd it w'd be indecent and y't my mother must be asked as well as I. He fell crying again, and seem'd so violently moved, that in pure humanity to a dying man (as well as to one I thought non compos) I w'd not directly persist in denying it strongly, but begg'd him to be easy upon y'e whole, and said that I would do all for him that I could with decency. These words and that reserve I can swear to; but y'r lordship sees ye whole fact (represented, upon my word, with ye strictest truth) upon which this idle woman – (Lady Kneller), w'd ground her answer, of w'ch I was accidentally informed by Mr Pigot.'

Alas, as a result of the conversation recorded in this letter, the 'idle woman' set in motion an action, through the Doctors' Commons, and tried to pull down the tablet Pope had erected to his father's memory over Lord Strafford's pew, and to fix in its place a large tablet bearing the names of Sir Godfrey Kneller and herself, with both their figures. The wrangle lasted for some time, pull devil, pull baker. In the end, Lord Strafford came in on Pope's side, and the poet won.

Pope wrote a very serene epitaph for Sir Godfrey Kneller's tomb in Westminster Abbey where they do bury fools. The epitaph runs:

> Kneller, by Heav'n, and not a master, taught,
> Whose art was Nature, and whose pictures Thought;
> Now for two ages having snatch'd from fate
> Whate'er was beauteous, or whate'er was great,
> Lies crown'd with princes' honours, poets' lays,
> Due to his merit, and brave thirst of praise.
>
> Living, great Nature feared he might outvie
> Her works; and dying, fears herself may die.

Doctor Johnson remarks that the fourth couplet 'is not only borrowed from the epitaph on Raphael, but is of very harsh construction'. The third couplet is shameless. I must confess that there are moments when I wonder why Pope believed Sir Godfrey Kneller to be non compos! Perhaps there was another reason than that given.

CHAPTER XVI

The Battle with Grub Street

THIS war, so protracted, and so ingenious, that the Siege of Troy seems but the occupation of an idle hour – this labyrinth of plots, so complicated that the Labyrinth of Crete is simple as a child's story in comparison – the history of these is so known that I shall attempt no elaborate explanation of it. No fresh light can be thrown upon the history, whose dullness is only equalled by that of the heroes it immortalized.

The history is as complicated as the plotting. It is known that long before the publication of *The Dunciad* Pope and Swift had determined upon some punishment of the Dunces; but why they should have troubled to attack them, we shall never know. Pope was irritable and nervous; he was aware of the persecution that Dryden had suffered, and he himself had been plagued to an intolerable extent, both on account of his genius and fame, an d of his personal deformity. But Swift's attitude in the matter is more difficult to understand.

Dennis, we know, had been very rightly designed for punishment since he attacked Pope on the score of his deformity. But there were other and less deserving victims.

In the spring of 1716, Pope met Edmund Curll, the most conspicuous publisher of the time. He met him once, and once only. There was scarcely any offence against decency that Mr Curll had not committed at one time or another. He had published libels, and lampoons, he had purchased and published stolen letters of eminent persons, and, when these eminent persons died, had printed histories of their lives which would have been unlikely to appeal to the heroes of those lives were they still in a position to resent anything. Indeed, Arbuthnot had christened Mr Curll one of the new terrors of death. His person, like his mind, lacked charm. He was described by a contemporary as tall, ungainly, and white-faced; his eyes were a light grey, large, projecting, goggle and purblind; he was splay-footed and 'baker-knee'd' (whatever that may mean). Nothing seemed to improve his character, nor daunt his courage – neither being imprisoned, nor pumped upon, nor pilloried, nor tossed in a blanket. All these events were taken in the course of the day's work..

In February or March, 1716, appeared Lady Mary Montagu's 'Court Poems', and three of those 'Town Eclogues' proved that the lady's friendship was as dangerous as it was boring. Curll was not the sole publisher; the whole business of the publication of these tiresome works was excessively complicated; a certain J. Robert, who issued them, affixed an advertisement to the pamphlet, in which he claims that the wits at the St James' Coffee-house believed it to be the work of a lady of quality; while at Button's, those equally qualified to judge had stated it to be the work of Mr Gay; but that 'a gentleman of merit' living at Chelsea, knew that such poems could come from no other hand than the great translator of Homer.

We can imagine the frenzy of rage into which Pope was thrown by the accusation that he could be the author of such doggerel. Not even his silly flirtation with the real author could prevent him from avenging himself. At this point, I find myself speculating whether this is not, in reality, the reason of his subsequent quarrel with Lady Mary. However this may be, he sent for Curll to the Swan Tavern in Fleet Street, and after a great deal of lying on Mr Curll's part, as to the publisher of the poems (he tried to blame Oldmixon, another hero of *The Dunciad,* but this gentleman denied the charge, as well as another publisher of the name of Pemberton), Pope rebuked him gravely, and then put an emetic in this enterprising business-man's sack.

The whole of Grub Street was in an uproar at such an outrage: Dennis flew to the defence of his peer, and proclaimed that Pope's action was 'so black, so double, and so perfidious, that perhaps a villain who is capable of breaking open a house is not capable of that.'

In these over-civilized days such a punishment may appear a little rough, but it seems an admirable way of dealing with offenders of this kind, since no argument or appeal to decency would have the slightest effect upon them. But it is to be regretted that Pope, in his eagerness to make the story known, wrote 'a full and true account of a horrid and barbarous revenge by poison, on the body of Mr Edmund Curll, bookseller, with a faithful copy of his last will and testament', followed by 'a further account of the most deplorable condition of Mr Edmund Curll, bookseller', and still worse, by 'a strange but true relation, how Mr Edmund Curll, of Fleet Street, stationer, out of an extraordinary desire of lucre, went into Fleet Street, and was converted from the Christian religion, by certain eminent Jews, etc.' All these publications are so disgusting as to be unreadable, and there is no trace of wit to be found in them.

From that moment, Curll took every revenge in his power; he published every libel, every forged letter, that came into his hands, if it related to Pope and his friends. In return, Pope has transfixed this ugly, purblind, and blundering moth, for all eternity, in the *Miscellanies* and *The Dunciad*. But the publisher, far from being dismayed, was delighted with his immortality, for did he not find himself transfixed in the company of Addison, and of the Duke of Marlborough?

Another victim was James Moore Smythe, the son of a rich man, and Pope's rival in his friendship with Teresa and Martha Blount. I imagine that Pope had always felt some resentment against this handsome and stupid young man; but the actual story of their warfare is so complicated, and so trivial, that nobody who is not accustomed to adjudicating in quarrels in the servants' hall, could be expected to unravel it. About 1716 appeared the verses on Moore, 'author of the celebrated Worm Powder.' Pope had accused Moore of plagiarizing from the verses he had written to Martha Blount, and of inserting these in his dull comedy *The Rival Modes*. The siege of Mr Moore Smythe was laid with the greatest care, and the trail of gunpowder was difficult to detect. The gunpowder, indeed, was disguised in a letter to the *Daily Journal*, 18th March, 1728, in which James Moore Smythe was supposed, on his side, to accuse Pope of plagiarism. It is, alas, more than probable that Pope wrote the letter himself, that he might have the opportunity of replying to it, and killing Mr James Moore Smythe. He did reply to it, in the enlarged edition of *The Dunciad* (1729), saying that he had given Mr Smythe permission to use the verses. The verses are undoubtedly by Pope, but there is some doubt as to the date when they were written. There are no such lines in the copy of the poem at Mapledurham, nor in the copy sent to Judith Cowper (with whom he was having a solemn flirtation at the moment), nor in a copy printed and published in 1726. Mr Carruthers believes that he inserted them in the verses addressed to Martha Blount in the *Miscellany*, in order to found and support his charge of plagiarism against Smythe, who probably intended none, since he was in the habit of making his characters deliver scraps of verse, and indeed, in the very next page to that in which the offending quotation appeared, had made one of his characters recite the following lines from the long-published *Essay on Criticism*:

> *Bell.* Nay, fly to altars, there I'll talk you dead,
> *Nell.* For fools rush in where angels fear to tread.

The quotation is given without quotation marks.

Pope's edition of Shakespeare, published in 1725 in six volumes quarto, and his translation of the Odyssey, were both causes of trouble with the higher and lower storeys in Grub Street. The edition of Shakespeare was the first, and perhaps the only, failure that Pope knew. It failed, that is to say, from the point of view of subscriptions. The edition, however, has many points of great interest, containing, as it does, alterations and suppressions of lines and passages which he believed to have been interpolated, or altered by the players, or by the course of time. He was the first to change the corrupt reading of the lovely lines on music in *Twelfth Night*:

> Oh! it came o'er my ear like the sweet *sound*
> That breathes upon a bank of violets.

to the far more lovely 'south', which must certainly have been the original reading. And in *Macbeth* he altered 'Tarquin's ravishing *sides*' to 'ravishing strides'. His essay on Shakespeare is just and illuminated, though it is not on fire with passion. For this work he received the sum of £217 12*s*.; for the supreme greatness of Shakespeare was not, at this time, acknowledged; he could not be understood by this age of elegance. The publication failed, and the highly-priced volumes were reduced in price. This was a delightful opportunity for Grub Street to assert itself; and in 1726, Mr Louis Theobald, platitudinous versifier, dramatist and translator, prepared his own immortality in *The Dunciad* by publishing a quarto called 'Shakespeare Restored, or a specimen of the many errors as well committed as unamended, by Mr Pope in his late edition.' Theobald was a bore; but he was a learned bore; he was well-read in black letter and in dramatic literature. Pope, in the edition of his own work, produced by Tonson, inserted a notice saying that Mr Theobald had not come forward until the edition of Shakespeare was published, and had then only found twenty-five words of which he could complain. And in the same year, Mr Theobald found himself enthroned as the principal hero of *The Dunciad*.

However he, in his turn, produced in 1733 (aided by Warburton and others), a complete edition of Shakespeare which showed a greater precision and learning than Pope's, and which soon eclipsed that edition altogether.

The trouble about Homer was of a different kind. In his *Proposals for the Translation of the Odyssey*, issued on 10th January, 1724-25, he had stated that the subscription was not entirely for his own use, but also for that of the two friends to whose help he was indebted. He did not claim to be the sole translator. But, at the end of the notes, he makes one of those friends (Broome) say: 'If my performance has merit either in these or in any part of the translation (namely, in the 6th, 11th, or 18th books), it is but just to attribute it to the judgment, and care of Mr Pope, by whose hands every sheet was corrected; his other and much more able assistant was Mr Fenton, on the 4th and 20th books.' Alas, only five books are mentioned here; but in sober truth, twelve were executed by the 'friends'. Fenton translated the 1st, 4th, 19th, and 20th books; Broome translated the 2nd, 6th, 8th, 11th, 12th, 16th, 18th, and 23rd. Besides this work, he was responsible for compiling the notes. The *Battle of the Frogs and Mice* was translated by Parnell. It must, however, be admitted that Pope *did* overhaul and correct the work of the 'friends' with great care.

They were not rewarded liberally. Warburton states that Broome received £600 for his work, and Fenton received £300. On the other hand, Spence seems positive that Fenton received only £240 and Broome £500.

There was a good deal of un-Christian feeling between the 'friends' – although one of these was a clergyman. Mr Fenton's opinion of Pope's much-vaunted heart would have surprised that great poet had he known it; the Reverend Mr Broome's opinion of Pope's Greek was equally unflattering. And as for Pope, only a year after this time, he enshrined Broome among 'the parrots who repeat another's words in such a hoarse, odd voice, as makes them seem their own'. These gentlemen were, comparatively speaking, unoffending. The same could not be said of Mr Colley Cibber, who was eventually to dethrone Mr Theobald as hero of *The Dunciad*. The feud between the laureate and Pope originated in 1716-17 over the serious matter of a mummy and a crocodile. This began with the production of Gay's comedy, *Three Hours after Marriage*. Pope and Arbuthnot had helped in the writing of this play, which was a failure, and was withdrawn after a run of seven nights. In the course of the play a crocodile and a mummy were introduced, and the audience, having borne considerable indecency and a great deal of silliness, found these alien characters too much for them, and rose and hissed the players.

Shortly afterwards, Colley Cibber took a principal part in the play of *The Rehearsal*. Into this play he introduced some mocking allusion to the offending mummy and crocodile, an allusion which was greeted by the audience with a roar of applause. Pope, who was present, became white with fury. 'In the swelling of his heart (said Cibber), after the play was over he came behind the scenes, with his lips pale, and his voice trembling, to call me to account for the incident; and accordingly fell upon me with all the foul language that a wit out of his senses could be capable. 'How durst I have the impudence to treat any gentleman in that manner", etc ... When he was almost choked with the foam of his passion, I was enough recovered from my amazement to make him (as near as I can remember) this reply: 'Mr Pope, you are *so particular a man,* that I must be ashamed to return your language as I ought to do; but since you have attacked me in so monstrous a manner, this you may depend upon, that as long as the play continues to be acted, I will never fail to repeat the same words over and over again." ' ...

But there were other causes of offence. Cibber's play, *The Nonjuror,* produced in the winter of 1717, was written for the purpose of satirizing the Roman Catholics and Nonjurors who had taken part in the 1715 Rebellion. The play was a huge success, and it was largely due to this that Cibber became poet laureate. It did not, however, please Pope.

After an almost unceasing warfare, which lasted for twenty-four years, Cibber found himself the hero of *The Dunciad,* having been enthroned in the place of Theobald, as a reward for telling a coarse story about the poet, and bringing against him the accusation that he had visited a house of ill-fame in the Haymarket. Whatever offence might be pardoned by Pope, this, at least, was never forgiven.

The Dunciad had been growing in the poet's brain for some years before its publication. In a letter to Swift, written in 1725, Pope complained of the hatred entertained towards him by bad people, and mentioned Gildon and Cibber as specimens (the former, in a worthless work called the *Complete Art of Poetry,* had depreciated Pope. He was, also, a friend of Namby-Pamby Philips. But, as he was by now dead, it would hardly seem to have been worth Pope's while to single him out for punishment). Swift advised the poet to be careful, lest the bad poets should outwit him 'as they have served the good poets in every age, whom they have provoked to transmit their names to posterity'.

Pope did not heed the warning, luckily for us, since his neglect of Swift's good advice has given us one of the greatest poems in our language. But I cannot believe that Swift ever wished him to pay attention to the warning. He must, at least, have seen the *Treatise on the Bathos or Profound* – (an amusing work which is singularly free from savagery, though the victims may have been unaware of this). And most undoubtedly both he, and Lord Bolingbroke, saw parts of the great work before its completion. The name by which Pope designed to have called *The Dunciad* was 'Dulness' or 'The Progress of Dulness', and the Dean, veering round from his former advice, urged the poet, in fact, worried him, to complete it.

The *New Dunciad,* published in 1742, contained actually the fourth book of *The Dunciad*; and, that he might introduce the offending Mr Cibber as hero, Pope had recast and changed the whole of *The Dunciad*. Alas, by now, this mighty war had taken on the aspect of a dying giant thrashing the mopping and mowing swirls of death-pale dust. Who would remember that dust now, if Pope had not given it life? Dennis was already in the grave; poor unoffending James Moore Smythe and his friendship with the Blounts and his meant or unmeant plagiarism, Blackmore and his offences against the Muse – where were these? The men and their works could not be told from each other, or from the wider dust. The wretched Arnall and Budgell, after God knows what starvation and despair, had committed suicide when their powers of endurance were sapped. Lady Mary Wortley devastated other and more deserving courtiers with her conversation. On the other hand, as Carruthers tells us, Namby-Pamby Philips was able to indulge his sense of his own importance to the highest degree, in the high post which he had obtained in Ireland, and in the Irish Parliament. Concanen was Attorney-General in Jamaica, and Welsted's prosperity was assured in the Ordnance Office. These must be, and were, properly punished.

But another, and less important warfare was carried on against the Dunces, in *The Grub Street Journal*. This paper, whose first number appeared on the 18th of January, 1730, was continued weekly until the end of 1737; it is believed by some to have been Pope's organ; other authorities consider this is doubtful. In it the critics, whilst pretending to admire the works of Grub Street, and to condemn those of Pope and his friends, in reality dealt with the former as Pope had dealt, in other years, with the unhappy Namby-Pamby. In the case of *The Grub Street Journal,* the shields from behind which Pope delivered his blows were Dr John Martyn, who had been Professor of Botany at Cambridge, and Dr Richard Russell, who wrote a *Treatise on Sea-Water*; but these gentlemen, it is believed by some, hid the identity of Pope. (Johnson says Savage had been invited to undertake the management of the paper. But this is uncertain.) In any case it is difficult to understand why respectable and rather earnest-minded scholars, whose lives had been spent in writing treatises in Latin on the subject of botany and the still more elusive subject of sea-water, should suddenly cast away their rôles, for the sake of avenging Pope upon his enemies, and should, like naughty little boys, take an immense delight in throwing filth and in hitting other learned gentlemen who had never offended them.

The poem appeared, in an imperfect edition, in May 1728, and soon afterwards made its appearance in the enlarged form, with the prolegomena of *Scriblerus,* notes variorum, and the preface which was believed to have been prefixed to the first five imperfect editions printed in London. The enlarged work, on its appearance, was surrounded by a fleet of pirated editions, just as a ship is surrounded by a school of porpoises, bobbing and floundering. Pope enjoyed the intrigues surrounding these editions, and his own mystifications about the authorship and the notes, and a million other matters. He even went so far as to assign over 'the Dunciad, an Heroic Poem' to the Earls of Burlington and Oxford, and Lord Bathurst, and these, in their turn, transferred it 'with the sole right and liberty of printing the same', to Pope's publisher, Lawton Gilliver. 'By this transaction', says Carruthers, 'the poet concealed his name, yet protected his property.' This left the poet free to disclaim anything he chose, claim anything he chose, hit anybody and deny that he had hit them, parry assaults, complain of injuries, protect his good name, and amuse himself in a million ways. We are left with the feeling that neither the poet nor his accommodating friends knew a moment's idleness.

The poem caused consternation and terror among the 'ragged regiment' of Grub Street; and the thought of that consternation and its reason is sad and pitiable: the members of the ragged regiment feared that the booksellers would no longer employ them; they foresaw a more gaunt starvation than even they had known hitherto. But they were not the only creatures who trembled, nor the only beings who were attacked. Pope, who was supposed to attack only those who were stricken with poverty, was no less savage with the Duchess of Newcastle, and with his former friend Lady Mary Wortley.

The quarrels I have mentioned are only outstanding examples among a hundred lesser ones; we could pursue each victim through the whole history of his warfare with Pope, and we could trace each quarrel to its primal cause. It would be dull and unnecessary. For in such learned and full works as those of Messrs Carruthers, and Elwin and Courthope, this has been done to its uttermost limit.

It is pleasant to turn from these petty quarrels to the great work they inspired, and to Pope's warm-hearted and generous *private* treatment of the inhabitants of Grub Street; to the thousand occasions when he relieved the misery of the ragged regiment, to his kindness to poor Savage, to whom he made an allowance, and whom he tried to save from himself. Of this wretched creature, Doctor Johnson said: 'his poverty ... was such as very few could have supported with equal patience ... He lived generally by chance, eating only when he was invited to the tables of his acquaintances, from which the meanness of his dress often excluded him, when the politeness and variety of his conversation would have been thought a sufficient recompense for his entertainment.

'He lodged as much by accident as he dined, and passed the night sometimes in mean houses, which are set open at night to any casual wanderers, sometimes in cellars, among the riot and filth of the meanest and most profligate of the rabble; and sometimes, when he had not money to support even the expenses of these receptacles, walked about the streets till he was weary, and lay down in the summer upon a hulk, or in the winter, with his associates in poverty, among the ashes of a glasshouse.'

His patrons were either dead, or estranged by his ungrateful behaviour and riotous life – he was left to his fate by all save Pope. And he, who has been accused of insulting poverty, of mocking at distress, whose heart is said to have been harder than a stone, could yet 'take more pains not to affront Savage than if my (Pope's) bread had depended upon him'. Pope was never tired of helping this unhappy creature, though all else had become wearied by him; neither time, nor thought, nor money were spared, if these could help the man he had befriended.

On 25th January, 1740–1 he wrote to his emissary Mallet: 'Surely nothing can be said *to*, or I fear done *for*, this poor, unhappy man, who will not suffer himself to have a friend. But I will immediately send him another ten pound (besides my own, which is paid to him)' – this refers to the allowance which Pope made to Savage – 'and take what money you can collect in repayment: if more, it shall be accounted to him, if less, I will be at the loss. I would not trouble Mr Louis; nor you further at present; and perhaps if you give it Dodsley he will take umbrage at that too. I have really taken more pains not to affront him than if my bread had depended on him. He would beg to be forgiven, if it was misfortune only, and not pride, that made him captious. All I can say is, I wish Providence would be kind to him in our stead, but till then he is miserable.''

Pope's letters to Savage were so delicate in feeling, so warm-hearted and so full of forbearance, that it is sad to think they were unheeded, or in any case, that they did not work the miracle for which the writer had hoped. Some of the letters have a despairing note: 'I once more tell you, that neither I, nor any one who contributed at first to assist you in your retirements, ever desired you should stay out of London, for any other reason than that your debts prevented your staying in it

'No man desired to confine you to the country, but that the little they contributed might support you better than in a town

'It was yourself who chose Swansea for your place; you no sooner objected to it afterwards (when Mr Mendez stopped his allowance, upon complaint that you had used him ill) but I endeavoured to add to it, and agreed to send remittances to any other country place you pleased. Indeed, I apprehended Bristol was too great a city to suit a frugal expense; however, I sent thither all I could, and now, with as good a will, I add this little more at your desire, which I hope will answer your end you propose of making easy your journey to London.'

It is one of the tragedies of Pope's life (and of the life of Savage), that when, as a last desperate attempt to pull Savage together, to save him from drink, from ungrateful behaviour, and from his general weakness of character, Pope wrote to him, saying he would withdraw his help until Savage should ask him to continue it, Savage, believing that this, his only friend, had deserted him, died, a few days after Pope's letter had reached him, in silence and despair.

Pope, on his side, had believed that Savage had betrayed his trust; and yet, believing that, he had written to Savage's jailer to ask the amount of those debts, that they might be paid. The letter arrived after Savage's death.

Indeed, Pope showed innumerable kindnesses toward Grub Street. He could even forget his vanity as an author, when the question arose of extending kindness and generosity to one of the ragged regiment. Here is another notable example of that unpraised benevolence.

In May 1738 appeared an anonymous poem called 'London'. The author of this poem, a starving and an unknown youth, received only ten guineas at its publication; but it had a rapid success, and was hailed as a great work by all the critics. Many of these, delighted to have the opportunity of belittling and insulting Pope, declared that this work by a new author far exceeded any work by the author of *The Dunciad*. But that great poet, who has been accused of every petty meanness and lack of generosity, far from resenting the appearance of this poem, was among the first to hail it with delight, and make enquiries about the anonymous author. It appeared that the writer of the poem was a shambling uncouth creature, stricken by hunger, wearing dirty linen (and sometimes no linen), and broken shoes, given to unaccountable eccentricities, grimacing and muttering as he walked, tearing food (when he was able to obtain it) like a bird or beast of prey. Pope set to work immediately to help this youth, taking endless trouble and setting every kind of machinery at work to obtain an academical degree and the mastership of a grammar school for him. Unhappily, his efforts failed, but that failure came from no lack of care on the part of Pope. It does not appear that Pope ever met this young man, whose name was Samuel Johnson.

CHAPTER XVII

Declining Years and Death

THE first part of the *Essay on Man* was published anonymously in 1732; and the mischievous poet found in this anonymity many opportunities for disconcerting the more pompous (or the more servile) among his friends. He wrote to Richardson, the portrait painter: 'I had a hundred things to talk to you of, and among the rest, of the "Essay on Man", which I hear so much of. Pray, what is your opinion of it? I hear some cry it extremely up, others think it obscure in part; and some (of whom I am sure you are not one) have said it is mine. I think I could show you some faults in it, and believe you can show me more; though upon the whole, it is allowed to have some merit, and I think so myself.'

The wary painter eluded him; but Mallet, I am glad to say, fell into the trap (if Ayre is to be believed – though Ayre does not mention Mallet by name). Pope conducted his victim towards the booby-trap by long and devious ways, asking him what new pieces were brought to light. The innocent Mr Mallet replied that nothing of any importance or worthy of notice had been published. It was true that there was a thing called an *Essay on Man,* but this was shocking poetry, it contained insufferable philosophy, and as for coherence or connection, there was none. The delighted poet claimed the offending poem immediately as his own, and the unhappy Mr Mallet left the house. Even Swift, as we may see from a letter written to him by Pope, was not convinced at first of the authorship, since the philosophy, in many places, resembled the metaphysical works of Lord Bolingbroke, though the *Essay on Man* was published before Lord Bolingbroke's treatises were written. There was, however, at one time some confusion as to which of the authors was first in the field.

Pope, during these years, was hard at work on poem after poem; but how threadbare, by this time, was the life in which those poems were composed; how needy and how starved was his heart. Before the publication of the *First Satire of the Second Book of Horace* (February 1733), Pope lost the man who was, perhaps, the most deeply loved of all his companions – dear John Gay. He died on the 4th of December, 1732, aged only forty-six years – of an inflammatory fever. Never again would Pope see that laughing and cheerful face, those eyes which still retained a childlike trust and innocence; never again would he and Swift tease the childlike creature about his love of good food, smart ribbons, and smart company. Pope was broken-hearted. As for Swift, those who looked over his papers when he, too, was gone, found the letter in which he received the news, endorsed with these words: 'On my dear friend Mr John Gay's death: received December the 15th, but not read till the 20th, by an impulse foreboding some misfortune.'

Gay had died in the house of the Duke and the Duchess of Queensberry, and these friends, who loved him as dearly as if he were their own child, gave him a funeral 'as splendid', said Arbuthnot, 'as if he had been a peer of the realm' – a funeral which would have delighted the innocent vanity that loved blue ribbons.

The Duchess never ceased to miss him: two years after this time, in a letter to Lady Suffolk, she wrote: 'I often want poor Mr Gay. Nothing evaporates sooner than joy untold, or even told, unless to one so entirely in your interest as he was, who bore an equal share in every satisfaction or dissatisfaction which attended us. I am not in the spleen, though I write thus: on the contrary, it is a sort of pleasure to think over his good qualities. His loss was really great, but it is a satisfaction to have known so good a man.'

Alas, the hunger of the waiting, watching dust was not appeased. It waited for Mrs Pope, that most loved of mothers. She was, by now, very old, and the small and happy flying moments were so quickly gone, that she could never seize them with her feeble and aged hand. They were gone before she could seize them, flown with her memories. The beat in her heart was slower than those flying moments, could never keep time with the cruel sweet moments that were passing. On the

7th June, 1733 she died. And this was the final blow to the hear of the son who had loved her so deeply.

Three days after this death in his heart, he wrote to Richardson: 'I thank God her death was as easy as her life was innocent; and as it cost her not a groan, nor even a sigh, there is ye upon her countenance such an expression of tranquillity, nay almost of pleasure, that it is even amiable to behold it. It would afford the finest image of a saint expired that ever painting drew and it would be the greatest obligation which even that obliging art could ever bestow upon a friend, if you would come and sketch it for me. I am sure if there be no very prevalent obstacle, you will leave any common business to do this, and I shall hope to see you this evening as late as you will, or to-morrow morning as early, before this winter flower is faded.'

Where could Pope rest his mind, or find peace, now that his winter flower, and his loved companion, were gone? He told Martha Blount that when he stayed with Lord Bathurst, he could hardly bear the memories of poor Mr Gay, and of another friend, Dean Swift, 'who is near dead, and quite lost to us'. And at Twickenham, whenever he passed his mother's room, the same misery overtook him.

Martha Blount, the beloved of his life, remained to him, but in his eyes alone was she unchanged. That lovely milk-white skin had grown hard and red, the cheerfulness and kindness which had been amongst her greatest charms, these had become bustling and incessant; she bored, worried and fatigued Pope's other friends, who wished her absent – a wish which was never realized.

Pope, meanwhile, though he had lost nearly all those who filled his heart, felt his fighting powers were unchanged. He continued his *Epistles*, and his chastisement of Lord Hervey and Lady Mary Wortley. He indulged in the most curious intrigues, more complicated even than those of his earlier years, planting altered letters in Lord Oxford's library, in the hope that they would be stolen and published, and plotting to withdraw them when he found they were too carefully protected.

In 1733 he had the heart to play a further trick on Mr Curll.

This gentleman, intending to publish a *Life of Pope*, advertised in the newspapers for information about the poet. On the 11th of October Mr Curll received a letter from a mysterious person signing himself P.T. This person claimed that he had, in former days, been an intimate acquaintance of old Mr Pope and of the poet; and he proceeded to tell Mr Curll a cock-and-bull story of old Mr Pope's noble birth.

Mr Curll was much excited by this letter, and, in answering it, received a further letter saying that the mysterious P.T. possessed a large collection of the poet's letters from his early life down to 1733; but that if Mr Curll wished to receive these, he must advertise the printing of them. Alas, at this point, Mr Curll shilly-shallied, and did not answer the letter for two years (until March 1735). In that year, he sent the advertisement of the prospective publication to Pope, and asked for a meeting to 'close all differences'; he offered, as well, to show him the letters. Pope placed an advertisement, immediately, in three papers, stating that he did not know P.T.; that he believed the letters were a forgery, and that he refused to have anything to do with E.C.

The whirl of intrigue then became so fast that the very contemplation of it makes me dizzy, with Mr P.T. offering to meet Curll and then not meeting him, with a thousand missives saying that the letters were printed at Mr P.T.'s own expense, etc. and that an old gentleman had transcribed them from Lord Oxford's library.

Then appeared on the scene 'a short squat man', calling himself Mr Smythe, and claiming to be a cousin of P.T.'s. This gentleman, who was in reality James Worsdale, an emissary of Pope's, had been determined to make the best of both worlds in the matter of his dress, uniting in it the authority of the law with the rectitude of the clergyman, since he wore a clergyman's gown with a large barrister's band of lawn round his neck. But even this absurd costume does not seem to have aroused any suspicions in the breast of Mr Curll.

In the end, 'Mr Smythe' and the diligent P.T. succeeded in forcing Mr Curll to advertise letters that had passed between Pope and Lord Halifax, Lord Burlington, etc.

This was exactly what Pope wanted, as Curll's advertisement was an infringement of that rule of the House of Lords which forbade the publication of a peer's letters without his consent. Pope drew attention to this advertisement by offering a reward of twenty guineas to R.S. and P.T. if they would come forward and discover the affair, and forty guineas if they could prove who was behind it. This resulted in the Earl of Jersey bringing the matter before the House of Lords, and in Mr Curll being summoned to attend before a judiciary court. P.T. was full of good advice to the unhappy Mr Curll, which would have landed him in endless trouble had he taken it. He did not take it, and told the House of Lords the whole story ... the books were examined, and it was then found that, in spite of the advertisement, the books contained not a single letter from a peer, and that therefore, there had been no infringement of any rule. Mr Curll emerged triumphant from the ordeal, bearing the bundle of books intact, and the House of Lords (according to Curll's statement) complained of being made the tools of Pope.

But that mischievous little creature had not finished with Mr Curll. The letters were published, and the edition pirated by other booksellers; and this gave the poet the opportunity he had waited for. He inserted a notice in the *London Gazette*, stating that as incorrect versions of his letters had been printed, and that as various letters which were not of his writing were advertised as his, he found himself under the necessity of publishing 'such of the said letters as are genuine, together with some others'.

Strangely enough, the (by now) greatly-advertised letters differed in no particular from those edited by Curll, yet differed very widely from those letters which had been written originally. There were alterations, there were omissions, the dates were changed, so were the incidents. In some cases, even the identity of the recipients of the letters was changed! As for the old gentleman who was supposed to have transcribed Mr Curll's edition of the letters from Lord Oxford's library, *his* identity will always remain a mystery, though less, perhaps, of a mystery than is the fact that he was able to insinuate himself, day after day, into Lord Oxford's library (presumably while the librarian was asleep) and copy those compromising and highly valued letters.

The published correspondence was hailed by the great world with excitement, as Pope had foreseen; and the letters made for the poet one new friend. This gentleman, Mr Allen, of Widcombe or Prior Park, near Bath, was so overcome with the obvious benevolence and beautiful character of Pope, as exhibited by the letters, that he sought his acquaintance, and, indeed, offered to print a genuine edition of the correspondence at his own expense; but this offer was declined. Mr Allen, the original of Squire Allworthy in Fielding's *Tom Jones*, was a warm-hearted and generous man; the friendship grew, Pope was a constant visitor at Prior Park, and Allen was indefatigable in his attempts to further Pope's undertakings.

In the summer of 1737 the poet visited Southampton and Portsmouth, Cirencester, Oxford and Bath. How could he remain at home, with his mother's voice, so weakened by age, so clouded by death, calling to him from the dusty corners of the room she inhabited no longer? He was restless, and his friends were taken from him by death, by banishment, by madness. Bolingbroke was in France, Gay was dead, Arbuthnot was dead and Jervas dying; Dean Swift was sunk in the silence of an incurable madness.

So Pope wandered from place to place, but in spite of his wanderings, his literary projects were never abandoned. In 1737 four of the *Imitations of Horace* appeared, and were followed in the next year, by the satirical dialogue *One Thousand Seven Hundred and Thirty-Eight* – afterwards renamed *An Epilogue to the Satires*.

These satires, and the attacks made upon the Court, resulted in Pope being threatened with prosecution, or at any rate receiving a warning; but the attacks made upon the Court did not alienate the Prince of Wales, who detested the King.

Meanwhile, Pope wandered, in 1739, from Rousham, the seat of Colonel Cotterell, near Oxford, to the house of Mr

Allen, and to the Hot Wells, near Bristol. In this year he edited a collection of Latin Poems by Italian authors, but without a preface or critical notes. He was at this time thinking of undertaking a History of English Poetry; but this, unfortunately, never came into being, though a plan of the history remains to us – a plan that is only a memorandum; it was printed first in Ruffhead's *Life of Pope*, 1769.

SKETCH FOR A HISTORY OF THE RISE AND PROGRESS OF ENGLISH POETRY

ÆRA I

Rymer. 2nd Part, pp. 65, 66, 67, 77.
Petrarch. 78 Catal: of Provencal Poets.
1 *School of Provence*. Chaucer's Visions, Romaunt of the Rose, Pierce Plowman. Tales of Boccace, Gower.
2 *School of Chaucer*. Lydgate, T. Occleve, Walt de Mapes, Skelton.
3 *School of Petrarch*. E. of Surrey, Sir Thomas Wyat, Sir Philip Sidney, G. Gascoyn. Translator of Ariosto's Com.
4 *School of Dante*. Mirror of Magistrates, Lord Buckhurst's Introduction, Gorboduc. Original of Good Tragedy, Seneca (his model).

ÆRA II

Spenser, Col. Clout, from the school of Ariosto and Petrarch, translated from Tasso.
5 *School of Spenser and from Italian Sonnets*. W. Brown's Pastorals, Ph. Fletcher's Purple Island, Alabaster, Piscatory. Ec. S. Daniel, Sir Walter Raleigh, Milton's Juvenilia, Heath-Habinton.
Translators from Italian. Golding, Ed. Fairfax, Harrington.
6 *School of Donne*. Cowley, Davenant, Randolph, Sir John Davis, Sir John Beaumont, Cartwright, Cleveland, Crashaw, Bishop Corbet, Lord Falkland.
Models to Waller. In Matter – Carew, T. Carey. In Versification – G. Sandys in his Par. of Job, Fairfax.
Originals of Hudibras. Sir John Mennis, Tho. Baynal.

Meanwhile, Pope's friendship with Warburton, whom he had met about three years previously, progressed rapidly, and the poet invited his friend to spend some time with him at the house of Mr Allen, near Bath. They remained there for six weeks, during which time Pope completed the fourth book of *The Dunciad*, which was published in March 1742, under the title of 'The New Dunciad as it was Found in the year 1741'. In the advertisement, Pope hinted that the manuscript had been found by accident in the library of a peer. (The mysterious old gentleman who had played such a strange part in the history of Mr Curll, had, presumably, insinuated himself into Lord Oxford's library again.)

The poem having been completed, Pope set off on a round of country visits. In September he stayed at the Duchess of Marlborough's country house at Windsor, and at Lord Cobham's house at Stowe, and in the summer of 1743 visited Bath once more, and from thence went to Prior Park, where Martha Blount was a fellow-guest.

Unfortunately, a violent quarrel took place between Mrs Allen and Martha; but the cause of the quarrel remains a mystery. For some eighteen years previously the life of Miss Blount had been more than difficult. Malicious persons had set afloat rumours that she was Pope's mistress – rumours that were denied by the poet with indignation and dignity. Suddenly, we do not know for what reason, Pope believed that Teresa Blount was responsible for inventing and spreading these scandals, and from that moment, his efforts to wrest Martha from the care of her mother and sister were almost unceasing. He wrote to the lady's godfather complaining that Teresa was in the habit of beating her mother (!) and ill-treating her sister, and urging that his beloved Patty must be removed from such a scandalous atmosphere, that she must live alone – it would be far better. It seemed, also, that Mrs Blount and Teresa had nearly succeeded in killing Martha as she lay ill. For had they not opened the windows and let in fresh air? Had they not insisted upon the floors being washed? Yet in spite of such monstrous conduct on the part of her parents and sister, Miss

Martha refused to leave home. Female credulity could hardly go further!

These stories may, or may not, have affected Mrs Allen's opinion of Miss Blount, whose proprietary manner towards the poet, together with her perpetual presence, affected the nerves of many of Pope's friends. In any case, the quarrel took place, and Pope left the house immediately, leaving Miss Blount to follow him. He left the house, he explained, because he could not countenance such behaviour as that exhibited by Mrs Allen towards Miss Blount. But we are left with a lurking suspicion that the poet was unwilling to face a field of battle which was so hotly contested by two ladies. I must admit, however, that he facilitated his friend's escape from the field of battle, once she had decided to leave it.

On the 12th of December, 1743, Pope made the will which provided Mrs Rackett with an opportunity for indulging in another lawsuit. He left to Martha Blount the sum of £1,000, all his household effects, and the residue of his estate after his legacies and debts had been paid. Mrs Rackett and her sons were to inherit all this after the death of Miss Blount. To Mrs Rackett he left £300 and a bond of £500 due by one of her sons; and he left £100 each to the other of her sons. Mrs Rackett was left, as well, in possession of the family pictures.

The time passed on swifter wings, the days were gone before he could catch at their lovely essence, the dream they contained. Yet he could still visit those he loved, although the beat in his heart fluttered like some bird that would escape, and must soon be gone.

'My dear Lords (he wrote to Bolingbroke and Marchmont), Yes, I would see you as long as I can see you, and then shut my eyes upon the world as a thing worth seeing no longer. If your charity would take up a small bird that is half-dead of the frost, and set it a-chirping for half an hour, I will jump into my cage, and put myself into your hands tomorrow at any hour you send. Two horses will be enough to draw me (and so would two dogs if you had them) ...'

On Easter Day (25th March, 1744), the poet wrote his last letter to the ever-beloved Martha Blount:

'Writing', he said, 'is become very painful to me, if I would write a letter of any length. In bed, or sitting, it hurts my breast; and in the afternoon, I can do nothing, still less by candlelight.' ... The letter ends with these words: 'I have little to say to you when we meet, but I love you upon unalterable principles, which makes me feel my heart the same to you as if I saw you every hour. Adieu.'

This letter contained, as well, the story of Pope's reconciliation with Mr Allen. For the shadow of a halcyon peace, a breathless calm, was already upon him.

The bird was fluttering, more and more wildly. Soon, very soon, it would be gone.

About three weeks before he died, Pope sent copies of the revised edition of his 'Ethic Epistles' to his friends: 'Here I am, like Socrates', said he, 'dispensing my morality among my friends just as I am dying.'

His friends left him scarcely at all ... Marchmont and the supposedly cynical and worldly Bolingbroke, in their love for him, could not bear to be absent from the dying man, for more than an hour. With them was Spence, and together they sat by the bedside, hoping against hope, holding him back with all their strength, from the world into which he was straying. Doctor Johnson relates a cruel and obviously untrue story about Martha Blount, accusing her of indifference towards that approaching death. 'As he (Pope) was one day sitting in the air with Lord Bolingbroke and Lord Marchmont, he saw his favourite Martha Blount at the bottom of the terrace, and asked Lord Bolingbroke to go and hand her up. Bolingbroke, not liking his errand, crossed his legs and sat still; but Lord Marchmont, who was younger and less captious, waited on the lady, who, when he came to her, asked, "What! is he not dead, yet?"'

How could this story be true of the friend who had comforted him through all his misery, strengthened him with her friendship in all his bodily weakness, borne unmerited scandal for his sake? The story is as cruel as the scandal was undeserved.

And Spence, unlike Doctor Johnson, quotes Warburton's remark that 'it was very observable during Pope's last illness, that Mrs Blount's coming in gave a new turn of spirits, or a temporary strength to him'. He, on his side, let no pain which he endured, no weakness which overcame his dying body, prevent him from planning for and ensuring the future of his beloved friend, that her life might be free from cares when he, who had loved her, was gone.

On Sunday, the 6th of May, the dying man became delirious, and four days afterwards said to Spence: 'One of the things that I have always most wondered at is, that there *should be any such thing as human vanity*. If I had any, I had enough to mortify it a few days ago, for I lost my mind for a whole day.'

He spoke, then, of that 'odd phenomenon' of seeing everything in the room as through a curtain, and of strange and unreal colours seen by him on the objects in his room. 'He said to me', Spence continues, ' "What's that?" pointing into the air with a very steady regard, and then looked down on me and said, with a smile of great pleasure, and with the greatest softness, " 'Twas a vision!" '

On the 15th of the month, he was visited by Lyttelton, and Pope, telling his friend that the doctor was pleased with some slight improvement in his condition, said: 'Here am I dying of a hundred good symptoms.' But his bodily sufferings, he said, were nothing compared to the fact that he could no longer think.

Bolingbroke wept over his dying friend: 'O Great God', he cried, through his sobs, 'what is man?'

Spence says that when he was telling Bolingbroke that the dying man, every time that he recovered, for a few fleeting moments, the possession of his mind spent those moments in saying something kindly about his present and his absent friends, as if his humanity outlasted his understanding, Bolingbroke replied: 'It has so! I never knew in my life a man that had so tender a heart for his particular friends, or a more general friendship for mankind. I have known him these thirty years; and value myself more for that man's love than ...' sinking his head and losing himself in tears.

A little while before Pope died, he whispered, 'I am so certain of the soul's being immortal, that I seem to feel it within me as it were by intuition'. And Ruffhead tells us that at four o'clock one morning the poet crept from his room, and was discovered by Warburton at the table in his library, writing, as if in great haste, for the moments left were so few. He was writing a paper on 'The Immortality of the Soul', but he, whose hope was centred on this, was led away once more and restored to his bed.

On the 27th the poet whispered over two of his own verses, from the *Imitation of Horace*, addressed to Colonel Cotterell – two verses which relate that his whole life had been

> Divided between carelessness and care.

Next day, he sat in his garden, in a sedan-chair, for three hours. How soon he must leave that garden, which had been to him a silent and all-understanding friend. This was the last time he would see that comforting friend, and now he must look at every flowering fruit-tree, at every humble and candid flower on the grass at his feet. Would they forget him? Those wise and all-seeing flower-eyes had never seen his deformity, but now, he fancied, they saw that he was dying; for this garden had been his refuge from pain; it understood and loved him.

The day before his death he was taken into Bushey Park. On his return, Hooke the historian, who was an earnest Catholic, asked the poet whether he should not send for a priest, that he might die as his father and mother had done. The dying man said: 'I do not suppose that is essential, but it will look right; and I heartily thank you for putting me in mind of it.'

The priest who performed the last office came from the dying man, as Hooke said, penetrated to the last degree with the state of mind in which he found his penitent, resigned, and with his soul and heart filled with the love of God and man. For Pope, whose weakness for the last years was such that he had to be dressed and undressed like a child, in his fervour for God, exerted his last power of movement that he might throw himself out of bed and receive the Last Sacrament kneeling on the floor.

After the priest had left him, Pope's dying voice said: 'There is nothing that is meritorious but virtue and friendship, and, indeed, friendship itself is but a part of virtue.'

The last beat in his heart ceased so quietly, so imperceptibly, that those he loved scarcely knew that he had left them. He died on Wednesday the 30th of May, having passed fifty-six years and nine days in this life.

He was buried near the monument to his parents in Twickenham Church, being carried to his grave by six of the poorest men of the parish, on Tuesday the 5th of June. A stone in the middle of the aisle of the church, bearing the letter P, marks the spot where he lies, quiet now, and with no memory of the broken shape that had hidden his great heart.

After Pope's death, Martha Blount remained true to his belief in her; but how hollow and breakable were some of the other friendships in which he had placed his trust. Pope's love for Bolingbroke was one of the deepest friendships of his life. But Bolingbroke found, after Pope's death, that the poet had ordered the publication of 1,500 copies of the statesman's *Letters on the Spirit of Patriotism, on the Idea of a Patriot King, and on the state of Parties,* instead of a few copies for private circulation only. This may have been a breach of trust, and it is true that the poet, as usual, had altered and omitted passages (this behaviour being a law of his nature); but that breach of trust was due to nothing but Pope's unreasoning admiration for his friend's powers; and Bolingbroke should have known this. Yet he could bring himself to hire Mallet to blacken his dead friend's character, and Mallet, the mean creature who had received a hundred benefits from Pope, to whom he owed such success as he had obtained, was willing, for the sum of £150, to blacken that dead benefactor's memory, now that he was safe from any reproach the poet could have uttered. The whole transaction can raise nothing but indignation in every right-thinking mind.

The publication of Mallet's and Bolingbroke's base attack

on Pope's memory called forth, as Carruthers tells us, 'a reply from Warburton ... This is an able and spirited vindication, and places Pope's conduct in its true light, as the result of an excessive and superstitious zeal for Lord Bolingbroke's glory' (page 399). 'It could not proceed', says Carruthers, 'from avarice, for the infirm health of Pope rendered it in the highest degree improbable that he would outlive his friend; it could not be the love of fame, for what reputation could be gained by printing the work of another? As little could Pope have dreamt that his conduct would be construed as treacherous, for he must have known that the impression would come into Bolingbroke's hands, the printer having been made acquainted with the name of the author. "His last illness was long and tedious", says Warburton, "and was known by him, as well as by his physicians, to be fatal: He might therefore have burned those fifteen hundred copies with a secrecy equal to the ostentation with which they were all destroyed in one common fire." No doubt', Carruthers continues, 'Pope expected to be able to overcome the false modesty of his friend, and obtain his concurrence to the publication; but even if he did not succeed in this, here was the invaluable treatise, secured for the honour and justification of his noble friend, "treasured up for a life beyond life", for the benefit of mankind.'

But he lies at peace, although the geese cackled and the jackals whined over his grave.

Pope's garden fell into the hands of Sir William Stanhope, and was so altered by him that the poet's ghost must wander bewildered among the ruins. But cuttings of his beloved willow beneath which he had sat so often, were sent by Sir William Stanhope to various parts of Europe, and in particular to the Empress of Russia, in 1789. It is said to be the ancestor of all the weeping willows in our gardens; but the tree itself is dead – it fell to the ground in 1801.

Horace Walpole, in a letter to Sir Horace Mann, lamented that, 'Sir William Stanhope bought Pope's house and garden. The former was so small and bad, one could not avoid pardoning his hollowing out that fragment of the rock Parnassus into habitable chambers – but would you believe it he has cut down the sacred groves themselves! In short, it was a little bit of ground of five acres, enclosed with three lanes, and seeing nothing. Pope had twisted and twirled, and rhymed and harmonised this, till it appeared two or three sweet little lawns opening and opening beyond one another, and the whole surrounded by thick impenetrable woods. Sir William, by advice of his son-in-law, Mr Ellis, has hacked and hewed these groves, wriggled a winding gravel walk through them with an edging of shrubs, in what they call the modern taste, and, in short, has desired the three lanes to walk in again – and now is forced to shut them out again by a wall, for there was not a Muse could walk there but she was spied by every country fellow that went by with a pipe in his mouth.'

How changed is that garden, from the time when a tiny hunchbacked figure, sad and dark as the lengthening shades of evening, sat beneath the trees; yet, should that lonely ghost return to it, I think it would be friendly to him still. And sometimes, on some ghost-lovely summer day, a shopkeeper and his son, walking in the Twickenham lanes, may meet that little ghost creeping along, a little shadow in rusty black with a cocked hat, and the boy, overcome with pity for one so small, and so bent with pain, will exclaim, 'Oh, poor man!' and his father will answer: 'That is not a poor man. That is the great and famous Mr Alexander Pope.'

CHAPTER XVIII

Some Notes on Pope's Poetry

IT is generally believed, by those whose appreciation of verse is a platonic one, that poetry springs from the poet's head, as Minerva sprang from the head of Jove. That is an easy explanation of the birth of our goddess, but it is not one which satisfies me. If we were to ask any of the poets of the past, we should without doubt be told that poetry is just as much a matter of physical aptitude as of spiritual. The poet feels, with his poetry, the same certainty yet excitement as a jockey feels with a racehorse. He has sensitive hands that feel the horse's mouth, that understand all the variations of speed, he has a body that is supremely fitted to ride the horse, a body that is light and that seems like part of this polished and victorious speed.

I believe that a poem begins in the poet's head, and then grows in his blood, as a rose grows among its dark leaves.

The poet feels the poem in the palm of his sensitive hands, understanding its exact weight (a most necessary part of the growth of the poem) letting the poem grow in his veins. He strokes it with his long fingers, as a sculptor divines the shape within the snow-cold, or sea-cold, marble that will soon discard, with his aid, all its outer sleep-wrappings, and stand revealed in its age-long beauty, one of a people of smiling statues, looking across an eternal and youthful sea.

The poet knows, through his sensitive hands, the difference between the sea-cold marble of the Ode, with all its divine variation of ivy-dark veins (cold as the satyrine forests) – veins with the shape of the Ægean waves within them, veins full of the light – the difference between this and the hot velvet petals of that rose the lyric – whose sound and whose music with its air-subtle variation makes the listener

Die of a rose in aromatic pain.

He feels in the veins of his hand, the shape and the texture of the poem before it has grown.

Poetry, too, is not only a result of this sensitiveness, but the form of the poem is dependent, very largely, on muscle. It is nearly always possible to judge of the poet's physique from his technique. Blanks, for instance, would have been impossible to a poet of Pope's tiny and weak body; but the stopped heroic couplet, with its sustaining rhymes, its outward cage (though that cage holds within it all the waves, and the towers and the gulfs of the world), this was born to be his measure. And it was because of his physical pain and weak physique that he, so wisely, perfected himself in the use of the couplet (the perfection is more miraculous, perhaps, than that of any other poetry), instead of attempting other and less suitable forms. He must, I think, have had strong and sensitive hands, otherwise he would not have attained to his supreme mastery of texture – that texture and understanding of the accumulation of quantities to which his extraordinary variation is due.

Professor Saintsbury has written so fully of the heroic couplet, that it would be a mere impertinence for one of so little learning as myself to discuss the couplet; but I would like, however, to examine the charge of monotony that has been brought against Pope.

Sir Leslie Stephen, in his *Life of Pope,* complains of the monotony of Pope's technique – as though the heroic couplet, with its infinite and subtle variation (especially in the hands of Pope) – were all of one depth, of one height, of one texture. How, for instance, can one compare the deep, sleepy richness, like that of some heavily-perfumed dark rose, of Keats' enjambed couplets, with the bucolic clumsiness of Chaucer's heroic couplets (as yet an unperfected form), or with the sylph-woven nets of dew of *The Rape of the Lock,* and the murky and hellish beauty of *The Dunciad*?

Let us take, for instance, these couplets from Chaucer's 'Portrait of the Monk':

> A Monk ther was, a fair for the maistrye,
> An out-rydere, that lovede venerye;
> A manly man, to been an abbot able.
> Ful many a deyntee hors hadde he in stable;

And, whan he rood, men mighte his brydel here
Ginglen in a whistling wynd as clere
And eek as loude as dooth the chapel-belle,
Ther as this lord was keper of the celle.

This has a splendid masculine quality, but, at the same time, a kind of bucolic roughness and an absence of subtlety. The cæsura or brake does not fall in its varying places of design, I imagine, or with any true sense of a feeling for its result. These enjambed couplets, when they are enjambed, have a country joviality, and are not like the full-blown enjambed couplets of Keats. This must not be taken in any way as a depreciation of that great poet Chaucer, since I yield to nobody in reverence for him. I mean, only, that the form was not, in that early time, perfected.

The heroic couplets of Waller, though they are very sweet and charming, are more pleasing in sense than in texture; for instance, the material of these couplets, from 'On St James' Park', is, whilst quite natural to the subject, and not at all at variance with it, not specially inherent in it:

While overhead a flock of new-sprung fowl
Hangs in the air, and does the sun control,
Darkening the sky; they hover o'er, and shroud
The wanton sailors with a feathered cloud.
Beneath, a shoal of silver fishes glides,
And plays about the gilded barges' sides;
The ladies, angling in the crystal lake,
Feast on the waters with the prey they take.

We can quite understand that Waller must have pleased Pope, but he can certainly not have taught him anything technically.

The heroic couplet, which is kept strictly within the limits of its outward structure, is as variable within those limits, as waves, as the air, with its light variations of wind, indeed, as variable as the earth itself, with its mountains and plains, its snows and gardens, towers, and gulfs. The reason why, to an insensitive ear, the heroic couplet seems monotonous, is because structure alone, and not texture, has been regarded as the maker of rhythm. In reality, both are the parents of rhythm in poetry; and variations in speed are certainly the result, not only of structure, but also of texture. Prosodists have been unable for obvious reasons, to discuss *all* the infinitely subtle variations and fluctuations of rhythm, and people of a coarse ear or taste in poetry have seized upon this silence as to these minute fluctuations and variations, as an excuse for denying or ignoring that the variations were there. Yet half the beauty and variation of English poetry is due to the prosodists' cunning and pretended deafness to the slightest of these fluctuations.

How faint they are, yet how significant – faint as the little air which comes to us from the feathers of the swan's wings, as he floats upon the lake. How slight, and how subtle are the changes of speed, or of depth, due to the difference in texture, and due to the fact that the English, in their cunning over the matter of poetry, have adopted the idea of equivalent syllables, that system which produces more variation than any other device. For is it really to be supposed that two words of one syllable each equal in speed one word of two syllables? The two-syllabled words, if unweighted by heavy consonants, move far more quickly. The system, therefore, of equivalent syllables gives variation to our poetry. Think, too, of the difference in speed caused by texture, by the use of heavy consonants, and especially the enormous effect on rhythm obtained by the variable use of rhyme.

I think I am right in saying that the rhythm and speed of a skilful and beautiful *un*rhymed poem differs from the rhythm and speed of a rhymed poem containing the same number and arrangement of feet, and that both the rhymed and unrhymed poems differ slightly in these respects from a poem ending with dissonances or with assonances, yet still containing the same number and arrangement of feet. It is a fact, too, that if assonances and dissonances are put at different places within the lines, and intermingled with equally skilfully placed internal rhymes, this has an intense effect both upon rhythm and in controlling and heightening speed; and the effect on rhythm and sometimes, though not always, on speed, is different to that of lines containing elaborately schemed internal rhymes without assonances or dissonances.

The truth is, that the texture of a poem has, in the past, been regarded as merely a matter of fatness or leanness – has been acknowledged only as producing richness, or sweetness, or harshness, in the poem; but the fact that texture is largely responsible for rhythm, for variations in the speed of the poem, this has not been acknowledged. Most of the technical experiments of our present time, are experiments in the effect that rhymes placed in an elaborate pattern throughout the poem (internally, outwardly, and at the beginning of lines), have upon rhythm, and the effect produced by variations of texture upon rhythm. But Pope's use of rhyme had not this variable effect, as he used the heroic couplet, nearly always, and seldom varied the heroic couplet by the use of a triplet, a fourteener, or an alexandrine, such as were used by Dryden:

> A needless Alexandrine ends the song,
> That, like a wounded snake, drags its slow length along.

The stupidly despised *Essay on Criticism* leads us to understand with what care and infinite subtlety Pope studied and worked at his texture:

> But when loud surges lash the sounding shore,
> The hoarse, rough verse should like the torrent roar:
> When Ajax strives some rock's vast weight to throw,
> The line too labours, and the words move slow:
> Not so, when swift Camilla scours the plain,
> Flies o'er th' unbending corn, and skims along the main.

The dipping and bending of that line is miraculous. No swallow ever flew more lightly.

The 'Ode on Saint Cecilia's Day' shows how stiff and unaccustomed Pope felt himself to be when he was not working in couplets. The poem contains beautiful lines, with occasional appalling lapses; it contains this splendour:

> Thy stone, O Sisyphus, stands still,
> Ixion rests upon his wheel,
> And the pale spectres dance!
> The Furies sink upon their iron beds,
> And snakes uncurl'd hang list'ning round their heads.

The first two lines are magnificent; the subsequent lines less so, but still fine; the poem contains also this lovely verse.

> By the hero's armed shades,
> Glitt'ring thro' the gloomy glades,
> By the youths that died for love,
> Wand'ring in the myrtle grove,
> Restore, restore Eurydice to life;
> Oh take the husband, or return the wife!

But the last line comes as a shock; it is difficult to see how so great a poet could reconcile himself to such bathos. The admiration for respectability which was such a moving power in his life, must have been at work here.

It is interesting to watch the perfecting of this sense of texture, from the groping beginning of it in the translation from Statius, to the greater accomplishment in the Pastorals, with the lovely use of liquids in the latter:

> So when the nightingale to rest removes,
> The thrush may chant to the forsaken groves,
> But, charmed to silence, listens while she sings,
> And all th' aërial audience clap their wings.

Here is no overburdening with heavy consonants; the lines are as soft and wet with dew as the leaves that hide the singing bird.

In *Windsor Forest* the power is greater, and so is the variation. For those who believe Pope is deficient in beauty, I will quote these lines:

> The shady empire shall retain no trace
> Of war or blood, but in the sylvan chace;

and

> O stretch thy reign, fair Peace! from shore to shore,
> Till conquest cease, and slavery be no more;
> Till the freed Indians in their native groves
> Reap their own fruits, and woo their sable loves,
> Peru once more a race of kings behold,
> And other Mexicos be roofed with gold.

If these lines are not beautiful, it is difficult to know what poetry in the English language may be so called.

As an example of Pope's so-called monotony, let us take the

difference between *The Rape of the Lock,* with its infinite variations, and *The Dunciad*, with its enormous variations of height and depth, speed, and heavy consciously-dulled sloth. *The Rape of the Lock,* this miraculous poem, which has been most foolishly described as a work in silver filigree, is light, variable and enchanting as a little summer wind blowing down the golden spangles of the dew from the great faunal trees – the whole poem might have been woven by the air-thin golden fingers of Pope's sylphs. This thin and glittering texture, how did it ever come into being? The lines differ in no wise from the wings of the sylphs, as they float above the barge:

> Some in the sun their insect-wings unfold,
> Waft on the breeze, or sink in clouds of gold;
> Transparent forms, too fine for mortal sight,
> Their fluid bodies half dissolved in light.
> Loose to the wind their airy garments flew,
> Thin glitt'ring textures of the filmy dew,
> Dipped in the richest tincture of the skies,
> Where light disports in ever-mingling dyes;
> While ev'ry beam new transient colours flings,
> Colours that change whene'er they wave their wings.

Those lines are the only fitting description of the poem itself; it is impossible to describe it in other terms. And yet Pope has been held to be deficient in beauty!

The only touch of shadow in those lines is the word 'waft', but I imagine that not in any other poem in the English language could such complete and dazzling control of texture be found, with the light and lovely liquids of the earlier lines, and the richer colour of the last two couplets. Compare the lines quoted above, with the description of the card-party, in the Third Canto, with the velvety softness, and depth and shade – like the shadow cast by a great tree on some hot afternoon.

> And parti-coloured troops, a shining train,
> Draw forth to combat on the velvet plain.
> The skilful nymph reviews her force with care:
> Let spades be trumps! she said, and trumps they were.

Now move to war her sable Matadores,
In show like leaders of the swarthy Moors.
Spadillio first, unconquerable lord!
Led off two captive trumps, and swept the board.

Compare this with the early morning whiteness of the First Canto, and see how far the charge of monotony can be brought against Pope.

The whole of *The Rape of the Lock,* excepting that part which deals with the Cave of Spleen, seems wet and shining with dew. Sometimes these 'thin glittering textures of the filmy dew' are 'dipt in the richest tincture of the skies' as in the description of the Sylphs which I have quoted already – sometimes the dew is shining like the pale flowers of the early light which are bunched outside Belinda's window – as in

'Twas he had summoned to her silent bed
The morning dream that hovered o'er her head,
A youth more glitt'ring than a birth-night beau,
(That ev'n in slumber caused her cheek to glow.)

Sometimes the dews are glittering night dews, as in these couplets:

Fairest of mortals, thou distinguished care
Of thousand bright inhabitants of air!
If e'er one vision touched thy infant thought,
Of all the nurse and all the priest have taught;
Of airy elves by moonlight shadows seen,
The silver token, and the circled green,
Or virgins visited by angel-pow'rs
With golden crowns and wreaths of heav'nly flowers;

In *The Rape of the Lock,* incidentally, Pope only used female rhymes twice, if 'flowers' may be held to be a female ending. (This is doubtful.) He has, however, this couplet ending with a female rhyme:

The meeting points the sacred hair dissever
From the fair head, for ever, and for ever!

It is interesting to notice the extra emphasis, like a cry, obtained by the use of an internal rhyme.

The clearest proof of the extraordinary subtlety of Pope's

use of texture, is that we actually notice the little cool shadows of that extra fraction of a syllable, so slight that it is hardly audible, contained in the rhymes of this couplet:

> A brighter wash; to curl their waving hairs,
> Assist their blushes, and inspire their airs;

The words 'airs', 'hairs' have a little wavering sound, like the slight breath of a summer air among young leaves. And this is not only the result of association. We find this tiny freshening sound several times in the poem.

The whole of *The Rape of the Lock* is fresh as the summer air blowing down the dew that tastes of the green leaves on which it has been lying, and this comes largely from the absence of female rhymes. It has not the honeyed sweetness of Keats' quicker poems, of the light

> What is more gentle than a wind in summer?
> What is more soothing than the pretty hummer
> That stays one moment in an open flower,
> And buzzes cheerily from bower to bower?
> What is more tranquil than a musk rose blowing
> In a green island, far from all men's knowing?
> More healthful than the leafiness of dales?
> More secret than a nest of nightingales?
> More serene than Cordelia's countenance?
> More full of visions than a high romance?

The honeyed quality of this comes very largely from the use of female rhymes with *light* vowel-sounds in the first couplet, and perhaps also in the second (though 'flower' is in reality a word, not of two syllables, but of one and three-quarter syllables) – contrasted with the richer vowel-sound in the third couplet.

It has been the fashion to regard only the tempests of fury, and not the strange murky and Tartarean beauty of *The Dunciad*, although it is one of the greatest poems in our language. Yet it is just as beautiful in its own way, and just as strange, as *The Ancient Mariner*. It has been held not to be, only because it is a satire, and people whose liking for poetry is a purely sentimental one, are unable to believe that beauty is not dependent upon subject alone.

How enormous are the opening lines, with the thick, muffled, dull thud of the alliterating M's:

> The mighty mother, and her son, who brings
> The Smithfield muses to the ears of kings.

The sound is thick, gross, and blind as stupidity itself. Then take the lines:

> Fate in their dotage this fair idiot gave,
> Gross as her sire, and as her mother grave,
> Laborious, heavy, busy, bold, and blind,
> She rul'd, in native anarchy, the mind.

The G sounds in the first and last word of the second line, give a designedly unwieldy lumbering gait to the line, a gait indicative of the subject; the next line, with its appalling deafening blows, caused by the alliterative B's, placed so close together, has an overwhelming effect of power.

If we compare those varying lines with those I have quoted from *The Rape of the Lock,* I do not see how it is possible, for any but the most insensitive, to uphold that Pope is monotonous.

As for beauty, there is a kind of smoky and appalling beauty throughout the poem, and such beauty as this, which has a kind of hell-born inspiration:

> So watchful Bruin forms, with plastic care,
> Each growing lump, and brings it to a bear.

we see his great technical genius in this:

> No meagre, muse-rid mope, adust and thin,
> In a dun night-gown of his own loose skin;
> But such a bulk as no twelve bards could raise,
> Twelve starv'ling bards of these degen'rate days.
> All as a partridge plump, full-fed and fair,
> She form'd this image of well-body'd air;
> With pert flat eyes she window'd well its head;
> A brain of feathers, and a heart of lead;

and in this:

> Now thousand tongues are heard in one loud din;
> The monkey-mimics rush discordant in;

'Twas chatt'ring, grinning, mouthing, jabb'ring all,
And noise and Norton, brangling and Breval,
Dennis and dissonance, and captious art,
And snip-snap short, and interruption smart,
And demonstration thin; and theses thick,
And major, minor, and conclusion quick.

The thick muffled deadness of the first couplet in the first quotation, the fatness and flatness of the second – this effect being produced by the softness of the consonants used, all this leads into the appalling trumpet-screams of the fifth and subsequent couplets. These lines can hardly be called monotonous. Nor can the poem which contains, together with these, such exquisite floating coolness as these lines:

To isles of fragrance, lily-silver'd vales,
Diffusing languor in the panting gales;
To lands of singing or of dancing slaves,
Love-whisp'ring woods, and lute-resounding waves.

and the colder, more remote beauty of

Lo! where Mæotis sleeps, and hardly flows
The freezing Tanais thro' a waste of snows,

(apart from the beauty of the vowel-sounds, the effect is produced largely by the little frozen air, dying away again, of the tribrach 'Tanais').

Contrast the cold beauty of that couplet, with the grave and majestic splendour of the last two couplets, and it will no longer be possible to call Pope monotonous:

Lo! thy dread empire, Chaos! is restor'd;
Light dies before thy uncreating word;
Thy hand, great Anarch! lets the curtain fall,
And universal darkness buries all.

Can these couplets be regarded as the same in rhythm – (if rhythm means anything to us at all) – as the Mæotis couplet? They cannot. The outward structure is the same; within that structure there is infinite variation. We might as well complain that the world is monotonous because it is round, and because it circles round the sun, as complain of the monotony of Alexander Pope.

One example of his 'monotony' is his use of the cæsura. Now the cæsura has, for the purposes of convenience, been held to be of uniform length and depth. But this is not so. And Pope places the cæsura, the pause (of varying depths) not only to vary the *music* of his verse, but so as to heighten the meaning. As when, in the *Epistle to Dr Arbuthnot,* he says:

> The dog-star rages! nay, tis past a doubt,
> All Bedlam, or Parnassus, is let out;
> Fire in each eye, and papers in each hand,
> They rave, recite, and madden round the land.

In this, the slightness of the pauses in the second line give the effect of a dishevelled procession streaming past one. In the fourth line, the fact that the first and second verb are alliterative, and rather long-sounding, with their hard R's, and that the third verb begins with a thick thumping M, gives the degree of irritation which was felt by the poet.

But to return to the cæsura. If we examine these lines from *The Dunciad,*

> One cell there is, conceal'd from vulgar eye,
> The cave of poverty and poetry.
> Keen, hollow winds howl thro' the bleak recess,
> Emblem of music caus'd by emptiness.

we shall find that the slightness of the cæsura, in the third line I have quoted – a cæsura so shallow as to be hardly perceptible, gives it a strange chilliness, which is added to by the little cold wind of the two words beginning with H in the third line, the last of these two words, because it is a one-syllabled word and has a long vowel-sound, being louder than the two-syllabled short-vowelled 'hollow'.

Compare the slightness of the cæsura here, with the violence of the pause, the violence of the antithesis in the last line of these couplets from the *First Epistle of the First Book of Horace*:

> To either India see the merchant fly,
> Scared at the spectre of pale poverty!
> See him, with pangs of body, pangs of soul,
> Burn through the tropic, freeze beneath the pole!

How perfectly he fits his substance to his meaning. Take, for instance, these lines, which convey, in spite of the perfect structure of the heroic couplet, a sense of the formlessness of primeval matter (the lines are from *The Dunciad*):

> 'Till genial Jacob, or a warm third day,
> Call forth each mass, a poem or a play:
> How hints, like spawn, scarce quick in embryo lie,
> How new-born nonsense first is taught to cry,
> Maggots half-form'd in rhyme exactly meet,
> And learn to crawl upon poetic feet.

These lines, and the eight lines which follow, have a perfectly deliberate, and most unpleasant, softness – the softness of corruption.

Compare this with the portrait of Lord Hervey in the *Epistle to Dr Arbuthnot* after that first terrible trumpet-scream of rage:

> Let Sporus tremble –

the lines have a dirty fluttering sound, to suit the dirty fluttering thing they portray. These lines, too, have a softness, but it is a different kind of softness to that of the lines I have quoted from *The Dunciad* – it is the softness, not of a shapeless thing, but of a fluttering insect at moments, of a serpent at others:

> Let Sporus tremble – A. What? that thing of silk,
> Sporus, that mere white curd of ass's milk?
> Satire or sense, alas! can Sporus feel,
> Who breaks a butterfly upon a wheel?
> P. Yet let me flap this bug with gilded wings,
> This painted child of dirt, that stinks and stings;
> Whose buzz the witty and the fair annoys,
> Yet wit ne'er tastes, and beauty ne'er enjoys:
> So well-bred spaniels civilly delight
> In mumbling of the game they dare not bite.
> Eternal smiles his emptiness betray,
> As shallow streams run dimpling all the way,
> Whether in florid impotence he speaks,
> And, as the prompter breathes, the puppet squeaks;
> Or at the ear of Eve, familiar toad,
> Half froth, half venom, spits himself abroad,

In puns, or politics, or tales, or lies,
Or spite, or smut, or rhymes, or blasphemies.
His wit all see-saw, between that and this,
Now high, now low, now master up, now miss,
And he himself one vile antithesis.
Amphibious thing! that acting either part,
The trifling head, or the corrupted heart;
Fop at the toilet, flatterer at the board,
Now trips a lady, and now struts a lord.
Eve's tempter thus the rabbins have expressed,
A cherub's face, a reptile all the rest.
Beauty that shocks you, parts that none will trust,
Wit that can creep, and pride that licks the dust.

In this, the dark consonants are more separated from each other than they are in the passage from *The Dunciad.* With the soft S's used in a pattern through the whole passage, and the viper-dart of

In puns, or politics, or tales, or lies,
Or spite, or smut, or rhymes, or blasphemies.

with the fluttering dirtiness of

Fop at the toilet, flatterer at the board,
Now trips a lady, and now struts a lord.

the whole passage is a triumph, not only of invention, but also of suitability and of command over the material. How miraculously he understands the different effects arising from the varied disposal of one-syllabled words among two-syllabled and three-syllabled words – and the effect that a line containing nothing but one-syllabled words may have, when placed among lines which contain artfully-placed and consciously-used double-and treble-syllabled words. There is no effect on rhythm and speed that can be gained by these variations, that has not been used by him to a miraculous extent.

In Pope's minor poems, there is not much to examine. Yet 'Eloisa to Abelard' although it is not one of Pope's most successful poems, has been, I think, rather under-rated, for it is in many ways a moving poem. Unfortunately, the skilled use of the antithesis, of which Pope and Dryden were our greatest masters, was not suitable to this subject:

> I mourn the lover, not lament the fault

this gives the emotion an epigrammatic effect which lessens and falsifies the emotion.

Yet how real and how moving is this:

> Ah hopeless, lasting flames! like those that burn
> To light the dead, and warm th' unfruitful urn.

The poem is very quiet and restrained, the restraint is moving; but I am not quite sure that it was *meant* to be as quiet as it is – that the quietness is not a result of Pope's ill-health – (his physical debility could never be guessed from *The Dunciad* or *The Rape of the Lock*!).

I am not qualified to judge of the Translations from Homer as *translations*. May I not, therefore, be allowed to regard them, not as translations, but as evidences of Pope's great poetic genius? The translation of the Odyssey is bathed in the azure airs of beauty that come to us from an undying sea. The lines and the heroes walk with the pomp and majesty of waves.

In the Odyssey we do not find the astonishing variations in texture that we find in *The Dunciad,* nor the incredibly subtle variations of *The Rape of the Lock*. The poem is more uniform, but had it been otherwise, the technique would have been unsuited to the matter. Again, in some lines we find the ancestry of Keats' *Endymion,* as in the first couplet of

> With unguents smooth the lucid marble shone,
> Where ancient Neleus sate, a rustic throne;
> But he descending to th' infernal shade
> Sage Nestor fill'd it, and the sceptre sway'd.

How magnificent is the dissonance, rather than the rhyme, of the middle couplet of

> Till the Cyclopean race in arms arose,
> A lawless nation of gigantic foes;
> Then great Nausithous from Hyperia far,
> Through seas retreating from the sound of war,

> The recreant nation to fair Scheria led,
> Where never science rear'd her laurell'd head:

An occasional, very occasional dissonance or assonance saves this otherwise flawless poem from monotony.

In Book VII we see the unperfected beginning of Pope's habit of the antithesis in

> These did the ruler of the deep ordain
> To build proud navies, and command the main;
> On canvas wings to cut the watery way;
> No bird so light, no thought so swift as they.

In 'To build proud navies' the double-syllabled word, 'navies', has the curious effect of seeming to shorten the value of the last foot, having indeed much the same effect as a female rhyme ending the line.

The poem has a thousand physical beauties, but these lie more in imagery and expression than in texture; for the texture is not very variable; the variety of the poem lies more in differences in colouring than in differences of texture. The poem indeed, seems cut out of various-coloured marbles. But there is a difference between the delicately veined marble of

> Some ply the loom; their busy fingers move
> Like poplar leaves when Zephyr fans the grove,

and the black basalt of

> Toss'd by rude tempest through a war of waves;

It is profoundly interesting to compare the altered and completed version of the Iliad with the first and uncorrected draft, and to speculate on the reasons for these corrections. If, for instance, we examine the corrections at the beginning of the first book – (I have already referred to the opening lines in another chapter) – the corrections of those lines which refer to the dead heroes, it is easy to see the reasons for those alterations. The corrected version stands thus:

> Whose limbs, unbury'd on the naked shore,
> Devouring dogs and hungry vultures tore,
> Since great Achilles and Atrides strove,
> Such was the sov'reign doom, and such the will of Jove.

The first line of the second couplet, in the uncorrected version, runs

> Since first Atrides and Achilles strove.

The reason for the alteration is obvious. There are too many sibilant sounds in the line; and 'Atrides and Achilles' gives no sense of heroic strength and combat, but of a weak thing falling, whereas 'Achilles and Atrides strove', with the long vowels of the two last words, gives just the effect of an heroic combat.

In the conclusion of Book VIII, v. 687, we find these multiple corrections of one couplet:

The corrected version, according to Dr Johnson, stands thus:

> As when the moon, refulgent lamp of night!
> O'er Heav'n's clear azure spreads her sacred light,

But in the 1715 edition the word is 'sheds', not 'spreads'.

This couplet has suffered many changes:

> As when in stillness of the silent night,
> As when the moon in all her lustre bright,
> As when the moon, refulgent lamp of night
> O'er heaven's clear azure sheds her silver light;
> pure spreads sacred

I shall never understand the reason for 'refulgent lamp of night', which seems to me appalling, but the reason for the alteration from 'pure' to 'clear' is that 'pure' has an echo to it, which makes it seem longer than a one-syllabled word, the reason for the change from 'sheds' to 'spreads' is too obvious to be commented on, the reason for the change from 'silver' to 'sacred' is that the length of the A in 'sacred' makes it seem like a clear and holy light shining over the scene.

In later editions the description of Tydides, inspired by Pallas (Book V), the last couplet but one reads thus:

> High on his helm celestial lightnings play,
> His heavy shield emits a living ray;
> Th' unweary'd blaze incessant streams supplies,
> Like the red star that fires th' autumnal skies.

The original draft of the first line of the first couplet ran:

> Bright from his beamy crest the lightnings play,

and the reason for the change is that the alliteration and the emphasis on one-syllabled words before the cæsura give the effect of height, because of their emphasis. The last line of the last couplet ran through these changes:

> The Goddess with her breath the flame supplies,
> Bright as the star whose fires in Autumn rise,
> Her breath divine thick streaming flame supplies,
> Bright as the star that fires the autumnal skies;

The reason for the change is partly because of the sound; but the splendour of

> Like the red star that fires th' autumnal skies

is a majesty equally of imagery and sound.

APPENDIX A

An Article from 'The Guardian', 21st May, 1713

Primoque a caede ferarum
Incaluisse putem maculatum sanguine ferrum. – OVID.

I CANNOT think it extravagant to imagine, that mankind are no less, in proportion, accountable for the ill use of their dominion over creatures of the lower rank of beings, than for the exercise of tyranny over their own species. The more entirely the inferior creation is submitted to our power, the more answerable we should seem for our mismanagement of it; and the rather, as the very condition of nature renders these creatures incapable of receiving any recompense in another life for their ill-treatment in this.

'Tis observable of those noxious animals, which have qualities most powerful to injure us, that they naturally avoid mankind, and never hurt us unless provoked, or necessitated by hunger. Man, on the other hand, seeks out and pursues even the most inoffensive animals, on purpose to persecute and destroy them.

Montaigne thinks it some reflection upon human nature itself, that few people take delight in seeing beasts caress or play together, but almost every one is pleased to see them lacerate and worry one another. I am sorry this temper is become almost a distinguishing character of our own nation, from the observation which is made by foreigners of our beloved pastimes, bear-baiting, cock-fighting, and the like. We should find it hard to vindicate the destroying of anything that has life, merely out of wantonness; yet in this principle our children are bred up, and one of the first pleasures we allow them, is the licence of inflicting pain upon poor animals: almost as soon as we are sensible what life is ourselves, we make it our sport to take it from other creatures. I cannot but believe a very good use might be made of the fancy which children have for birds and insects. Mr Locke takes notice of a mother who permitted them to her children, but rewarded them or punished them as they treated them well or ill. This was no other than entering them betimes into a daily exercise of humanity, and improving their very diversion to a Virtue.

I fancy, too, some advantage might be taken of the common notion, that 'tis ominous or unlucky to destroy some sorts of birds, as swallows and martins; this opinion might possibly arise from the confidence these birds seem to put in us by building under our roofs, so that it is a kind of violation of the laws of hospitality to murder them. As for robin-red-breasts in particular, 'tis not improbable they owe their security to the old ballad of 'The Children in the Wood'. However it be, I don't know, I say, why this prejudice, well improved and carried as far as it would go, might not be made to conduce to the preservation of many innocent creatures, which are now exposed to all the wantonness of an ignorant barbarity.

There are other animals that have the misfortune, for no manner of reason, to be treated as common enemies wherever found. The conceit that a cat has nine lives has cost at least nine lives in ten of the whole race of 'em: scarce a boy in the streets but has in this point outdone Hercules himself, who was famous for killing a monster that had but three lives. Whether the unaccountable animosity against this useful domestic may be any cause of the general persecution of owls (who are a sort of feathered cats) or whether it be only an unreasonable pique the moderns have taken to a serious countenance, I shall not determine. Though I am inclined to believe the former; since I observe the sole reason alleged for the destruction of frogs is because they are like toads. Yet amidst all the misfortunes of these unfriended creatures, 'tis some happiness that we have not yet taken a fancy to eat them: for should our countrymen refine upon the French never so little, 'tis not to be conceived to what unheard-of torments, owls, cats, and frogs may be yet reserved.

When we grow up to men, we have another succession of sanguinary sports; in particular hunting. I dare not attack a diversion which has such authority and custom to support it, but must have leave to be of opinion, that the agitation of that exercise, with the example and number of the chasers, not a little contribute to resist those checks, which compassion would naturally suggest in behalf of the animal pursued. Nor shall I say with Monsieur Fleury, that this sport is the remain of the Gothic barbarity; but I must animadvert upon a custom yet in use with us, and barbarous enough to be derived from the Goths, or even the Scythians: I mean that savage compliment our huntsmen pass upon ladies of quality, who are present at the death of a stag, when they put the knife in their hands to cut the throat of a helpless, trembling and weeping creature.

> Questuque cruentus,
> Atque Imploranti similis.

But if our sports are destructive, our gluttony is more so, and in a more inhuman manner. Lobsters roasted alive, pigs whipp'd to death, fowls sewed up, are testimonies of our outrageous luxury. Those, who (as Seneca expresses it) divide their lives betwixt an anxious conscience and a nauseated stomach, have a just reward of their gluttony in the diseases it brings with it: for human savages, like other wild beasts, find snares and poison in the provisions of life, and are allured by their appetite to their destruction. I know nothing more shocking, or horrid, than the prospect of one of their kitchens covered with blood, and filled with the cries of creatures expiring in tortures. It gives one an image of a giant's den in a romance, bestrow'd with the scattered heads and mangled limbs of those who were slain by his cruelty.

The excellent Plutarch (who has more strokes of good-nature in his writings than I remember in any author) cites a saying of Cato to this effect: 'That 'tis no easy task to preach to the belly which has no ears. Yet if', says he, 'we are ashamed to be so out of fashion as not to offend, let us at least offend with some discretion and measure. If we kill an animal for our provision, let us do it with the meltings of compassion, and without tormenting it. Let us consider, that 'tis in its own nature cruelty to put a living creature to death; we at least destroy a soul that has sense and perception.' In the life of Cato the Censor, he takes occasion from the severe disposition of that man to discourse in this manner. 'It ought to be esteemed a happiness to mankind, that our humanity has a wider sphere to exert itself in, than bare justice. It is no more than the obligation of our very birth to practise equity to our own kind, but humanity may be extended through the whole order of creatures, even to the meanest: such actions of charity are the overflowings of a mild good nature on all below us. It is certainly the part of a well-natured man to take care of his horses and dogs, not only in expectation of their labour while they are foals and whelps, but even when their old age has made them incapable of service.'

History tells us of a wise and polite nation that rejected a person of the first quality, who stood for a judiciary office, only because he had been observed in his youth, to take pleasure in tearing and murdering of birds. And of another that expelled a man out of the Senate for dashing a bird against the ground which had taken shelter in his bosom. Every one knows how remarkable the Turks are for their humanity in this kind: I remember an Arabian author, who has written a treatise to show, how far a man, supposed to have subsisted in a desert island, without any instruction, or so much as the sight of any other man, may, by the pure light of nature, attain the knowledge of philosophy and virtue. One of the first things he makes him observe is, that universal benevolence of Nature in the protection and preservation of its creatures. In imitation of which, the first act of virtue he thinks his self-taught philosopher would of course fall into is, to relieve and assist all the animals about him in their wants and distresses.

Ovid has some very tender and pathetic lines applicable to this occasion.

> Quid meruistis oves, placidum pecus, inque tegendos
> Natum homines, pleno quæ fertis in ubere nectar?
> Mollia quæ nobis vestras velamina lanas
> Præbetis; vitaque magis quam morte juvatis.

Quid meruëre boves, animal sine fraude dolisque,
Innocuum, simplex, natum tolerare labores?
Immemor est demum, nec frugum munere dignus,
Qui potuit, curvi dempto modo pondere aratri,
Ruricolam mactare suum –
Quam male consuevit, quam se parat ille cruori
Impius humano, vituli qui guttura cultro
Rumpit, et immotas præbet mugitibus aures!
Aut qui vagitus similes puerilibus hædum
Edentem jugulare potest! –

Perhaps that voice or cry so nearly resembling the human, with which Providence has endued so many different animals, might purposely be given them to move our pity, and prevent those cruelties we are too apt to inflict on our fellow creatures.

There is a passage in the book of Jonas, when God declares his unwillingness to destroy Nineveh, where methinks that compassion of the Creator, which extends to the meanest rank of his creatures, is expressed with wonderful tenderness – 'Should I not spare Nineveh the great city, wherein are more than six thousand persons ... And also much cattle?' And we have in Deuteronomy a precept of great good-nature in this sort, with a blessing in form annexed to it in those words. 'If thou shalt find a bird's nest in the way, thou shalt not take the dam with the young: But thou shalt in any wise let the dam go, that it may be well with thee, and thou may'st prolong thy days.'

To conclude, there is certainly a degree of gratitude owing to those animals that serve us; as for such as are mortal or noxious, we have a right to destroy them; and for those that are neither of advantage or prejudice to us, the common enjoyment of life is what I cannot think we ought to deprive them of.

This whole matter, with regard to each of these considerations, is set in a very agreeable light in one of the Persian fables of Pilpay, with which I shall end this paper.

A traveller passing through a thicket, and seeing a few sparks of a fire, which some passengers had kindled as they went that way before, made up to it. On a sudden the sparks caught hold of a bush, in the midst of which lay an adder, and set it in flames. The adder entreated the traveller's assistance, who, tying a bag to the end of his staff, reached it, and drew him out: he then bid him go where he pleased, but never more be hurtful to men, since he owed his life to a man's compassion. The adder, however, prepared to sting him, and when he expostulated how unjust it was to retaliate good with evil, I shall do no more (said the adder) than what you men practise every day, whose custom it is to requite benefits with ingratitude. If you can deny this truth, let us refer it to the first we meet. The man consented, and seeing a tree, put the question to it in what manner a good turn was to be recompensed? If you mean according to the usage of men (replied the tree) by its contrary, I have been standing here these hundred years to protect them from the scorching sun, and in requital they have cut down my branches, and are going to saw my body into planks. Upon this the adder insulting the man, he appealed to a second evidence, which was granted, and immediately they met a cow, The same demand was made, and much the same answer given, that among men it was certainly so. I know it (said the cow) by woeful experience; for I have served a man this long time with milk, butter and cheese, and brought him besides a calf every year: but now I am old, he turns me into this pasture, with design to sell me to a butcher, who will shortly make an end of me. The traveller upon this stood confounded, but desired, of courtesy, one trial more, to be finally judged by the next beast they should meet. This happened to be the fox, who, upon hearing the story in all its circumstances, could not be persuaded it was possible for the adder to enter in so narrow a bag. The adder to convince him went in again; when the fox told the man he had now his enemy in his power, and with that he fastened the bag, and crushed him to pieces.

APPENDIX B

A Letter to A Noble Lord

ON OCCASION OF SOME LIBELS WRITTEN AND PROPAGATED AT COURT IN THE YEAR 1732–3

Nov. 30, 1733.

MY LORD – Your Lordship's Epistle has been published some days, but I had not the pleasure and pain of seeing it till yesterday: pain, to think your Lordship should attack me at all; pleasure, to find that you can attack me so weakly. As I want not the humility, to think myself in every way but *one* your inferior, it seems but reasonable that I should take the only method either of self-defence or retaliation, that is left me against a person of your quality and power. And as by your choice of this weapon, your pen, you generously (and modestly too, no doubt) meant to put yourself upon a level with me, I will as soon believe that your Lordship would give a wound to a man unarmed, as that you would deny me the use of it in my own defence.

I presume you will allow me to take the same liberty in my answer to so candid, polite, and ingenious a nobleman, which your Lordship took in yours, to so *grave, religious,* and *respectable* a clergyman. As you answered his Latin in English, permit me to answer your verse in prose. And though your Lordship's reasons for not writing in Latin, might be stronger than mine for not writing in verse, yet I may plead two good ones, for this conduct: – the one, that I want the talent of spinning *a thousand lines in a* day (which I think is as much time as this subject deserves), and the other, that I take your Lordship's verse to be as much prose as this letter. But no doubt it was your choice, in writing to a friend, to renounce all the pomp of poetry, and give us this excellent model of the familiar.

When I consider the great difference betwixt the rank your Lordship holds in the *world*, and the rank which your writings are like to hold in the learned world, I presume that distinction of style is but necessary, which you will see observed through this letter. When I speak of *you*, my Lord, it will be with all the deference due to the inequality which Fortune has made between you and myself: but when I speak of your *writings*, my Lord, I must, I can, do nothing but trifle.

I should be obliged indeed to lessen this respect, if all the nobility (and especially the elder brothers) are but so many hereditary fools, if the privilege of lords be to want brains, if noblemen can hardly write or read, if all their business is but to dress and vote, and all their employment in court, to tell lies, flatter in public, slander in private, be false to each other, and follow nothing but self-interest. Bless me, my Lord, what an account is this you give of them? and what would have been said of me, had I immolated, in this manner, the whole body of the nobility, at the stall of a well-fed prebendary?

Were it the mere excess of your Lordship's wit, that carried you thus triumphantly over all the bounds of decency, I might consider your Lordship on your Pegasus, as a sprightly hunter on a mettled horse; and while you were trampling down all our works, patiently suffer the injury, in pure admiration of the noble sport. But should the case be quite otherwise, should your Lordship be only like a boy that is run away with; and run away with by a very foal; really common charity, as well as respect for a noble family, would oblige me to stop your career, and to help you down from this Pegasus.

Surely the little praise of a *writer* should be a thing below your ambition: you, who were no sooner born, but in the lap of the Graces; no sooner at school, but in the arms of the Muses; no sooner in the world, but you practised all the skill of it; no sooner in the court, but you possessed all the art of it! Unrivalled as you are, in making a figure, and in making a speech, methinks, my Lord, you may well give up the poor talent of turning a distich. And why this fondness for poetry? Prose admits of the two excellences you most admire, diction and fiction; it admits of the talents you chiefly possess, a most fertile invention, and most florid expression; it is with prose, nay the plainest prose, that you best could teach our nobility to vote, which you justly observe, is half at least of their business: and give me leave to prophesy, it is to your talent in prose, and not in verse, to your speaking, not your writing, to your art at court, not your art of poetry, that your lordship must owe your future figure in the world.

My Lord, whatever you imagine, this is the advice of a friend, and one who remembers he formerly had the honour of some profession of friendship from you: whatever was his real share in it, whether small or great, yet as your Lordship could never have had the great *loss* by continuing it, or the least interest by withdrawing it, the misfortune of losing it, I fear, must have been owing to his own deficiency or neglect. But as to any actual fault which deserved to forfeit it in such a degree, he protests he is to this day guiltless and ignorant. It could at most be but a fault of omission; but indeed by omission, men of your Lordship's uncommon merit may sometimes think themselves so injured, as to be capable of an inclination to injure another; who, though very much below their quality, may be above the injury.

I never heard of the least displeasure you had conceived against me, till I was told that an imitation I had made of Horace had offended some persons, and among them your Lordship. I could not have apprehended that a few *general strokes* about a *Lord scribbling carelessly, a pimp,* or a *spy* at court, a *sharper* in a gilded chariot, etc. – that these, I say, should be ever applied as they have been, by any malice but that which is the greatest in the world, the malice of ill people to themselves.

Your Lordship so well knows (and the whole court and town through your means so well know), how far the resentment was carried upon that imagination, not only in the nature of the libel you propagated against me, but in the extraordinary manner, place and presence, in which it was propagated, that I shall only say, it seemed to me to exceed the bounds of justice, common sense, and decency.

I wonder yet more, how a lady, of great wit, beauty, and fame for her poetry (between whom and your Lordship there is a natural, a just, and well-grounded esteem), could be prevailed upon to take a part in that proceeding. Your resentments against me indeed might be equal, as my offence to you both was the same; for neither had I the least misunderstanding with that lady, till after I was the author of my own misfortune in discontinuing her acquaintance. I may venture to own a truth, which cannot be displeasing to either of you; I assure you my reason for so doing, was merely that you had both *too much wit* for me; and that I could not do with *mine*, many things which you could do with *yours*. The injury done you in withdrawing myself could be but small if the value you had for me was no greater than you have been pleased since to profess. But surely, my Lord, one may say, neither the revenge, nor the language you held, bore any proportion to the pretended offence: the appellations of *foe* to *human kind*, an *enemy* like the *devil* to all that have *being*; *ungrateful, unjust,* deserving to be *whipped, blanketed, kicked,* nay *killed*: a *monster, an assassin,* whose conversation every man ought to *shun*, and against whom all doors should be shut; I beseech you, my Lord, had you the least right to give, or to encourage or justify any other in giving such language as this to me? Could I be treated in terms more strong or more atrocious, if during my acquaintance with you I had been a betrayer, a backbiter, a whisperer, an eaves-dropper, or an informer? Did I in all that time ever throw a false die, or palm a foul card upon you? Did I ever borrow, steal, or accept either money, wit, or advice from you? Had I ever the honour to join with either of you in one ballad, satire, pamphlet, or epigram on any person living or dead? Did I ever do you so great an injury as to put off my own verses for yours, especially on those persons whom they might most offend? I am confident you cannot answer in the affirmtive; and I can truly affirm, that ever since I lost the happiness of your conversation, I have not published or written one syllable of or to either of you; never hitched your names in a verse, or trifled with your good names in company. Can I be honestly charged with any other crime but an omission (for the word *neglect*, which I used before, slipped from my pen unguardedly) to continue my admiration of you all my life, and still to contemplate, face to face, your many excellences and perfections? I am persuaded you can reproach me truly with no great faults, except my natural ones, which I am as ready to own, as to do all justice to the contrary beauties in you. It is true, my Lord, I am short, not well-shaped, generally ill-dressed, if not sometimes dirty. Your Lordship and Ladyship are still in bloom; your figures such, as rival the Apollo of Belvidere, and the Venus of Medicis; and your faces so finished, that neither sickness nor passion can deprive them of *colour*. I will allow your own in particular to be the finest that ever *man* was blest with. Preserve it, my Lord, and reflect that to be a critic would cost it too many frowns, and to be a statesman too many wrinkles! I further confess, I am now somewhat old; but so your Lordship and this excellent Lady, with all your beauty, will, I hope, one day be. I know your genius and hers so perfectly tally, that you cannot but join in admiring each other, and by consequence in the contempt of all such as myself. You have both, in my regard, been like – (your Lordship, I know, loves a *simile*, and it will be one suitable to your quality) – you have been like two princes, and I like a *poor animal* sacrificed between them to cement a lasting league; I hope I have not bled in vain; but that such an amity may endure for ever! For though it be what common understandings would hardly conceive, two *wits* however may be persuaded that it is in friendship as in enmity, the more *danger* the more honour.

Give me the liberty, my Lord, to tell you, why I never replied to those *verses on the imitator of Horace*. They regarded nothing but my *figure*, which I set no value upon; and my morals which, I knew, needed no defence. Any honest man has the pleasure to be conscious, that it is out of the power of the wittiest, nay the greatest person in the kingdom, to lessen him *that way*, but at the expense of his own truth, honour, or justice.

But though I declined to explain myself just at the time when I was sillily threatened, I shall now give your Lordship a frank account of the offence you imagined to be meant to you. *Fanny* (my Lord) is the plain English of *Fannius*, a real person, who was a foolish critic, and an enemy of Horace, perhaps a noble one; so (if your Latin be gone in earnest) I must acquaint you, the word *Beatus* may be construed;

> Beatus Fannius! ultro
> Delatis capsis et imagine.

This *Fannius* was, it seems, extremely fond both of his *poetry* and his *person,* which appears by the pictures and statues he caused to be made of himself, and by his great diligence to propagate bad verses at court, and get them admitted into the library of Augustus. He was moreover of a delicate or effeminate complexion, and constant at the assemblies and operas of those days, where he took it into his head to slander poor Horace:

> Ineptus
> Fannius, Hermogenis laedat conviva Tigelli;

till it provoked him at last to name him, give him a lash, and send him whimpering to the ladies.

> Discipularum *inter jubeo plorare cathedras.*

So much for *Fanny*, my Lord. The word *spins* (as Dr Freind, or even Dr Sherwin could assure you) was the literal translation of *deduci*; a metaphor taken from a *silk-worm,* my Lord, to signify any slight, silken, or (as your Lordship and the ladies call it) *flimsy* piece of work. I presume your Lordship has enough of this, to convince you there was nothing personal but to that Fannius, who with all his fine accomplishments had never been heard of, but for that Horace he injured.

In regard to the right honourable Lady, your Lordship's friend, I was far from designing a person of her condition by a name so derogatory to her as that of *Sappho*; a name prostituted to every infamous creature that ever wrote verse or novels. I protest I never applied that name to her in any verse of mine, public or private; and I firmly believe, not in any letter or conversation. Whoever could invent a falsehood to support an accusation, I pity; and whoever can believe such a character to be theirs, I pity still more. God forbid the court or town should have the complaisance to join in that opinion! Certainly

I meant it only of such modern Sapphos, as imitate much more the lewdness than the genius of the ancient one; and upon whom their wretched brethren frequently bestow both the name and the qualification there mentioned.

There was another reason why I was silent as to that paper – I took it for a *lady's* (on the printer's word in the title-page), and thought it too presuming as well as indecent, to contend with one of that sex in altercation. For I never was so mean a creature as to commit my anger against a lady to paper, though but in a private letter. But soon after, her denial of it was brought to me by a noble person of real honour and truth. Your Lordship indeed said it was your Lordship's; some thought the beautiful bye-blow had two fathers, or (if one of them will hardly be allowed a man) two mothers; indeed, I think both sexes had a share in it, but which was uppermost, I know not. I pretend not to determine the exact method of this witty fornication; and if I call it yours, my Lord, it is only because, whoever *got* it, you brought it forth.

Here, my Lord, allow me to observe, the different proceeding of the ignoble poet, and his noble enemies. What he has written of *Fanny, Adonis, Sappho,* or who you will, he owned, he published, he set his name to. What they have published of him, they have denied to have written; and what they have written of him, they have denied to have published. One of these was the case in the past libel, and the other in the present. For though the parent has owned it to a few choice friends, it is such as he has been obliged to deny in the most particular terms, to the great person whose opinion concerned him most. Yet, my Lord, this epistle was a piece not written in haste, or in a passion, but many months after all pretended provocations, when you were at full leisure at Hampton Court, and I the object singled, like a deer out of season, for so ill-timed and ill-placed a diversion. It was a deliberate work, directed to a reverend person, of the most serious and sacred character, with whom you are known to cultivate a strict correspondence, and to whom it will not be doubted but you open your secret sentiments, and deliver your real judgment of men and things.

This, I say, my Lord, with submission, could not but awaken all my reflection and *attention*. Your Lordship's opinion of me as a *poet*, I cannot help; it is yours, my Lord, and that were enough to mortify a poor man; but it is not yours alone. You must be content to share it with the gentleman of the Dunciad, and (it may be) with many more innocent and ingenious men. If your Lordship destroys my *poetical* character, they will claim their part in the glory: but, give me leave to say, if my *moral* character be ruined, it must be wholly the work of your Lordship: and it will be hard even for you to do, unless I myself co-operate.

How can you talk (my most worthy Lord) of all Pope's Works as so many *libels*, affirm that *he has no invention* but in *defamation*, and charge him with *selling another man's labours printed with his own name*? Fye, my Lord, you forget yourself. He printed not his name before a line of the person's you mention; that person himself has told you and all the world in the book itself, what part he had in it, as may be seen in the conclusion of his notes to the Odyssey. I can only suppose your Lordship (not having at that time *forgot your Greek*) despised to look upon the *translation*; and ever since entertained too mean an opinion of the translator to cast an eye upon it. Besides, my Lord, when you said he *sold* another man's works, you ought in justice to have added that he *bought* them, which very much alters the case. What he gave him was five hundred pounds: his receipt can be produced to your Lordship. I dare not affirm that he was as well paid as some writers (much his inferiors) have been since; but your Lordship will reflect that I am no man of quality, either to buy or sell scribbling so high, and that I have neither place, pension, nor power to reward for *secret services*. It cannot be, that one of your rank can have the least envy to such an author as I: but were that possible, it were much better gratified by employing not your own, but some of those low and ignoble pens to do you this mean office. I dare engage you will have them for less than I gave Mr Broom, if your friends have not raised the market. Let them drive the bargain for you, my Lord; and you may depend on seeing, every day in the week, as many (and now and then as pretty) verses, as these of your Lordship.

And would it not be full as well, that my poor person should be abused by them, as by one of your rank and quality? Cannot Curll do the same? nay, has he not done it before your Lordship, in the same kind of language, and almost the same words? I cannot but think the worthy and discreet clergyman himself will agree, it is improper, nay unchristian, to expose the *personal* defects of our brother; that both such perfect forms as yours, and such unfortunate ones as mine, proceed from the hand of the same Maker, who fashioneth his vessels as he pleaseth, and that it is not from their shape we can tell whether they are made for honour or dishonour. In a word, he would teach you charity to your greatest enemies; of which number, my Lord, I cannot be reckoned, since, though a poet, I was never your flatterer.

Next, my Lord, as to the *obscurity of my birth* (a reflection copied also from Mr Curll and his brethren), I am sorry to be obliged to such a presumption as to name my family in the same leaf with your Lordship's: but my father had the honour in one instance to resemble you, for he was a younger brother. He did not indeed think it a happiness to bury his elder brother, though he had one who wanted some of those good qualities which yours possessed. How sincerely glad could I be, to pay to that young nobleman's memory the debt I owed to his friendship, whose early death deprived your family of as much wit and honour as he left behind him in any branch of it. But as to my father, I could assure you, my Lord, that he was no mechanic, neither a hatter, nor, which might please your Lordship yet better, a cobbler, but, in truth, of a very tolerable family; and my mother of an ancient one, as well born and educated as that Lady, whom your Lordship made choice of to be the mother of your own children; whose merit, beauty, and vivacity (if transmitted to your posterity) will be a better present than even the noble blood they derive only from you; a mother, on whom I was never obliged so far to reflect, as to say she spoiled me; and a father, who never found himself obliged to say of me that he disapproved my conduct. In a word, my Lord, I think it enough that my parents, such as they were, never cost me a blush; and that their son, such as he is, never cost them a tear.

I have purposely omitted to consider your Lordship's criticisms on my *poetry*. As they are exactly the same with those of the forementioned authors, I apprehend they would justly charge me with partiality, if I gave to you what belongs to them; or paid more distinction to the same things when they are in your mouth, than when they were in theirs. It will be shewing both them and you (my Lord) a more particular respect, to observe how much they are honoured by your imitation of them, which indeed is carried through your whole epistle. I have read somewhere at school (though I make it no vanity to have forgot where), that Tully naturalized a few phrases at the instance of some of his friends. Your Lordship has done more in honour of these gentlemen; you have authorized not only their assertions, but their style. For example, *a flow that wants skill to restrain its ardour – a dictionary that gives us nothing at its own expense – As luxuriant branches bear but little fruit, so wit unpruned is but raw fruit – While you rehearse ignorance, you still know enough to do it in verse – wits are but glittering ignorance – The account of how we pass our time – and the weight on Sir.* R *W.–'s brain – you can ever receive from no head more than such a head* (*as no head*) *has to give*: your Lordship would have said, *never* receive instead of *ever*, and *any head* instead of *no head*: but all this is perfectly new, and has greatly enriched our language.

You are merry, my Lord, when you say, *Latin* and *Greek*

> Have quite deserted your poor John-Trot head,
> And left plain native English in their stead;

for (to do you justice) this is nothing less than *plain English*. And as for your *John-Trot head*, I cannot conceive why you should give it that name; for by some papers I have seen signed with that name, it is certainly a head very different from your Lordship's.

Your Lordship seems determined to fall out with everything

you have learned at school: you complain next of a *dull dictionary*

> That gives us nothing at its own expense,
> But a few modern words for ancient sense.

Your Lordship is the first man that ever carried the love of wit so far, as to expect a *witty dictionary*. A dictionary that gives us anything but words, must not only be an expensive but a very extravagant dictionary. But what does your Lordship mean by its giving but a *few modern words* for *ancient sense*? If by *sense* (as I suspect) you mean *words* (a mistake not unusual), I must do the dictionary the justice to say, that it gives us just as many modern words as ancient ones. Indeed, my Lord, you have more need to complain of a bad grammar than of a dull dictionary.

Dr Freind, I dare answer for him, never taught you to talk

> Of Sapphic, Lyric, and Iambic Odes.

Your Lordship might as well bid your present tutor, your tailor, make you a *coat, suit of cloaths,* and *breeches*: for you must have forgot your logic, as well as grammar, not to know, that sapphic and iambic are both included in lyric; that being the *genus*, and those the *species*.

> For all cannot invent who can translate,
> No more than those who clothe us, can create.

Here your Lordship seems in labour for a meaning. Is it that you would have translations, originals? for it is the common opinion, that the business of a translator is to translate, and not to invent; and of a tailor to clothe, and not to create. But why should you, my Lord, of all mankind, abuse a tailor? not to say, blaspheme him; if he can (as some think) at least go halves with God Almighty in the formation of a beau. Might not Dr Sherwin rebuke you for this, and bid you remember your Creator in the days of your youth?

From a *tailor*, your Lordship proceeds (by a beautiful gradation) to a *silkman*:

> Thus *P–pe* we find
> The gaudy *Hinchcliff* of a beauteous mind.

Here too is some ambiguity. Does your Lordship use *Hinchcliff* as a proper name? or as the ladies say a *hinchcliff* or a *colmar*, for a silk or a fan? I will venture to affirm, no critic can have a perfect taste of your Lordship's works, who does not understand both your male phrase and your female phrase.

Your Lordship, to finish your climax, advances up to a hatter; a mechanic, whose employment, you inform us, is not (as was generally imagined) to cover people's heads, but to dress their brains. A most useful mechanic indeed! I cannot help wishing to have been one, for some people's sake. But this too may be only another lady-phrase: your Lordship and the ladies may take a head-dress for a head, and understand, that to adorn the head is the same thing as to dress the brains.

Upon the whole, I may thank your Lordship for this high panegyric; for if I have but dressed up Homer, as your tailor, silkman, and hatter, have equipped your Lordship, I must be owned to have dressed him marvellously indeed, and no wonder if he is admired by the ladies.

After all, my Lord, I really wish you would learn your grammar. What if you put yourself awhile under the tuition of your friend *W- - m*? May not I with all respect say to you, what was said to another Noble Poet by Mr Cowley, *Pray, Mr* Howard, *if you did read your grammar, what harm would it do you*? You yourself wish all lords would *learn to write*; though I do not see of what use it could be, if their whole business is to *give their votes*: it could only be serviceable in signing their protests. Yet surely this small portion of learning might be indulged to your Lordship, without any breach of that *privilege* you so generously assert to all those of your rank, or too great an infringement of that *right* which you claim as *hereditary*, and for which, no doubt, your noble father will thank you. Surely, my Lord, no man was ever so bent upon depreciating himself!

All your readers have observed the following lines:

How oft we hear some witling pert and dull,
By fashion coxcomb, and by nature fool,
With hackney maxims, in dogmatic strain,
Scoffing religion and the marriage chain;
Then from his common-place-book he repeats,

> The lawyers all are rogues, and parsons cheats,
> That vice and virtue's nothing but a jest,
> And all morality deceit well-drest;
> That life itself is like a wrangling game, etc.

The whole town and court (my good Lord) have heard this witling; who is so much everybody's acquaintance but his own, that I will engage they all name the same person. But to hear *you* say, that this is only – *of whipt cream a frothy store*, is a sufficient proof, that never mortal was endued with so humble an opinion both of himself and his own wit, as your Lordship: for, I do assure you, these are by much the best verses in your whole poem.

How unhappy is it for me, that a person of your Lordship's modesty and virtue, who manifests so tender a regard to religion, matrimony, and morality; who, though an ornament to the court, cultivate an exemplary correspondence with the clergy; nay, who disdain not charitably to converse with, and even assist, some of the very worst writers (so far as to cast a few conceits, or drop a few antitheses, even among the dear joys of the *Courant*); that you, I say, should look upon Me alone as reprobate and unamendable! Reflect what I was, and what I am. I am even annihilated by your anger: for in these verses you have robbed me of *all power to think*, and, in your others, of the very *name* of a *man*! Nay, to show that this is wholly your own doing, you have told us that before I wrote my last Epistles (that is, before I unluckily mentioned *Fanny* and *Adonis* whom, I protest, I knew not to be your Lordship's relations), *I might have lived and died in glory*.

What would I not do to be well with your Lordship? Though, you observe, I am a mere *imitator* of *Homer, Horace, Boileau, Garth,* etc. (which I have the less cause to be ashamed of, since they were imitators of one another), yet what if I should solemnly engage never to imitate your Lordship? May it not be one step towards an accommodation, that while you remark my *ignorance in Greek*, you are so good as to say, you have *forgot your own*? What if I should confess I translated from Dacier? That surely could not but oblige your Lordship, who are known to prefer French to all the learned languages. But allowing that in the space of twelve years' acquaintance with Homer, I might unhappily contract as much Greek as your Lordship did in two at the university, why may not I forget it again as happily?

Till such a reconciliation take effect, I have but one thing to entreat of your Lordship. It is, that you will not decide of my principles on the same grounds as you have done of my learning; nor give the same account of my want of grace, after you have lost all acquaintance with my person, as you do of my want of Greek, after you have confessedly lost all acquaintance with the language. You are too generous, my Lord, to follow the gentlemen of the Dunciad quite so far, as to seek my utter perdition; as Nero once did Lucan's, merely for presuming to be a *poet*, while one of so much greater quality was a *writer*. I therefore make this humble request to your Lordship, that the next time you please to write to me, speak of me, or even whisper of me, you will recollect it is full eight years since I had the honour of any conversation or correspondence with your Lordship, except just half an hour in a lady's lodgings at court, and then I had the happiness of her being present all the time. It would therefore be difficult even for your Lordship's penetration to tell, to what, or from what principles, parties, or sentiments, moral, political, or theological, I may have been converted, or perverted in all that time. I beseech your Lordship to consider the injury a man of your high rank and credit may do to a private person, under penal laws and many other disadvantages, not for want of honesty or conscience, but merely perhaps for having too weak a head, or too tender a heart. It is by these alone I have hitherto lived excluded from all posts of profit or trust: as I can interfere with the views of no man, do not deny me, my Lord, all that is left, a little praise, or the common encouragement due, if not to my genius, at least to my industry.

Above all, your Lordship will be careful not to wrong my moral character with THOSE under whose protection I live, and through whose lenity alone I can live with comfort. Your

Lordship, I am confident, upon consideration will think, you inadvertently went a little too far when you recommended to THEIR perusal, and strengthened by the weight of your approbation, a libel, mean in its reflections upon my poor figure, and scandalous in those on my honour and integrity: wherein I was represented as '*an enemy* to the human race, a *murderer* of reputations, and a *monster* marked by God like *Cain*, deserving to wander accursed through the world'.

A strange picture of a man, who had the good fortune to enjoy many friends, who will be always remembered as the first ornaments of their age and country; and no enemies that ever contrived to be heard of, except Mr John Dennis, and your Lordship; a man, who never wrote a line in which the religion or government of his country, the royal family, or their ministry, were disrespectfully mentioned; the animosity of any one party gratified at the expense of another; or any censure passed, but upon known vice, acknowledged folly, or aggressive impertinance. It is with infinite pleasure he finds, that some men, who seem ashamed and afraid of nothing else, are so very sensible of his ridicule: and it is for that very reason he resolves (by the grace of God, and your Lordship's good leave)

> That, while he breathes, no rich or noble knave
> Shall walk the world in credit to his grave.

This, he thinks, is rendering the best service he can to the public, and even to the good government of his country; and for this at least, he may deserve some countenance, even from the GREATEST PERSONS in it. Your Lordship knows of WHOM I speak. Their NAMES I shall be as sorry, and as much ashamed to place near yours, on such an occasion, as I should be to see you, my Lord, placed so near their PERSONS, if you could ever make so ill an use of their ear as to asperse or misrepresent any innocent man.

This is all I shall ever ask of your Lordship, except your pardon for this tedious letter. I have the honour to be, with equal respect and concern, My Lord,

Your truly devoted servant,

A. POPE

INDEX